1970
Murmansk
SCANDINAVIA
ARENTS SEA
NORTH CAPE
BEAR I.
20°
VEST SPITSBERGEN IS.
0°
JAN MAYEN
70°
60°
ICELAND
20°
KING FREDERIK VIII LAND
PEARY LAND
GREENLAND
Angmagssalik
40°
ELLESMERE I.
Thule
BAFFIN BAY
Godthaab
DAVIS STRAIT
80°
60°
DEVON I.
PRINCE WILLIAM LAND
BAFFIN I.
BOOTHIA PEN.
NORTH MAGNETIC POLE 1961
SOUTHAMPTON I.
Scale
miles
0
500
palacios
MERICA

Victor, Paul-Emile
Man and the Conquest of the
Poles

RECD

DATE DUE	BORROWER'S NAME	

By PAUL-ÉMILE VICTOR

APOUTSIAK
AVENTURE ESQUIMEAU
LA GRANDE FAIM
BORÉAL
BANQUISE
COUTUMES ET TECHNIQUES DE LA PISTE BLANCHE
POÈMES ESKIMO
PÔLE SUD
GROENLAND
TERRE ADÉLIE
LA VOIE LACTÉE
L'HOMME À LA CONQUÊTE DES PÔLES
CONTRIBUTION À L'ETHNOLOGIE DES ESKIMO D'ANGMAGSSALIK

Translated into English:

MY ESKIMO LIFE
THE GREAT HUNGER
MAN AND THE CONQUEST OF THE POLES

PAUL-ÉMILE VICTOR

MAN AND THE CONQUEST

TRANSLATION BY SCOTT SULLIVAN

OF THE POLES

SIMON AND SCHUSTER • NEW YORK • 1963

PUBLISHED BY SIMON AND SCHUSTER, INC.
ROCKEFELLER CENTER, 630 FIFTH AVENUE
NEW YORK 20, N. Y.

FIRST PRINTING

LIBRARY OF CONGRESS CATALOG CARD NUMBER: 63-12568
MANUFACTURED IN THE UNITED STATES OF AMERICA
BY H. WOLFF BOOK MANUFACTURING CO., INC., N. Y.

CONTENTS

ILLUSTRATIONS

THE BEGINNINGS

THE CONQUEST

1

THE FIRST MAN

IN THE FOURTH CENTURY B.C., Marseilles was already a prosperous, diversified city. Her remarkable geographical situation, at the crossroads of the trading routes of Gaul and the Mediterranean, made her a clearinghouse for ideas and an ideal point of observation. The town listened with delight to the tales of Alexander the Great's exploits as he overwhelmed the Greek world, a world of which she herself was one of the jewels. She calmly watched the decline of her neighbor Carthage on the opposite shore of the Mediterranean; though Carthage was still strong—she would not finally fall and disappear until 146 B.C.—Marseilles was no longer afraid of her.

Amid the din of travelers' and traders' chariots, in the hurly-burly of her markets tottering beneath the weight of goods like pewter and amber with their magic names, facing out on the port —even then an old one—where the deep-bellied trading ships and the impressive three-tiered warships with their battering rams danced under the mistral, a man was dreaming of distant voyages. His name was Pytheas.

The Mediterranean, stretched out at his feet, held no interest for him. It was farther, beyond the Pillars of Hercules, toward the unknown and mysterious seas beyond the setting sun, that he dreamed of sailing, but not merely to seek his fortune there; his passion was not gain, but knowledge. He had never believed in the strange tales of the Carthaginian Himilco, who, a hundred years earlier, had steered a course toward the north of the ocean and had spoken with terror of "frightful sea-monsters, floating grasses and thick black waters." Pytheas knew that he had lied in order to discourage future competition; the Carthaginians had no desire to tempt the Greeks, whom they knew to be curious and adventurous. Nor did Pytheas believe in what was then thought and taught about the world: that beyond the populated countries, there stretched a dark region where the elements grew confused and bordered on the edge of the void.

For Pytheas knew that the world was round.

His family, though scarcely well-to-do, had insisted on giving him a solid education, no doubt perceiving that, even as a child, he had great scientific aptitude. He had studied with the famous mathematician, Eudoxus of Cnidus, a student of Plato; and it was from him that Pytheas had learned that the world was round. It was Eudoxus too, who, upon his return from a trip to Egypt, established a new and more accurate basis for reckoning the year's length; he was the first man to set it at 365¼ days.

But there can be little doubt that what impressed the young Pytheas most were the extraordinary calculations by which his master attempted to determine the length of the terrestrial meridian. Eudoxus calculated the angle of deviation between his own town, Cnidus, and an Egyptian town situated on approximately the same meridian by measuring the altitude of the same star above the horizon in both places. After evaluating the distance between the two towns, he was able to deduce the length of the meridian:

38,700 or 43,500 miles (depending on what value we assign to the *stadium*, Eudoxus's linear unit).

His master's feat was to change the course of the young Pytheas's life; his own passion for astronomy was real indeed, and he decided to devote his life to it.

The Greek geographer Strabo (b. *c.* 63 B.C.)—though he is extremely harsh in his appraisal of Pytheas, going so far as to call him a liar—nevertheless recognizes him as an astronomer of high merit. This is the very least that can be said of a man who, for the first time, applied the principles of astronomy to geography, calculating the latitude of his own city, Massilia—or Marseilles—with an error of only a few minutes.

In geography the word "latitude" is understood to indicate the angular distance between any given point and the equator, expressed in degrees of the circumference of the globe. In other words, it is the angle that a line perpendicular to the horizon of a given point makes with the plane of the global equator. Since the latitude of any point is counted starting from the equator, it is, therefore, 0° at the equator and increases as one moves away from it. It is, naturally, the same for all points on the same parallel.

The highest possible latitude is 90°—the latitude of the North Pole and of the South Pole—a latitude which was to be chipped away at, degree by degree, through the course of centuries. It is easy to imagine Commander Peary's delight, when, on April 6, 1909, he took a reading of the sun's altitude and realized he had reached latitude 90° north. He was at the Pole.

There are several methods for reckoning latitude; most of the polar explorers after 1731 used the *sextant*, an instrument which enables one to determine the latitude at any given point. In the time of Pytheas, however, other, longer and less precise methods had to be employed. We are familiar with the method used by the astronomer from Marseilles, thanks to the accounts of the historians and geographers of antiquity (Strabo, Polybius, Eratosthenes and Pliny) who remarked upon it.

Pytheas used the *gnomon*, the first astronomical instrument ever invented; it had been known and used by the Egyptians, the Chinese, and even the Peruvians, since the dawn of time. On the market square, he set up a sort of obelisk several yards high on which he had ruled off a scale with 120 equal gradations. He reproduced these same gradations (equal in length) on the ground. Then there was nothing left for him to do but to observe the varying lengths of the shadow cast by the gnomon.

One can readily imagine the amused comments of the Marseilles crowd watching Pytheas measuring the sun's shadow and making careful notes on his tablets—the amusement being all the greater for the fact that the operations continued for several months. In fact, we know that Pytheas measured the sun's shadow on the day of the summer solstice (the longest day) and on the day of the winter solstice (the shortest day). He noted that the day of the summer solstice, the length of the shadow represented 41⅘ divisions out of the total of 120 inscribed on the gnomon. From this fact, he concluded that the obliquity of the ecliptic[1] at this period was of the order of 23° 49′.

Moreover, when both the declination and the meridian altitude of the sun are known for a given point, the latitude of that point can then be determined. Pytheas arrived at the figure 43° 13′ north latitude for his own city; his calculations were of astonishing accuracy, Marseilles's exact latitude being 43° 17′ 4″ north.

In fact, observations made by means of the gnomon could not have given the sun's altitude with absolute accuracy. The shadow would never have been sufficiently well defined. Later, attempts were made to remedy this difficulty by placing a plate pierced by a circular hole at the top of the gnomon; the sun's image was projected through the hole, but there still remained a considerable penumbra.

Nor could Pytheas do anything about errors due to parallax, to refraction and to the semidiameter of the sun. The result of his calculations remains none the less extraordinary for that.

It is known that later, during the course of his voyage (or voy-

---

[1] The ecliptic is the great circle of the celestial sphere which the sun seems to describe in the course of its apparent annual orbit around the earth. This circle is so named because an eclipse can occur only when the moon is in the same plane. The obliquity of the ecliptic is the angle that the plane of this circle makes with that of the equator. It is to the oblique position of these two planes in relation to each other that the alternation of the seasons is due. If the ecliptic coincided with the equator, there would be neither summer nor winter, and the lengths of day and night would always be equal, and the same for every point on the earth.

ages) to the Far North, Pytheas reckoned the latitudes of the countries he visited; those who have reported his voyage to us—in order to criticize it—have felt no need to make precise note of these findings. It is probable that Pytheas, being as ingenious as he was, invented a more manageable and practical instrument than the gnomon to take with him on his voyage. But we can only suppose this.

In any case, the gnomon was to remain in wide use for centuries; the tallest gnomon recorded in history was constructed at Samarkand in 1437 by the astronomer Ulug Beg; it was 176 feet high.

But Pytheas did not stop his astronomical observations at this point. He spent long nights studying the stars; he even discovered that Polaris (the North Star) did not give an exact indication of true north. The precise reckoning of true north was to haunt the man from Marseilles. It was no doubt indispensable for him to achieve it in order to adjust the sundial he carried with him on his voyage.

Nansen[2] suggests that Pytheas knew how to determine the latitude of a point directly, by measuring the altitude of the Pole above the horizon; it was doubtless in making this sort of measurement that he discovered that Polaris was not precisely fixed.

These nighttime measurements could obviously not have been made with the gnomon, which makes it seem likely that Pytheas had at his disposal some mysterious new instrument.

By discovering that the true Pole did not coincide with any given star, he obviously invalidated the teachings of his master Eudoxus, who had never questioned the theory of the polar star. In any event, when Pytheas embarked on his famous voyage toward the Arctic Circle, he knew that the North Pole formed a nearly perfect rectangle with three nearby stars; it is believed that these were the β (beta) of Ursa Minor, or the Little Bear, the χ (chi) and the α (alpha) of Draco, or the Dragon.

Pytheas was unquestionably a man of science who made use of his knowledge in a practical way, by applying it to navigation. He must even have possessed a solid reputation as a scientist and astronomer in his own city; for how else can we explain the fact that he was put in charge of an expedition, if he did not enjoy the full confidence of the people? Certainly, Pytheas, the astronomer and

---

[2] Fridtjof Nansen, *In Northern Mists* (Vol. I).

scientist, was thirsty for knowledge. He dreamed of traveling over the face of the earth to continue his observations in different latitudes, and thus to verify his conception of the world. But we know from the *Histories* of Polybius (*c.* 205–*c.* 125 B.C.) that Pytheas was poor. Scientific research has never made anyone rich.

Another historian, Pytheas's chief detractor, Strabo, writes that it "seems incredible for an individual possessing no means whatever to undertake on his own initiative an expedition of such far-reaching extent."

Pytheas doubtless realized that, to satisfy the demon driving him toward travel and scientific discovery, he would have to go by way of commerce. We must note here that this marriage between commerce and science has lasted for centuries since Pytheas's time, and that, up to a certain point, we owe the conquest of the poles to it. The merchants of Marseilles who paid for amber and tin at their weight in gold could not easily dismiss the idea of going to search for them at their source. But this was at the time a hazardous and a perilous enterprise; all the more so as the Carthaginians, although in their decline, still kept a vigilant guard posted in the Strait of Gibraltar, then known as the Pillars of Hercules.

But the temptation was too strong and the anticipated profits too great to halt the Phocaean spirit of enterprise; about 330 B.C., a naval expedition commanded by Pytheas left Marseilles. It set sail for the unknown, to become the first polar expedition in history.

We know practically nothing about the circumstances in which this expedition was organized. We cannot say whether Pytheas himself was its promoter or whether he personally fitted it out. It is certain that the merchants of Marseilles participated in its financing, but it seems logical that the town government, which was very powerful at the time, granted its patronage and no doubt partly underwrote it. We cannot rule out the possibility of an official expedition organized by the state at the request of the business community either. In this case, the distinguished astronomer would have been asked to accompany the expedition as some sort of pilot; his science and his learning, of which the whole town must have been talking (a man who measured the sun's shadow in Marseilles could not have helped being famous), must have seemed sure guarantees on a voyage into the unknown.

It must be remembered that formerly, down to quite modern

times, the commander of a ship was not specifically a navigator. That role was confided to a "pilot" whose duty was to direct the ship on her course, while the commander himself performed only the functions of authority.

Pytheas, then, might well have been the first great pilot; being the only lettered man on board, he was naturally expected to write the account of the voyage; this account (now entirely lost) may have been responsible for the erroneous belief that Pytheas was in command.

About this voyage—one of the most mysterious in antiquity—one point alone remains certain: Pytheas took part in it and played an important role. He certainly looked after the practical organization and the scientific equipment; no one who is aware of his rigorous standards in scientific matters can doubt that this preparation was minutely and very seriously carried out.

The choice of a ship must certainly have been his greatest problem. It is useful to recall at this point that we do not know (how many things we do not know about this strange voyage!) if the expedition consisted of one or of several vessels.

Prudence would have led Pytheas to set out with two ships at least; the terrifying reputation the Carthaginians had given the Ocean could only have reinforced such a decision. Nor could the Phocaean merchants, who were extremely rich, well have refused to make this extra expenditure, in view of the commercial stakes involved.

No information at all has come down to us on this subject. We know only that the Carthaginian navigator Hanno—who lived, according to some, about 1000 B.C. and, according to others, about 500 B.C.—undertook a long voyage along the African coast with sixty vessels, each with fifty oarsmen, a precedent which might have convinced Pytheas not to set out with only a single ship. In any case, the ship, or ships, used by Pytheas were very much of the same type; the uncertainty and the perilousness of the voyage dictated a ship that was sturdy, powerful and well armed.

We can imagine Pytheas walking in the Old Port of Marseilles (then called Lacydon), among the innumerable trading barks of every nationality, and the impressive war vessels. He must in the end have chosen whatever was the best-constructed warship of the period, for he could not possibly have been unaware of the dangers the expedition faced. He ran the risk of violent encounters not only with the Carthaginians—who were not in the least eager to see commercial competition arise on the part of the Phocaeans —but also with the unknown peoples he might meet in the course of the voyage. Pytheas's expedition must, therefore, have been heavily armed, thanks to its warships, though this does not rule out the possibility that several trading ships intended to carry home booty or to transport soldiers may also have been included.

The ships used by the Greeks during this period were of two types: men-of-war (νῆες, *naves bellicae*) and merchant or transport ships (φορτηγικά, ὁλκάδες, πλοῖα, *naves onerariae, mercatoriae*). These latter could be recognized by their rounded sides, from which was derived the name "rounds" (στρογγύλαι, *rotundae*) which was often given them; they were powered by sails and were quite slow. The men-of-war were, however, very slim and deserved the epithet (νῆες μακραί *naves longae*) which was given them by several authors of the period. They were operated by oars, which gave them speed as well as great ease in handling; their speed was as great as that of the steamships at the end of the nineteenth and the beginning of the twentieth century. The galleys were equipped with auxiliary sails for use in favorable winds, but these sails were not so designed that the ship was able to beat up windward.

Triremes (galleys with three tiers of oars) were in current use in Pytheas's day; indeed, in 400 B.C., Dionysius, the tyrant of Syracuse, had *quadriremes* (four-tiered galleys) built, and even *quinqueremes*.[3] By the time of the death of Alexander the Great, galleys of four, five and six tiers were in current use.

The Greeks went on using the trireme for a long time, because of its speed, lightness and low tonnage. However, in 330 B.C. (the time of Pytheas), they possessed many quadriremes and quinqueremes as well, and it was at about this time that they gave up building triremes to turn exclusively to the construction of quadriremes.

We may suppose then, with some chance of hitting on the truth,

---

[3] Callisthenes speaks of a "tessaraconter," which is generally defined as a ship with forty banks of oars, but which may have been a ship requiring forty rowers to each oar. In any case, the tessaraconter was an impressive vessel; Callisthenes's vessel would have carried a crew of 8000, if it ever existed.

that Pytheas's flagship was a trireme. In fact, this same sort of ship was, for centuries, standard.

The Egyptian galleys of 1500 B.C. measured 130 feet by 16. The Venetian galleys of the fourteenth century were of the same dimensions, as was the *réale* of Louis XIV; it was the "human motor" which imposed these limits.[4]

These ships were all seven or eight times as long as they were wide; this "coefficient of narrowness" was recognized as a necessary factor in obtaining maximum speed.

Pytheas's ship, if we are to believe the authors of antiquity who speak of it, was about 155 feet long and about 20 feet wide. It was larger than Christopher Columbus's famous caravel. It must have had a displacement of between four and five hundred tons, including twenty tons of stones as ballast.

The triremes' prows were decorated with sculptures, and each bore the particular emblem associated with the ship's name. Below the prow was a boarding ram, like the one with which Assyrian galleys were equipped. The care of the prow was entrusted to a special overseer (the *proreus*), who also commanded the oarsmen. Over the prow stood a high platform for the soldiers (between ten and fifty of them).

The stern was built very high so that the crew could beach the ship easily when darkness fell. The poop stood higher than the other parts of the deck; it was there that the helmsman stood. It was also on the poop that the image of the god who protected the ship was painted. The commander and whatever important persons happened to be aboard had a cabin set up for them in the stern. At the center of the galley rose a mast (sometimes two), carrying the large rectangular auxiliary sail.

However, the vessel was propelled principally by the oarsmen (*remiges*). These formed a class distinct from the sailors (*nautae*), who were in charge of maneuvering the ship, and the sea-borne soldiers (*classiarii*). They sat on small benches, the lowest row of which was called *θάλαμος* in Greek, the highest *θρᾶνος*, and the middle *ζυγόν*.

A *trireme* carried about 170 to 200 oarsmen.[5] The handle of

---

[4] A. Thomazi, *Les Navires*.

[5] The question of how the banks of oarsmen were disposed has been much discussed, but no definite conclusion has been arrived at.

each oar was made partly of lead, in order to facilitate its balance and make it more manageable. The rudder was simply an extra oar, fitted with a broad scoop and attached beside the poop; in general, the ship carried twin rudders joined by a bar, which was controlled by the helmsman.

It must be noted that these ships, designed as they were for navigation in the Mediterranean in warm and agreeable weather, were normally without any provision whatever against cold or ice. The ram with which Pytheas's ship was probably equipped could, nevertheless, have proved useful in facilitating her passage through the ice; it is likely that an experiment along these lines was made.

What is more certain is that Pytheas was aware that he was going to visit cold and misty regions; he knew the climatic zones, and he knew that the farther north he would go, the greater the declination of the sun would be—and as a result, the colder the climate by comparison with Marseilles.

How, then, can we suppose that he did not provide equipment which would enable his men to withstand the elements? The authors who have given us accounts of Pytheas's voyage—accounts which they have presumably modeled on Pytheas's own—make no mention of any special suffering due to the cold. Yet Pytheas and his men were the first in history to have gone beyond the Arctic Circle. The prudent man from Marseilles then, must have provided warm clothing, and doubtless had the inside of the ship specially fitted out, so that rain and storms could not reach his oarsmen.

Even a brief description of Pytheas's ship would not be complete without a word mentioning the set of compartments placed under the bridge for storing various sorts of equipment (weapons, clothing, food), as well as for the officers' cots; the galley slaves generally lived chained to their benches, especially when it really was slaves that were used, as is logical to suppose in this case.

The scientific equipment Pytheas took with him must not have been very extensive. It was doubtless rather cumbersome, especially if it included a gnomon. But we have already seen that Pytheas probably had at his disposal an instrument both more sophisticated and less cumbersome with which to measure the altitude of the stars and to determine the latitude.[6] To do this, he needed to

---

[6] It has been suggested that this may have been what was later to be known as the "Ptolemaic rule," a sort of long-stemmed pair of compasses, called a

take readings on the days of the two solstices and was therefore obliged to make long stops at the ports he visited. In order to determine the longest and the shortest day, he had no guide but his own judgment; thus, he carried with him machines "to measure time." This reference could not possibly indicate merely the sundials with which the ship was certainly provided. (Archimedes used one on the ship *Hiero* a century later.) Pytheas must also have had water clocks and hourglasses at his disposal. The working of the hourglass is well known even in our own day. The water clock was also in current use and had been since very early times. An intact specimen of the water clock, or *clepsydra*, has been found in the temple of Amon at Karnak. It is thought to date from the fifteenth century B.C. It is a vase with an opening through which the water runs. On the inner face are inscribed the hour markings, with the seasonal variations in the length of the hours indicated; the most interesting markings are those which correspond to the summer and winter solstices, as well as the spring and autumn equinoxes.

Pytheas must have taken along a full series of clepsydras of all sizes and shapes for use in his scientific observations. We ought to note here that the clepsydra, which had been used in Greece mainly for timing speeches before the Tribunal, had not reached a very high state of development in Pytheas's day. It was only two centuries later that certain essential improvements were made on it by Ctesibius of Alexandria. Pytheas had to settle for the approximate readings provided by his clepsydras, though they could hardly have satisfied his strict scientific standards; but he had no other method of measuring time by day and night.

Thus Pytheas's scientific equipment must have been quite modest; he had to count above all on his own eyes, his memory, his sense of observation and his intelligence.

This was, in the fullest sense, a great adventure on which he was about to embark. So there must have been many a curious and dazzled well-wisher in the Old Port of Marseilles that spring morning, come to watch Pytheas and his fleet as they departed for the unknown seas of the Far North.

---

triquetrum by the Romans. The altitudes measured by it were arrived at by measuring the distance between the legs of the compass; they were expressed in cubits (a Roman cubit equaled 17.5 inches; an Egyptian, 20.7 inches).

In the fourth century B.C., navigation was, more than anything else, an art; radar, the gyroscopic compass, the inertial navigator had not yet converted it into a rigorous scientific discipline. Sailing was a personal matter between the sea and man—man practically without external aids, without even the compass.

The Phocaeans knew their own sea well; its narrow dimensions allowed them to voyage in a series of short runs, and despite the Mediterranean's unpredictable behavior, the sailors of the period were able to make their way anywhere between Alexandria and the Pillars of Hercules.[7] This was all the more remarkable in view of the fact that the Greeks, theoretically, permitted navigation only during the fine weather from March to November.

The pilots, with nothing but the heavenly bodies, the sun and the stars, and a sounding line to guide them, generally hugged the coast by day. When evening came, they beached the boat and waited till dawn to depart again. But the Phocaeans were also aided by their sense of navigation—an intangible but real quality.

So Pytheas reached the Pillars of Hercules. For him they formed a gateway opening out on the unknown, on the terrible Ocean. Indeed, the strait was very like a gateway: a narrow passage 40 miles long, 8½ miles wide, jealously guarded by the Carthaginians, whose task was facilitated by the dominant west winds and by the violent current that ran from the Ocean into the Mediterranean.[8]

Pytheas thus had to force his passage through the strait one way or another. It has been suggested that the government of the powerful city of Massilia might have negotiated this passage with the Carthaginian government, which was in considerable difficulties of its own at the time.[9] But this scarcely seems likely, since Car-

---

[7] Numerous lighthouses stood along the Mediterranean coast, the most famous one unquestionably being that of Alexandria, which was considered one of the seven wonders of the ancient world.

[8] The variation in level between the Atlantic and the Mediterranean is so marked that it once gave rise to a project for constructing a gigantic dam at Gibraltar, shutting off the Mediterranean entirely. The electric current produced by the dam could serve the whole of Europe. But this idea is still no more than an idea, fortunately.

[9] Examples of such negotiation are to be found throughout world history. At the height of the American War of Independence, for example, when the French and English were on opposing sides, Louis XVI granted the famous Captain Cook a "passport" to be used in case of any unforeseen en-

thage had no intention whatever of doing anything that might favor a commercial competitor; at this period, of course, the idea of a purely scientific expedition was unheard of. The Phocaeans would have needed powerful arguments, flavored with a good pinch of bribery, to have extorted the right of free passage from the Carthaginians.

It is easier to imagine that Pytheas, enterprising and determined as he was, should have forced the strait by night. The guard was reduced then, as it was admitted by all concerned that nighttime navigation was extremely perilous, especially in a bottleneck of this kind. Moreover, the speed of his vessels would have protected the Massilian adventurer from pursuit.

Another hypothesis has been put forward to explain this passage. It has been suggested that Pytheas's mission was to establish communications with the British Isles (producers of tin) and the Nordic countries (producers of amber), but to do this without passing by way of Gibraltar.[10] He would, in this case, have made his way by land from Marseilles to the mouth of the Loire, where large shipyards already existed at this period.[11] He would have bought a vessel there, fitted her out and taken on a pilot familiar with navigation in the British Isles. This supposition is a bit fragile, of course, but it cannot be ruled out *a priori.*

Sailing out into the Atlantic, Pytheas was able to confirm his belief that the Carthaginian legend, according to which the Ocean was a shadowy, scorching region, peopled with monsters and choked with sea grasses, was, in effect, no more than a legend. Faithful to his old Mediterranean principles, Pytheas probably gave the order not to sail out of sight of the coast; it was thus that he must have discovered, with a certain amount of astonishment, the existence of tides, which up to then were unknown by the Greeks, but which were now easily to be observed along the Atlantic coast. This phenomenon must have deeply fascinated Pytheas, and as a man of science, he sought an explanation for it.

He found one, moreover, since even his detractors admit that he

---

counter; an order was even issued to all French ships to assist Cook's two ships, the *Resolution* and the *Discovery*, if the occasion should arise.

[10] Captain P. Celérier, *Histoire de la navigation.*

[11] A rather prosperous Greek colony had been set up there; Pytheas must have visited it in any case.

was the first astronomer to establish a relationship between lunar attraction and the tides.

Skirting the Sacred Promontory (Cape St. Vincent), which marked the limit of the world known to the Greeks, Pytheas stood out resolutely for the northeast. He crossed the Bay of Biscay and put in at the island of Ushant (Île d'Ouessant). Continuing his scientific observations, he noted that at this point—almost on the parallel of 49 degrees north—the longest day was sixteen hours long.[12] This would allow us to suppose that he was at Ushant in the month of June, the month in which, in this part of the world, the longest day falls.

Having no doubt parleyed with the fishermen of Ushant, and having possibly even taken one of them aboard as a pilot, Pytheas then set sail for England. On the itinerary he followed, the experts frankly disagree. Some think he first landed in the county of Kent (Caesar's Cantium); others maintain that he went directly to Cornwall where the tin mines were located.

Pytheas was not satisfied merely with circumnavigating England; he organized long and frequent expeditions into the interior of the country. At this period, it was in a state of savagery: immense primeval forests loomed among fearful bogs, and human life was possible only in the highlands. Pytheas noted that the people were quite hospitable, that they cultivated wheat and other cereals, possessed domestic animals, iron tools and weapons, and chariots made of wood reinforced with metal and trimmed in gold and bronze. The English of this era threshed their wheat in covered granges and distilled a barley liquor that was most agreeable to the palate. Pytheas noted the ingenious way in which the natives mined their tin. The Greek historian Timaeus, a contemporary of Pytheas who read his account of the journey, reports his observations:

> The bed is of rock, but contains earthy interstices, along which they cut a gallery. Having smelted the tin and refined it, they hammer it into knucklebones and carry it in a six-day journey to a neighboring island called Ictis.[13] They wait till the ebb-tide has

[12] For the Greeks, this system of giving the length of the longest day was a way of expressing latitude.

[13] This is believed to refer to Mont St. Michel (Vilhjalmur Stefansson, *Great Adventures and Explorations*).

drained the estuary, after which the Gallic traders carry loads of it away on wagons.

The part of England in which Pytheas was obviously most interested was the far north. He noted that the closer he came to it the more human and animal life diminished and the more the vegetation changed. He lost no time in sailing to a group of islands then known as Orkan, which later came to be called Orkney, or Orcades. "Orkan" derives from the Celtic word *orc*, which designates a sort of large, very bellicose cetacean (the grampus) that frequents those parts.

In the north of England Pytheas continued his astronomical observations and noted that at this latitude the longest day of the year was eighteen "equinoctial hours." (It ought to be explained here that the Greeks divided the day into twelve hours, however long it might actually be. The "hours" were thus of unequal duration. On the days of the equinoxes, the hours corresponded to our present hours of sixty minutes, and these were known as "equinoctial hours.")

Pytheas's observations were utilized especially fruitfully by the great geographer Hipparchus in his "climate tables."

It was certainly among the islands of the north of England that Pytheas first heard of a mysterious country called Thule, situated somewhere in the icy regions. It is over this land, later christened *Ultima Thule*, that so many inconclusive arguments have raged. For there is not a single specialist in Northern studies—and in some others as well—who has not advanced his own suppositions and commentaries on the subject.

The origin of the word "Thule" is itself extremely nebulous. Sir Clements Markham[14] derives it from *Thyle*, *Thull*, *Tell*, meaning "limit" or "boundary" in Old Saxon. Nansen,[15] who has produced an astounding work of exegesis on the subject, is more circumspect in his judgment. He mentions the Saxon word, but also speaks of a Gothic word, *Tiele* or *Tiule*, also meaning "boundary." He then quotes Professor Alf Torp, who for his part refuses to give a precise origin for "Thule," on the grounds that the extremely confused situation does not permit anyone to make a final

---

[14] Sir Clements Markham, *The Lands of Silence*.
[15] F. Nansen, *op. cit.*

pronouncement; several different roots, deriving from ancient Nordic dialects and signifying "boundary," "frozen sea," "sun," or "darkness," could all have given rise to the word "Thule." It has even been claimed that Thule was named for Tyle, the capital of a Celtic colony established in Thrace in the third century B.C.

Leaving aside several hundred other theories to explain the origin of the word, let us attempt to limit ourselves to noting simply that Pytheas made his way to an unknown land, called Thule, lying practically on the Arctic Circle, at a latitude which he was the first explorer in the world to pass. (The Arctic Circle[16] is a small circle parallel to the plane of the equator now lying at latitude 66° 33′ N. Above the Arctic Circle, the sun no longer appears above the horizon every day of the year; the duration of the polar night increases as one approaches the Pole, up to the ultimate point where it lasts six months.)

Pytheas, since he speaks of the midnight sun, certainly must have crossed the Arctic Circle (which then lay at 66° 15′ N.). "The Barbarians," he wrote, "showed us the place where the sun goes to rest. For it was the case that in these parts the nights were very short: in some places two, in others three hours long, so that the sun rose again a short time after it had set."

All the ancient authors, whether favorable to Pytheas or not, place Thule within the Arctic Circle, or in immediate proximity to it.

"Concerning the island of Thule," writes Cleomedes, "which is said to have been visited by the philosopher Pytheas of Marseilles, it is claimed that the circle described by the sun at the summer solstice is above the horizon and coincides, at that place, with the Arctic Circle. In these regions, when the sun is in Cancer, the day lasts a month, if, that is, the whole of Cancer remains visible." Strabo, Pliny, Servius, Mela, Dionysius Periegetes, Solinus and all the other commentators on Pytheas's writings agree: Thule is the land of the midnight sun.

The bedazzlement of the astronomer Pytheas, when he was confronted by these phenomena, is easy to imagine. It is also easy to

---

[16] "Arctic" derives from the Greek ἄρκτος meaning "bear." This name indicates the region of the North Pole, because the constellation of the Little Bear is very close to it.

picture his chagrin at the fact that he possessed no instrument capable of measuring the temperature, for the cold must have been intense.

"Thule," writes the Greek Strabo, Pytheas's principal detractor, "is situated quite close to the frozen seas."

"Within one day's sailing from Thule," reports Pliny, "one encounters the frozen sea, called by some *Cronium*." [17] For, it must be pointed out that the intrepid Pytheas wished to advance even farther north, beyond Thule; but he was halted by the frozen sea, which he describes with considerable astonishment: the "sea lung," a sort of mixture of air, water and earth.

"Pytheas claims he saw it with his own eyes, this substance resembling a lung," writes Strabo incredulously. Without any doubt, this refers to the edge of the ice pack, the brash ice, where a thick fog often envelops the mixture of ice and glassy water whipped up by the sea swells.

His progress halted, Pytheas decided to return to England. The great question that obviously remains is: Where exactly did the mysterious Thule lie? This question is likely to go unanswered for a long while. Innumerable studies, treatises, books and essays have been devoted to it, but no one, up to the present, has been able to make a pronouncement of entire certainty in the light of the documents in our possession. Everyone tries to place Thule according to his own convictions. The great experts on the "Thule question" may be divided into three warring camps.

The "Norwegian" camp has as its standard-bearer the great Fridtjof Nansen. In his remarkable *In Northern Mists*, an extremely minute and well-documented study of the first polar explorations, he makes no secret of his belief that Thule was Norway: his Scandinavian heart could never reject this idea. A precise and learned man, Nansen asserts nothing in a peremptory manner; he merely demolishes one by one the arguments opposed to the Thule-Norway thesis. To the same camp belongs the Greek historian Procopius, who lived in the sixth century A.D.

---

[17] Still another word which often appears in the ancient authors and whose origin is only imprecisely known. Does it derive from the Greek *Cronos* (the god Saturn), from the Celtic, from the Gallic *Croni*, or from the Old Irish? No one really knows.

The "Icelandic" camp is a good deal larger; it has picked up numerous adherents, of whom Professor Broche is by no means the least important.[18]

Pytheas's voyage from England to Thule is said to have taken six days: at a speed of 80 nautical miles (about 92 land miles) per day, his ship could quite easily have reached Iceland. Marthe Emmanuel [19] reports Commander Charcot's convictions on the matter. It took him an average of from four to five days to sail from Stornoway (in the Hebrides) to Iceland, and his *Pourquoi-pas?*, a three-masted bark with a weak auxiliary engine, sailed scarcely faster than Pytheas's galley.

The probability of the Thule-Iceland thesis is increased by the fact of Pytheas's having run against the ice pack near Thule. For the ice pack is not to be met with on the western coast of Norway, which is washed by the Gulf Stream. Nansen admits this and suggests that Pytheas never did see the ice but was merely reporting the accounts of native inhabitants; this seems hardly likely, however, on the part of a man of science like Pytheas.

There exists a third camp—this one more timid in its convictions than the other two—which identifies Thule with Jan Mayen Island, still farther north, at latitude 71° N. But the weather conditions along the coast of this island are so bad that it is difficult to imagine Pytheas's galley withstanding the storms that smashed the *Pourquoi-pas?* on the reefs of Iceland.

The great explorer Stefansson[20] has examined the theses of all three schools and seems to lean toward the Thule-Iceland position. In any event, we are still certain that Pytheas of Marseilles was the first great polar explorer in history. Thus, the French polar tradition goes back a long way.

Having returned to Marseilles after his voyage—which lasted several years, and during which he sailed far into the Baltic Sea in search of amber—he devoted himself to the writing of his book, *On the Ocean*, recounting his travels, his observations and his conclusion.

The book is now lost and we know only what the historians (principally Strabo) tell us about it; moreover, Strabo quotes from

---

[18] E. Broche, *Pythéas le Massaliote*.
[19] Marthe Emmanuel, *La France et l'exploration polaire*.
[20] Vilhjalmur Stefansson, *Ultima Thule*.

it only to demonstrate the impossibility of any such voyage. For antiquity, Pytheas was to remain nothing but "the great liar," and Eratosthenes and Hipparchus alone were to take his astronomical observations seriously.

In fact his voyage was the most fertile in scientific results of any made before Henry the Navigator. The tally of those results is impressive indeed: the reckoning of latitudes, the confirmation of the theory of the earth's sphericity, the crossing of the Arctic Circle, the geographical and ethnological descriptions, the explanation of the phenomenon of the tides, the probable preparation of documents and charts of great interest to later navigators, and, without any doubt at all, fruitful commercial transactions. This feat was accomplished in a simple oared galley designed for use in the Mediterranean, and without even the aid of a compass.

Here, then, we have an extraordinary page in the great book of human exploration, and the hostility of philosophers like Polybius and Strabo, who have unfortunately distorted his writings, can do nothing to detract from the glory of Pytheas of Marseilles, the first and one of the greatest polar explorers in history, in whose honor his home town has built a statue on the pediment of its Chamber of Commerce: surely the least of his distinctions.

2

THE VIKINGS

PYTHEAS'S GLORY in antiquity was of brief duration. The commercial success of his mission—he had traced both amber and tin back to their sources—doubtless earned him great fame in his own fair city of Marseilles, and it was with a peaceful heart that he was able to sit down to the writing of his book. It is very easy to imagine him at this juncture, recounting his voyage, as only the people of Provence could do—even then!

Then one day Pytheas died, as did the longest-lived of the men who had accompanied him. There were no longer any witnesses to the voyage. The jealous were now free to rip apart his writings, and they worked unceasingly to demolish them—an easy task, considering how fantastic Pytheas's whole account must have seemed to his contemporaries. Polybius and then Strabo displayed the greatest possible zeal in this enterprise; they made Pytheas out to be "the greatest liar of all mankind." It is a happy fact that our century has rehabilitated Pytheas (he remained forgotten down to our day), even though his book, or books, have been lost.

Thus, we know of his voyages only through the quotations of his detractors, and we are ignorant even of the date on which he sailed. It is supposed that he was a contemporary of Aristotle and Alexander the Great.

Although numerous authors in antiquity quote from him, not only Pytheas but the Arctic too was forgotten, and it was to remain clouded for centuries in the thickest of mists. Eratosthenes and Hipparchus, both of them true scientists in the modern sense of the word, were the only figures in antiquity to take Pytheas's descriptions seriously. Eratosthenes, a mathematician and geographer born in Cyrene in 276 B.C., carried on Pytheas's astronomical work. He was inspired by the Arctic traveler's discoveries to draw up the first world map, using the various latitude readings that Pytheas had made on the spot. Eratosthenes was to live in the eyes of history as the man who first succeeded in measuring the terrestrial meridian. With the aid of a very deep vertical well, he first located the position of the noon sun over Syene (Aswan), Egypt; at the same instant, he had an aide measure the zenithal angle at Alexandria. Knowing exactly (just how, we do not know) the distance —406 miles—between the two towns, and knowing the difference in latitude, by means of the angular divergence, he deduced the length of the meridian: 24,800 miles, a result of overwhelming precision.

One picturesque detail: Eratosthenes was not only a thinker—he was awarded the prize for the pentathlon, which went to the athlete winning the five contests at the Olympic Games.

(In passing, we must note the illogicality of the terms "longitude" and "latitude," which we owe to the Romans, who were familiar with only a small part of the world, and a part which was laid out more nearly along an east-west axis than along a north-south axis. They thus decided to use the term *longitudo* to indicate distances read along the "longer" dimension of the world they knew and *latitudo* for distances read along the "shorter" dimension.)

The second man to take Pytheas seriously was Hipparchus of Nicaea (in Bithynia), who lived between 160 and 125 B.C. He created mathematical astronomy and trigonometry, discovered the precession of the equinoxes, calculated the eclipses of the sun and the moon with precision; and it was he who imposed the conventional division of the circle into 360 degrees. Above all, he was the inventor of the astrolabe, an instrument that enables one to observe the positions of heavenly bodies and facilitates the reckoning of latitudes.

Oddly enough, this invention was soon forgotten. Later the Chinese reinvented it in their turn and passed it on to the Arabs, who finally communicated it to the great navigators of the Renaissance. It was thanks mainly to the astrolabe that Columbus and his contemporaries were at last able to navigate safely on the high seas, basing their new science on the "altitude" of the heavenly bodies.

In spite of a few allusions in Virgil, Tacitus and Cicero, the Arctic was in fact rather rapidly forgotten after Pytheas.

While the Greeks had arrived at a rational conception of the sphericity of the earth and had been aware of the existence of the polar regions, the High Middle Ages fell back into ignorance. The intransigence of the Fathers of the Church played a significant part in this situation; science was required to conform to the teaching of the Bible. Still, paradoxically enough, the first polar explorers after Pytheas were Gaelic monks of the sixth century. These astounding men, riding in tiny, hide-covered boats, discovered the Faroe Islands, Jan Mayen Island, Iceland and perhaps even North America.

And when the first *drakkar*, its prow ornamented with an enormous bronze dragon, beached on the shores of Iceland twelve centuries after Pytheas, those monks were there, with their churches, their bells, books and croziers. The Viking era began under the sign of the cross.

The Viking era is of capital importance in the conquest of the poles. Admirable navigators and great adventurers, the men of the North were the first true explorers of the polar lands of the North Atlantic. The tale of their exploits and of their turbulent voyages through the lacy pattern of the islands of the north of England, in

Iceland, in Greenland and in North America is just as much a part of legend as of history. Indeed, we derive this tale from a source more poetic than historical, the "sagas," composed by the Scandinavian skalds, or bards, of the eleventh and the thirteenth centuries, dedicated to the glory of the mythological and historical traditions of the peoples of the North. Luminous but imprecise, sometimes entirely false, these accounts nevertheless furnish us with much information on the voyages of these "men of the bays." (*Vikingr* is thought to derive from the word *vik*, "bay," joined to the suffix *ingr*, "man.")[1]

Fortunately, we have other, surer sources, notably archaeology, runic inscriptions and a few ancient books. Archaeology, as we shall see, enables us to form an exact notion of the technical means the Vikings had at their disposal. Runic inscriptions are scattered more or less everywhere, in Greenland and Iceland as well as in Scandinavia; in 1898, some were even discovered in the United States, on the famous Kensington (Minnesota) Rune Stone. Their origin is mysterious and their meaning magical; their very name places them: it signifies "secret" (*runar*).

This taste for the secret and the mysterious, it must be added, is to be met with in all the explorer races: the oral tradition laid hold on their exploits and sprinkled them with the powdered gilt of legend. The voyagers thereby received their reward in glory, and the people's thirst for the marvelous was also satisfied; everyone was happy, except, of course, the historians, who through these fantastical tales and these distorted accounts have attempted to reestablish the truth.

The consensus of all the studies of the exegetes is that, from the very earliest times, the men of the North, the "Norsemen," also called "Normans," had the wanderlust.[2]

In about 830, the historian-monk Dicuil wrote his *Liber de Mensura orbis terrae*, in which he mentions the story of the Irish monks of St. Columbanus, who were forced to flee, in about 793, before the Norman pirates. Their flight took them to Iceland, to Greenland, and even to Labrador.

Dicuil speaks of Thule (Iceland in this case) in the same way

---

[1] "Viking," according to Nansen, might also derive from a Celtic word meaning "warrior."

[2] Certain Scandinavian pirates are believed to have arrived in Italy and in Sicily as early as 455.

and in nearly the same words as Pytheas: "One day's sail to the north of this island, the monks found the frozen sea."

There exist numerous semihistorical, semilegendary sources for the voyages of the Vikings; we may take our choice from among the *Kongsspejl* (*The Mirror of the King*), composed in about 1200 for the education of a Norwegian prince, the *Saga of Eric the Red*, the fantastical *Legend of St. Brendan* and the *Book of the Icelanders* by the first Icelandic writer, Ari the Learned (1067-1148).

The first even slightly accurate account is that of the voyage to Lapland made by the Norwegian Othere toward the end of the ninth century, which has been recorded for us by King Alfred the Great with the greatest exactitude and objectivity.

The discovery of Jan Mayen Island is credited (but with reservations) to Saint Brendan and his companion Saint Malo (sometimes MacLow)[3] in the sixth century.

In the same period, a monk named Cormac, in search of "the solitude of the sea," settled in Iceland—if we are to believe the word of Adamnan, the abbot of Iona.

The Thordarsson Saga mentions the arrival of a Swede named Gardar, son of Svavar, in Iceland in about 860. On his way to the Hebrides, where he was to take possession of the heritage left him by his stepfather, Gardar was deflected from his route by bad weather and made for Iceland, where "there was a harbor" and where he spent the winter. This same saga recounts the voyage, in about 861, of a certain Naddod (or Naddoc), who christened Iceland the "land of the snows."

Ari the Learned, in his *Book of the Icelanders*, attributes the discovery of Iceland to a Norwegian named Ingolf, who—along with Harold Fairhair[4]—was seven years old "870 winters after the birth of Christ." He settled in the south, at Reykjavik, the name of which signifies "bay of mists." According to the traditional story, Ingolf threw the back of his ceremonial chair into the sea and landed at the exact spot where the waves washed it up. Nevertheless, the credit for writing the first authentic account concern-

---

[3] Commander Charcot identifies this island with the island mentioned in the *Legend of St. Brendan*, a 900-verse poem which recounts the peregrinations of the saint and his companion.

[4] King of Norway (863-930).

ing the Arctic goes to King Alfred, whom Markham[5] unhesitatingly describes as "the most truly great, the wisest and the best monarch who ever ruled over any country." To relax from his royal preoccupations, Alfred undertook the translation of Orosius's *Historiarum adversus paganos libri VII*. A fifth-century historian and theologian, born in Spain, and a disciple of Saint Augustine, Orosius had compiled an account of all the disasters of the human race from Adam down to the year 417.

King Alfred had no hesitation about making corrections and additions, one of which, it turned out, was an account of the Arctic voyage of the Viking Othere,[6] which he appears to have got directly from the voyager himself.

Othere, or Ottar Jarl, is described as being an extremely rich man, the owner of six hundred reindeer and many head of cattle (cows, sheep, pigs, et cetera), and as receiving an enormous income from the furs and hides that the Lapps paid him in tribute. Othere even traded in whalebones, being a redoubtable whale hunter as well. He told the tale of his adventures and voyages to King Alfred, who doubtless got great pleasure out of hearing about them. He was the first man known to have passed—in 874—the North Cape, the farthest boundary of Europe. He sailed the Barents Sea and the White Sea, reached the mouth of the Dvina (according to Nordenskjöld) and, if one is to take Nansen's word, followed the coast of the Kola Peninsula as far as Kandalaksha.

Othere described the lands and the scattered and savage people he discovered. (He was also a hunter; he bagged sixty walrus in two days as well as whales ninety-eight feet long.) His account, as recorded by Alfred, is sober and concise. It is very probably the first truly historical account of a polar exploration.

The Viking Othere died almost a Frenchman. According to the Comte de Gobineau, who was proud to claim him as an ancestor, Othere is supposed to have settled in the county of Bray, on the banks of the river Epte.[7]

The most serious author after Alfred the Great was the canon Adam of Bremen, who, in about 1067, wrote a chronicle of the Nordic countries, expressing the dismay of his contemporaries be-

---

[5] Clements Markham, *The Lands of Silence.*

[6] Also spelled Oder, Ohtere and Ottar.

[7] Gobineau, *Histoire d'Ottar Jarl.*

fore "the immensity of the abyss where the confines of the world are lost in the mists." He was familiar with the epic of Eric the Red and his sons, who had opened the great era of Viking expansion toward Greenland.

These Vikings were not peaceful travelers; they were what are commonly called in our day "toughs." Thorvald Aswaldsson was the first to be forced to leave Norway, as the result of a murder he had committed. Having heard reports of a new land from the skipper of an Icelandic ship, Gunnbjörn, who had discovered it while escaping from a storm, Aswaldsson decided to set off in search of it. His son Eric—who was to become famous under the name Eric the Red—had a model to live up to. And he did; he too set off in search of the same land when he was forced to flee Iceland as a result of two murders that he had committed in his turn. Thus it was that Greenland was discovered; it was given its present name by Eric, who hoped to attract other immigrants to settle in a country that "bore such a beautiful name." Without knowing it, Eric the Red invented the art of tourist advertising, in the year 981.

Eric spent three years in Greenland, where he found evidence of its having been formerly inhabited. He returned to Iceland and succeeded in persuading a large number of Icelanders to emigrate to the new land, taking their weapons and their baggage with them.

He headed a fleet of twenty-four *drakkars,* piled on board which were fifteen hundred colonists with all their worldly goods, their furniture, their cattle and their horses; this was the largest polar expedition in history and was not to be exceeded in point of size till Operation High Jump, carried out by Admiral Byrd and the United States Navy in 1946, at the South Pole.

Of Eric's twenty-four ships,[8] only fourteen completed the voyage. The colonists settled on the southwest coast of Greenland, the coast with the best climate. They built two centers, 125 miles apart. The population never rose above 3,000. They pushed back the frontier to the north, at the same time hunting seal and walrus. They built artificial nests to trap eider duck (these have been

---

[8] Marthe Emmanuel, in *La France et l'exploration polaire,* raises this figure to thirty-five.

found as far as 80° N.). It is thought that they made contact with the Eskimos.[9]

Eric the Red's life ended better than it had begun; he retired to his farm and enjoyed the veneration of all around him. He had three sons (Leif, Thorstein and Thorvald) and a daughter, Freydi,[10] who, according to the *Saga of the Greenlanders*, was "proud and brave."

The peculiar character of the sagas, their lack of precision, their fantasy, do not permit us to determine with clarity the sequence of the various voyages made by Eric the Red's successors. In any event, the Norsemen deprived Christopher Columbus of the distinction of being the discoverer of the New World, for they visited it long before he did. Bjarni Herjulfsson, Leif Ericsson and Thorfinn Karlsefni led expeditions to Labrador and Maryland as well as to Baffin Island.

Eric's colonists kept up regular maritime communications with Iceland and particularly with Norway. It was during a voyage from Iceland to Greenland that Bjarni Herjulfsson was thrown off course by a storm and driven toward the Labrador coast.

Leif Ericsson set out in turn to find the country where Bjarni had landed. He even bought the latter's boats from him, and set off to try his luck. Old Eric the Red refused to come along; he preferred to stay and grow old in his own colony. It was during the course of this voyage that Leif discovered a rich new land, where the vine flourished uncultivated, and to which he gave another "well-chosen name": Vinland (or Wineland). The sagas often follow the word "Vinland" with the words "the Good" or "the Beautiful!" We must mention, however, that *vin* in Old Norse means "pasture lands" and that we must take care not to fall into an etymological error, in spite of the mention of the wild vines.

However this may be, since Leif made a note of the abundant salmon in the region, we are able to place Vinland with some accuracy; for the southern boundary of these fish lies at the 41st

---

[9] The most northerly of the runic inscriptions, found at Kingigtorsuak (72° 55′ N.), is believed to date from this period.

[10] The saga also gives her the name Gudrid; nothing, however, prevents us from supposing that Eric may have had two daughters; or the second name may refer to his daughter-in-law, who lived with him after her husband's death, and who subsequently was married to Thorfinn Karlsefni.

parallel, while the northern boundary of the wild wheat that Leif also saw and commented on lies at the 44th parallel; we may therefore permit ourselves to suppose that Vinland lay in the region between Boston and New York.[11]

Bjarni had "seen" and Leif had "explored," but it was Thorfinn who "exploited" the region, by organizing commercial voyages, by cultivating the newly discovered land with Irish slaves and by carrying on trade with the natives he met, probably Indians.

The enterprise became more complicated when Leif was converted to Christianity and thus came into conflict with his father, Eric. In 999, after a voyage to the Hebrides (where he married a girl named Thorgunna), Leif received an order from the Norwegian king, Olaf I Tryggvesson, commanding him to evangelize among the colonists. Christianity spread very rapidly. Three centuries later, there were eighteen churches in Greenland and 330 in Iceland; this widespread adoption of the new faith served the Norwegian cause, since, in 1261, the people of Greenland and, in 1262, the people of Iceland officially recognized the suzerainty of Catholic Norway over their territories.

Some years later, toward the end of the thirteenth century, the last ship departed from Greenland on its way to Norway; the Viking empire fell totally into oblivion, and no one has ever been able to explain the disappearance of Eric's two thousand colonists.

It was from Rome that the first cry of alarm rose, when it was noticed that the Bishopric of Greenland, although an important one, had not yet paid in its tithe to the coffers of the Papacy.[12]

The Pope's various emissaries "having found no one," it was decided to send an expedition in 1355. "Everywhere," says the Norwegian king's report, which was transmitted to Rome, "the land is like a desert . . . there remain only a few goats, sheep, cows and calves, in a wild state. Not a man is left, neither Christian nor pagan. . . ."

This expedition searched thoroughly over all the places where there was the slightest hope of finding the lost colonists, including America; inscriptions discovered in the nineteenth century in Minnesota and in the Mississippi valley seem to support the authenticity of this astonishing voyage, which recalls the wave of expedi-

---

[11] Michel Mollat, *Le Moyen Age.*

[12] Louis Kervran, *Les Celtes ont découvert l'Amérique au VIe siècle.*

tions that set out in the middle of the nineteenth century in search of Sir John Franklin.

In 1721, Scandinavia returned officially to Greenland in the person of Hans Egede, a missionary who wanted to come to the aid of the Greenland Christians; he found none, but he did not fail to evolve his own theory on the disappearance of the colonists. In his opinion, it was due to the lack of supplies from Europe, following the break in communications with Norway. The Eskimos took advantage of this situation to exterminate them. This supposition has not been altogether accepted.

Digging carried out by Paul Norlund in 1921 resulted in the discovery of a large number of bodies, remarkably preserved by the cold. All of them showed signs of dwarfing, weakness in the bones and sterility. Hans Egede had also found bodies; he had noted that the faces were "broad," the noses "flattened" and the skin "brown"; this gave birth to the theory that the colonists had been assimilated by the Eskimos.

Along with Nansen,[13] Stefansson[14] declares himself unable to explain the catastrophe. Both of them refuse to credit that the Black Plague of 1347 could have wiped out the Europeans without touching the Eskimos. Moreover, Norlund has demonstrated that European survivors were still alive in 1520.

Egede's theory, according to which a general cooling of the climate might have occurred after the colonization and disorganized the colonists' food supply to the point of exterminating them, does not find favor with Stefansson, who demonstrated between 1906 and 1918 that the white man could perfectly well live and feed himself in the Far North, all the more so in the southwest of Greenland.

Archaeological studies will perhaps tell us one day whether the extinction of the Viking colonists was caused by a change in climate, by the plague, by Eskimo attacks, or by the arrival of European "barbarians" who killed the colonists or led them off into captivity.[15]

---

[13] Fridtjof Nansen, *In Northern Mists.*

[14] Vilhjalmur Stefansson, *Unsolved Mysteries of the Arctic.*

[15] A document exists which proves that an agreement was made in 1432 between King Henry VI of England and the Scandinavian King Eric, bearing on the restitution of prisoners taken by the English in Eric's "dependent" territories.

In any event, the history of the first period of Arctic discovery finished in the most utter mystery. The Viking era had produced the discovery and exploration of vast hostile territories, from the White Sea to Labrador, from Baffin Island to Smith Strait.

Sir Clements Markham's admiration for the Norsemen (his ancestors, he says)[16] is shared by all specialists on the poles; all of them are dumfounded by the size and the extent of the Viking conquests, achieved as they were with such ridiculously limited technical means.

If we have only an imperfect idea of the voyages, the explorations and the achievements of the Vikings, we do possess much information on the practical means (boats, chariots, weapons, tools) they had at their disposal, and with which they wrote their epic.

For the Viking, the boat was more precious than the horse; it was the object of all his attention, and his reason for living.

One can readily imagine the emotions of the peaceful seaboard peoples as they watched the hideous dragons' heads approaching their shores, erect above the water's surface, and concealing behind them the fearful Vikings. These dragons' heads which decorated the prow of the "Sea-chargers" gave the ships their name: *drakkars*.

The *drakkar* was so much venerated and so precious that when a king or a chief died, the Vikings buried him with the boat he had commanded. To this custom we owe the happy fact that today we possess several examples of the *drakkar* in an almost perfect state of preservation.

In 1880, Nikolas Nikolaysen, president of the Antiquarian Society of Oslo, conducted diggings in the little Norwegian town of Gokstad; he succeeded in bringing to light a magnificent *drakkar* in a remarkable state of preservation, thanks to the clay in which the ship had been placed. With infinite precautions and despite numerous difficulties (the wood deteriorated on contact with the air), Nikolaysen ended by unearthing a veritable archaeological treasure.

First he found, along the sides of the boat, the skeletons of twelve horses and six dogs, as well as bronze horseshoes and dog collars. Then the ship itself was freed. It was 79 feet long. The

---

[16] *Op. cit.*

keel measured 64 feet; above, seventeen timbers had been mortised in; these supported sixteen planks on each side, the planks bound to the timbers with willow strips (not nailed), thus giving the whole construction an extraordinary elasticity, capable of withstanding the most furious assaults of the sea. Chinks were filled with three-stranded cowhair rope.

The ship was made of oak, with one deck only of fir. Sixteen sealable portholes opened on each side; thirty-two shields of 35 inches in diameter hid these portholes, and their black and yellow paint was perfectly preserved. In the stern, the rudder oar was in place, as were the thirty-two driving oars.

The burial chamber, which had been placed beside the guyed mast, was found, sacked by vandals; it was clear, moreover, that the robbers had broken into the sepulcher shortly after its erection. Nikolaysen and his assistants, in spite of all this, collected an ample number of objects and furnishings: belt buckles in various metals, clothes hooks, buttons, bits of cloth, leather purses, chiseled trays, and even a full chess set.

They also found small kegs, copper cauldrons, wooden bowls and water casks. The anchor was in place, as were the three small lifeboats. The digging also turned up an awning with carved stanchions, and a sleigh. The experts were of the opinion that the find dated from the year 850; it is today the pride and joy of the museum of the University of Oslo.

The second discovery of a *drakkar* was even more important. It occurred in 1903, and was the astonishing result of the minute and laborious work of Professor Gabriel Gustafson.

He had had first to overcome the greed of the Oseberg farmer on whose land the ship lay buried. A law had to be voted by the Norwegian parliament forbidding the export of archaeological treasures to prevent the peasant from selling it to Americans. Through the intervention of the future King Gustavus VI Adolphus, of Sweden,[17] himself a passionate student of prehistory, it was possible to compensate the farmer, and work on the digging could begin. It turned out to be of capital importance for the advance-

---

[17] From 1815, Norway as an independent kingdom had been united with Sweden in the person of the Swedish king; his sovereignty was acknowledged by the Norwegians, while they maintained their own constitution and their own parliament. This personal union was terminated by the Norwegian Storting in 1905; Sweden and its king, Oscar II, acquiesced.

ment of our knowledge of the technical means used by the Vikings, even though the burial chamber, which contained the skeletons of two women, had been pillaged, as at Gokstad.

Hundreds of objects were unearthed, among which were two iron cauldrons, a frying pan, hatchets, knives, a pocket wheat mill, two beds with their bedclothes, comforters, a large quantity of sheets and pillows, a keg full of wild apples, ladles, chests, platters, a saddle, carved bedsteads, a roll of tapestry, three looms, one for wool, one for lace, one for cord. The ship itself was 69 feet long, with only 30 oars; thus, it was slightly smaller than the Gokstad ship, which dated from the same period (*c.* 850).

But this discovery became the more important when there was found within the ship the remains of a four-wheeled chariot and four carved and painted sledges, alongside the skeletons of the ten horses which must have drawn them.

This *drakkar*, removed and reconstructed with remarkable skill by Professor Gustafson and his assistant Professor Haakon Shetelig, is presently to be found in the National Museum at Oslo; it is one of the most precious treasures of the Norwegian people, and of all humanity. Unfortunately, the robbers had made off with all the objects in precious metals, going so far as to chop off the ring-laden hand of the dead queen buried in the Oseberg *drakkar*.

We had to wait till 1939 for the rediscovery of an intact burial-boat at Sutton Hoo (in Suffolk, England). This *drakkar* dated from about 700; it was of more modest size and less well preserved. Robbers had visited it at the time it was set up, but had not been able to find the burial chamber.

A Saxon chieftain lay there surrounded by his treasures: a gilded iron helmet, a sword with a gold handle decorated with precious stones, a shield decorated with gold leaf. He was dressed in his full regalia, with solid-gold buckles and hooks. The burial chamber also contained a solid-gold purse with forty pieces of gold, a great quantity of gold and silver vessels, bronze cauldrons, and solid-silver drinking horns, their handles and mountings incrusted with precious stones.

Professor A. W. Brögger, Professor Gustafson's successor after the latter's death in 1915, devoted himself to the study of these discoveries and compared them with the sagas. He arrived at the conclusion that the half-paralyzed man who lay in the Gokstad *drakkar* was King Olaf and that the Oseberg *drakkar* contained the remains of Queen Aasa, the mother of Harold Fairhair, whose cruelty had forced Othere to flee to the Far North, the Barents Sea and the White Sea.

The crucial importance of the discoveries made at Gokstad, Oseberg, and Sutton Hoo is obvious. Thanks to them, we know what an extraordinary ship it was that the Vikings used in their Arctic conquests.

With its forty tons' capacity and its draft of only 35 inches, the *drakkar* kept an extraordinary hold on the sea at a speed of eight or nine knots: this was the speed attained by the *Viking*, which was built in 1893 on the exact model of the Gokstad *drakkar*, and which crossed the Atlantic with ease.

The Vikings were remarkable navigators; they made their way without compasses or even the slightest astronomical instrument with which to establish their position. It is generally supposed that the Norwegians knew of the compass only from the thirteenth century on; that they should have used it earlier seems improbable, since the sagas mention voyages made entirely blind through the mists. The Vikings thus relied on the sun, the moon and the stars whenever possible. But the seas they frequented were, as we know, extremely foggy.

One can imagine, then, what their sense of direction must have been like in order to make Greenland from Norway "blind," without even touching at Iceland. They must have been sensitive to the slightest changes in the wind, and they must have known how to navigate by running before the sea. They must have known how to interpret the smallest sign, like the humidity of the air, smells, colors, animal life, ocean currents. It is known that they carried birds with them, notably crows, which they released at sea in order to learn the direction of the land.

They certainly had a highly refined notion of time, though they possessed no clocks. On land, they told time thanks to various markings made on the walls of their houses, taking into account variations due to the seasons; at sea they could count only on their instinct, which allowed them to "feel" the latitude, reckoning from the length of the days and nights.

Nevertheless, it is not out of the question that they should, in the twelfth century, have had at their disposal a special instrument with which to measure the altitude of the heavenly bodies. It has been suggested that they observed the size of the shadow on the gunwale under certain conditions, from which they were able to calculate the sun's altitude even at sea. It is reasonable to suppose that on their voyages of discovery they used the "line abreast" system—that is, that the boats deployed themselves in a line, one in sight of the next—and that they could thus explore a vast extent of sea. Observation of the habits of the whale and of the movement of icebergs must also have aided them in their calculations. Thus, with no other tools than their own instinct and audacity and their exceptional talent for navigation, the Vikings were the sole masters of the northern seas for centuries.

3

THE RENAISSANCE

AFTER THE VIKINGS' marvelous, if practically useless, Arctic adventures, the Far North fell back into oblivion. Indeed, a sort of calm seemed to settle over the world, as if it needed time to catch its breath before the great explosion of activity of the Renaissance. Because of an almost total lack of communications—maps, printing, et cetera—the Norsemen's exploits remained unknown for a very long time; Stephen Borough (or Burrough), in 1553-54, believed that he was the discoverer of the North Cape, which the Viking Othere had rounded more than seven centuries earlier.

But beneath the shadows, the Middle Ages were making ready for the future. Thanks to lonely travelers, merchants and missionaries, and to the nomadic barbarian hordes, whole separate worlds were beginning to take note of each other's existence. While Islam, Christendom and the Chinese Empire traded ideas, information, merchandise and crossbow arrows, while the alchemists bent over their esoteric "*elixir vitae*" and their "philosopher's stone," certain men were gradually preparing for the great adventure of their planet: the irresistible conquest of knowledge and of the elements which was to reach its apotheosis some centuries later in the Russian cosmonauts' prodigious leap into space, while at almost the same time, an American atomic submarine burst through the ice at the North Pole with one thrust of its hull.

In the Middle Ages (which are arbitrarily held to end with the fifteenth century), the technical means available to man to carry on the conquest were partial, limited and slow.

It was only in the eighth century that the Arabs introduced paper into the Western world; in 751 they set up their first paper mill in Samarkand, where they employed Chinese slaves to produce paper from linen and hemp rags.

It was at about the same time that a new method of harnessing appeared among the desert caravans: the shoulder harness, which revolutionized the world by doing away with slavery, regarded as a necessity before that time. Man also learned to join the planks of his ships with nails; until then the timbers always had to be bound or mortised together. Certainly, except for the Vikings' admirable *drakkar*, the boats of the Middle Ages were ponderous and scarcely suited to the requirements of great voyages of exploration, as the elegant caravel was later to be.

Cannon did not yet exist; all that was required to convert a simple merchant ship into a man-of-war was to take soldiers aboard. The world had to wait till the end of the Middle Ages to see any progress in naval architecture.[1] Hull structures had by then become more resistant, and the "castles" fore and aft sturdier; then the "carrack," or galleon, made its appearance. Navigators had learned to use the compass and the astrolabe, but sailing, depending as it still did on very limited technical means, nevertheless remained an adventure; the Arab geographers had only just begun to make maps and charts, always incomplete and often false.

---

[1] See G. Fouille, *L'Histoire des bateaux.*

Certain men undertook astonishing nautical adventures, almost blind, but we know very little, alas, about them. The Basques and the Celts fished regularly off Labrador and Newfoundland and at the mouth of the St. Lawrence; but to avoid competition, the route, the currents, the winds and the techniques used were kept jealously guarded secrets, transmitted only from captain to captain. Thus the post of "pilot" [2] grew up, an institution that was to be put to such extensive use by the great discoverers like Columbus.[3] Louis Kervran points out [4] that a half century before Columbus's discoveries a royal edict had granted the abbey of Kerity-Paimpol exclusive right to the tithe on fish and other products imported to France from the distant lands of North America. These "anonymous" explorers must certainly have made some interesting discoveries, but they kept their findings secret; the time was approaching, nevertheless, when interest was to be rekindled along with the thirst for knowledge that was to inflame the Renaissance.

The Middle Ages practically forgot that the earth was round; since the earth was flat, there was obviously little point in thinking about the poles.

Certainly the Northern peoples, the Danes, the Frieslanders, the Swedes, were not cut off from the rest of the "*oecumen*." [5] They are known to have kept in communication with the Eastern countries. (The word "Russia" is, it might be pointed out, thought to derive from the Finnish word *Ruotsi-laiset*, used to designate the Swedes.) But no more than the southern border of the Arctic regions was ever involved in these relations.

The Arab philosopher Ibn Batuta, known as the "traveler of the era," must certainly have reached Arctic Siberia in about 1332. In his account of the voyage, he speaks of the huge fur-lined cloaks he had to wear, of the horsehide boots lined with wolfskin, and of the water which "freezes instantaneously, even when heated." He also speaks—doubtless for the first time in history—of

---

[2] The word "*pilotois*" from which "pilot" is derived is a Basque word meaning "magician."

[3] Columbus availed himself of the services of the brothers Pinçon from Dieppe; some think the credit for choosing the direction Columbus eventually took should go to them.

[4] *Les Celtes ont découvert L'Amérique au VIe siècle.*

[5] The Northern Hemisphere, the Southern Hemisphere being called the *anticthon*. *Oecumen* from the Greek οἰκυμένη: the whole inhabited earth.

"dog sledges which lead to the land of shadows." Here, of course, we are dealing with nothing more than a single isolated case which bears no relationship with the leading preoccupations of the period. Nevertheless, it indicates the extent of the Arab civilization at that time, a civilization to which the European sailors who were soon to set out for the Arctic owed a great debt.

The Arabs contributed not only navigational instruments but also a series of maps, which, despite their inaccuracy, display a universalistic conception of geography. The cartographers of the Middle Ages (the Arabs as well as the others) obviously were lacking in accurate information; they were satisfied to reproduce the maps of the ancients, while modifying them in the light of travelers' accounts.

We need do no more than glance at the world map made by the greatest Islamic geographer, Al Idrisi (in the eleventh century), in order to realize this. His world map-disc, though reasonably accurate for North Africa and for Chinese Asia, quickly goes wrong when it comes to the other parts of the world.

The world map in the great *Chronicles of Saint Denis*, which was drawn up in the time of King Charles V of France (d. 1380), bears witness to the geographers' ignorance; they continued to believe that the world was composed of three continents: in the north, they placed "Paradise," a fact which was later to amuse many polar explorers.

In the Middle Ages, the cartographers placed the East at the top of the map; we shall have to wait till the first serious voyages of exploration before we see the science of cartography make any real progress; at this period it was little more than a mental exercise, and too often an exercise of the imagination, sometimes with tragic consequences.

In order to convince ourselves of this, we have only to consider the errors of the Zenos. Two Venetian brothers, Niccolò and Antonio Zeno, were said to have accomplished a voyage to the North in the fourteenth century. Their descendants published an account of this "voyage" accompanied by a rather fantastical map. In it, all the lands are shifted from five to six degrees to the north (which in itself is not very serious, although it does, in any case, show that Pytheas knew how to measure latitude better than the brothers Zeno). But the sheer inventions and the geographical "finds" included on this map held extremely serious difficulties in store for the first English explorers who were to make use of it.

This very problematical "voyage" of the Zenos is one of the two voyages which are known (or supposed) to have been taken in the fourteenth century, the second being that of the young Franciscan, Nicholas of Lynn. In his Essay on the Astrolabe, Chaucer speaks with much respect of his contemporary Nicholas.

It was in about 1360 that the young Nicholas—of whose life, travels, and even origin we have very little knowledge—undertook a long cruise to the north. It is thought that he visited southern Greenland, discovered the ruins of ancient Viking colonies and met the Eskimos. He is thought also to have written an account of this voyage and drawn a map, going so far as to represent the North Pole as a magnetic rock surrounded by narrow waterways, the extremely violent currents of which smashed up boats in the neighborhood.

Nansen makes a great deal of the works of Nicholas of Lynn, which served as inspiration to many geographers, including Claudius Clavus, a Dane, the author of the earliest dated (1427) and signed map of the Nordic regions, along with a commentary. Greenland is represented on this map with astonishing precision.

Then suddenly, after so many years of inactivity and darkness—of retirement, as it were—the world awoke from its slumber; men became conscious of their planet. On all sides, there was an explosion of passion, adventure, creation. A kind of frenzy developed which was to last for two centuries and which ended in the organized conquest of our globe.

In the fifteenth and sixteenth centuries men became aware of new needs, both material and spiritual, and they set about doing everything in their power to satisfy them. They discovered spices and the perfumed products of the East, and they decided that they could no longer do without them; cooking, which had previously been a dull and tasteless business, the science of "pharmacy," and the religious liturgy, all suddenly needed pepper, cloves, cinnamon, nutmeg, ginger, camphor, incense. Silk (which cannot be destroyed by moths), gold and the precious stones attracted general attention. The Church, for its part, dreamed of setting out to the land of the infidel, to impose her faith on him. States became conscious of their national missions, and power. Commerce, politics, religion and the military instinct joined in the common endeavor.

This period of expansion, of explosion and adventure is summed up in one of the most beautiful tools that man has ever forged for himself: the graceful, the proud, the admirable caravel.

The Renaissance is the "age of the caravel." [6] The progress now being made in naval matters was considerable; ships were better; navigation was more precise, sailors were better qualified, organization was more rational; long-range navigation was born.

When Cabot, Cartier, Chancellor, Frobisher, Davis, Barents and their companions set off to attack the Arctic seas, and when, in the course of man's conquest of the poles, they began to chip away at the latitude, degree by degree, minute by minute, they would have at their disposal a far more carefully conceived, more precise and more ample technical arsenal than did their ancestors the Vikings, though even so it would be a long time before they succeeded in bettering their predecessors' achievements.

Christopher Columbus's famous *Santa Maria*[7] has long been a familiar image in the popular mind; it can serve us as a prototype for the ships of this period. A little less maneuverable than the oared galley, a bit lighter than the rounded commercial vessel, the caravel was a magnificent instrument, "easy to defend" and capable of beating up windward; this ability to sail against the wind—which was not possessed by the older sailing vessels—was in large measure responsible for the great voyages of discovery.

The *Santa Maria* was 128 feet long, 26 feet wide, drew 10 feet of water and had a capacity of 100 tons. She had three masts, with the mainmast in the center; a crows-nest for the watch was placed two thirds of the way up this large mast. The use of square sails, which were less cumbersome than the triangular Latin sail then still in use on other vessels, allowed both more varied and more reliable handling.

The crew and any passengers huddled together on the deck, where they slept,[8] ready to carry out any urgent maneuver that might be required; only the captain had a cabin, where he kept his instruments and his charts. The hold carried the cargo and provisions. These last were not particularly appetizing; the staple

[6] Jean Amsler, *La Renaissance*.

[7] Columbus's flagship was in fact called the *Marigalante*, but the Genoese rechristened her the *Santa Maria* and dedicated her to the Virgin.

[8] The hammock was not yet in use; it was to be imported from the West Indies.

was salted meat and dried vegetables washed down with strictly rationed drinking water. Still, when Columbus left on his great voyage, he calculated the needs of his crew on the basis of two thirds of a pound of meat or fish, a pound of biscuits, and two quarts of wine per man, per day. He carried cheese, oil and vinegar with him as well.

The weapons, which had been greatly improved, thanks to the ceaseless wars of the Middle Ages, were, principally, the cannon,[9] the harquebus, the crossbow and the side arm (sword, or lance). The boats also carried breastplates and helmets in case of skirmishes with unfriendly natives.

The principal improvement incorporated in the caravel was the rudder, which replaced the directing oar (or pair of oars) at the stern.

Of course, the rudder was by no means as highly refined or as sensitive as modern rudders are. It consisted of two essential parts: the main piece and the cheek. The main piece was a strong piece of oak which was attached to the keel by pintles or hinges. The cheek was fixed to the main piece just at the point where the latter entered the water; it was the projecting part of the rudder, and was composed of planks solidly fitted together.

The rudder's head entered the body of the ship through an opening called the rudder tube or "partner"; this head was pierced by a square hole (or mortise) into which was inserted the bar (or tiller).

This bar was set up on the lower deck on the vessel (on the orlop deck of a frigate, on the only deck of the caravel); the sailors on the latter managed the bar with the help of lines called tiller ropes. This was what was called "steering with a free bar." Rapidly, however, a new piece of apparatus came into use: the steering wheel.

Ships were in the habit of carrying a spare rudder in their hold, for the storm's shattering of this now-essential instrument was a frequent occurrence. Indeed, in combination with the sails, the rudder was henceforward to allow the sailors to breast the high seas

---

[9] At the beginning, the heaviest piece of artillery was fired over the ship's bow. Two or three smaller pieces fired a broadside from very close in; as the time required to reload was very long, only one round was fired, and the rest was left to the boarding party.

and to navigate against the winds without having to wait for a favorable breeze.

In this period of renewed maritime activity, a second type of ship was to be launched on the seas: the carrack, or galleon. The carrack was not to become as famous as the caravel, but its usefulness was beyond argument. It was essentially a combat ship, a ship of great bulk which was to hold its place till the seventeenth century, when it would be dethroned by the man-of-war. Heavy and cumbersome, the carrack carried a crew of from two to three hundred, and sometimes as many as five hundred passengers; in other words, it was not the ship for long-distance expeditions, still less for those to the Pole.

Henry the Navigator's[10] Portuguese sailors, Dias, Vasco da Gama and Magellan, all used caravels. The English navigators had ships similar to the caravel.

It is true that in 1514 the English built an enormous carrack, the *Great Harry*, armed with cannon of various caliber, nineteen of bronze and three hundred of iron. She was 164 feet long and displaced nearly two thousand tons; she carried a crew of 700. This extravagant vessel did not often go to sea, and she burned in 1552.

The history of the *Grande Françoise*, which was built at about the same time, was still more astounding; her size was so prodigious (the interior fittings included a chapel and a windmill) that she could not be got out of the port of Le Havre and had to be demolished in 1545. Houses were built out of the wood saved from her demolition. Such monsters were of little practical use, and when Sir Hugh Willoughby set out for the Barents Sea in 1553, following the route of the Viking Othere, his ship, the *Bona Esperanza*, carried 36 crewmen and displaced only 120 tons.

Along with the rudder, it was the compass that enabled navigation to take its giant step forward.

The compass took a good while to make its way around the world; it is generally felt that the Chinese had already invented it by 1200 B.C. Klaproth[11] has demonstrated that Chinese sailors were

[10] Henry the Navigator (1394-1460) was the son of John I of Portugal; born at Oporto. He was the patron of numerous voyages and expeditions.

[11] Heinrich Julius Klaproth (1783-1835), a great German Orientalist and

using it in 120 A.D. But it was not till the twelfth century that the compass made its appearance in Europe, passing at the time of the Crusades from the Arabs, who had learned of it from the Chinese, into the hands of the Christians.

The documents on this subject are extremely scanty; the most significant is a French poem by Guyot de Provins, a troubadour who wandered over the face of Europe toward the end of the twelfth century. In about 1190, he composed a "Bible," from which the following extract is taken:

Un art font qui mentir ne puet
Par la vertu de la marnière;
Une pierre laide et brunière
Où li fers volontiers se joint,
Ont, si esgardent le droit point:
Puis c'une aguile i ont touchié
Et en un festu l'ont couchié
En l'erre la mettent sans plus;
Et li festu la tient desus.
Puis se tourne la pointe toute
Contre l'estoile . . .
Quant la mer est obscure et brune,
Quant ne voit estoile ni lune,
Dont font à l'aguile alumer,
Puis n'ont-ils garde d'esgarer;
Contre l'estoile va la pointe . . .[12]

---

traveler; he wrote a long study on the origins of the compass in his *Mémoires relatifs à l'Asie.*

12 *They practice an art that cannot lie*
Thanks to the mariner's needle;
An ugly brownish stone
To which iron is drawn of its own accord
They have; they have taken note of just the right spot;
Then they have rubbed a needle there,
And they have set it in a straw;
They put it in the water without more ado,
And the straw keeps it afloat.
Then the point turns straight
Toward the star . . .
When the sea is dark and brown,

(In the beginning, the compass went by the name "guidestone," "lodestone," "mariner's needle" or "*marinette*"; it consisted of a thin magnetized needle supported by two straws floating on water in a pan. Sometimes the needle was inserted into a single straw; in any event, whenever an observation was to be made, the whole instrument was set afloat.)

It seems that Flavius Giosa of Amalfi, a Neapolitan sailor who lived toward the end of the thirteenth century, deserves the credit for having turned the compass into a precise and practical instrument; he mounted the magnetized needle on a pivot and enclosed the whole in a box:—hence the French word for compass, *boussole*, from the Italian *bossola*, meaning "box."

A lightweight cardboard disc was added, which turned with the needle; its circumference was divided into the thirty-two points of the compass, or rhumbs: the compass rose. The box or "binnacle" was set within gimbals so that it might be affected as little as possible by the ship's pitch and roll. This was already, at the very beginning of the Renaissance, the true marine compass, whose principal features were to remain unchanged to our day.

Users of the compass were not slow in noting certain anomalies in its behavior. The needle does not indicate the Geographic Pole; this is the "declination" (the angle between the geographical meridian and the magnetic meridian) which was discovered, so it is said, by Christopher Columbus himself. The realization of this phenomenon even gave him the hope that he might be able to measure longitude with it.

The notion of a Magnetic Pole took shape only much later; the North and South Magnetic Poles were, in fact, discovered before the geographic poles (the North Magnetic Pole in 1831, while the Geographic Pole was to be conquered in 1909; the South Magnetic Pole in 1909, while the Geographic Pole was not reached till 1911). It was also much later before anyone finally noticed that the masses of iron on board ships made the magnetized needle vary in its true heading.

When neither star nor moon is to be seen,
Then they light up the needle,
And they do not fear to stray off course;
The point turns straight toward the star . . .

With the compass to determine direction, it was still necessary, if one was to navigate the ship accurately, to have a means of estimating the distance already traveled. This was a difficult task; the ship's log had not yet been invented—it would not be till the seventeenth century.

Speed was estimated by the pilot, thanks to his own experience with winds, currents and the particular feel of his ship. As for time, it was measured by the hourglass (the chronometer did not yet exist); this method was all the more inaccurate since the helmsman, wishing to cheat a little on the length of his watch or "quarter," often turned the hourglass before it was empty; those who indulged in this practice were known as "sand eaters."

As a result of all this, it is clear that no map could be other than imprecise and fantastical. The appearance and the general acceptance of the compass was the determining factor in the widespread blossoming of maps for navigators. The maps of the Middle Ages were generally false, and the sailors placed their greatest trust in the "*portulan,*" or "*portolano,*" [13] a book giving the lay and description of the harbors and the coasts, as well as the directions of the currents and tides.

The first map drawn up according to information obtained by the compass goes back to 1300. It is known as the "Pisan Map" and does not include anything beyond Flanders and the south of England. The rest of the world was still unknown, and it was the explorers themselves who, often at the cost of their lives, were to sketch in its contours.

On these abbreviated maps, the point of reference was the compass rose; the system of parallels and meridians invented by Hipparchus in the second century could not be maintained, because of the difficulty of determining the longitudes.

Latitudes themselves were difficult to specify; they were to be found by observing, with the aid of an astrolabe, the altitude of the North Star.

The astrolabe (from the Greek: ἀστήρ, "star," plus λαμβάνω, "to take") was created by Hipparchus in the form of two, or several, circular hoops with a common center and inclined with

---

[13] These treatises on navigation, called *portulans* by the Genoese and the Venetians, were called "pilots" by the English and "sea charts" (*routiers de mer*) in Dieppe.

relation to one another so as to allow the user to observe the various circles of the sphere at the same time. In this form the instrument was called an "armilla." Ptolemy stripped it down to a single plane surface which he called a planisphere; hence the modern name for the stereographic projection of the sphere on the plane of one of its great circles.

The astrolabe, despite its many inscriptions which may make it appear complicated, is a simple instrument, which enables the user to measure the angle that a heavenly body makes with the horizon.

This instrument was to remain in use till the invention of the sextant toward the middle of the eighteenth century: England piously preserves Sir Francis Drake's astrolabe, which dates from 1572, at Greenwich.

Small, heavy astrolabes were built so that they should not be blown away by the winds; the English astrolabes used by the first polar explorers were about eight inches in diameter, and all of them included a ring through which the right thumb was passed when a reading was to be taken.

The compass, the astrolabe, a few inaccurate maps and naval documents, and the hourglass: such was the armor of the Renaissance polar explorer.

4

THE FIRST ENGLISHMEN

When in 1485 the King of France, Charles VIII, lent two thousand of his bravest soldiers to the young Earl of Richmond, he did not expect that he would thereby help to make England the first nation to explore the polar regions. For the Earl of Richmond defeated his foes at Bosworth Field and mounted the English throne as Henry VII; the Wars of the Roses ended in the victory of the red rose over the white. And for England there began a long period of internal peace, during which she devoted herself to her commerce, under the guidance of a king who had a very strong feeling for money and neglected nothing that might serve him in amassing it.

The riches of Spain and Portugal prevented the English from sleeping easy; more than one of them dreamed of reaching the fabled Indies without having to confront the Spanish and the Portuguese. As the Norwegians had declined in power over the past few centuries, the northern route alone lay open to the English, who set out to attack it with typically British courage and endurance.

A thoroughly hardened heart was required of anyone who set sail for a North which popular legend had peopled with frightful monsters and insurmountable dangers:

> The Middle Ages had filled it with "whales, or sea-oxen, as big as mountains" which overturned ships; sea-grasses, which, when they rose to the surface could "founder a vessel, no matter how large"; "shrimp or crabs of majestic size" that took hold of swimmers and killed them; sea-monsters with heads ringed in horns which were "horrible to look at, and all the more so for their flaming gaze"; or "ducks born from the fruit of some tree or other."

These monsters slowly disappeared from popular belief, but they gave way in the explorer's mind to the horror of the polar night and the frozen sea; the first Arctic pioneers carried their fear with them. This fear lasted for centuries, and hardly had man succeeded in overcoming it when the poles themselves were conquered. At the beginning, the notion of wintering in the Arctic seemed little more than a folly. Everyone was terrified of the interminable Arctic night; the discoverers were satisfied to make brief summer excursions by boat into these regions in their attempts to find the famous "great passage" to the Indies and to fabled Cathay. Stefansson estimates that this period of summer forays lasted till 1820, the time of the "great approach." [1]

Fear diminished little by little, as knowledge of the region increased. Certain experiences which were forced on the explorers by circumstance demonstrated that it was possible to survive the Arctic winter; it became a usual occurrence for ships to be icebound, and it was realized that man could easily subsist. When Stefansson set out on his immense voyage in the Beaufort Sea in 1913, carrying no provisions at all, *he was no longer afraid;* this

---

[1] Vilhjalmur Stefansson, *The Friendly Arctic.*

was only a year or two after Peary and Amundsen had planted their flags at the two poles.[2]

Still, it is not hard to imagine how entirely different the situation must have been in 1497, four centuries earlier, on board the first English ships to set sail for the North, the *Matthew*, commanded by John Cabot, whose name had once been Giovanni Caboto and who had first seen the light of day at Genoa; Cabot set off the race for the poles.

It is generally thought that he was the "first," modern polar explorer but that has not been conclusively demonstrated. Indeed, patient scholarship[3] has indicated that in 1472 the two kings Alfonso V of Portugal and Christian I of Denmark served as patrons to an expedition whose aim was to "explore the ancient Viking route." Joâo Corterreal was one of the leaders of this voyage; it reached Newfoundland by way of Iceland, the east coast of Greenland and Labrador. As a result, Corterreal bore the title of Discoverer of La Terra do Bacalhão (the "Land of the Codfish").

It has also been said that, at about the time of the Corterreal expedition, Columbus himself traveled in the north. Some historians suppose that he too was seeking the "great passage" and was trying to find it by going west when he discovered America. Nor is there anything to prove that he did not come to Iceland in 1476 to consult the pilots who knew the codfishing route. Christopher Columbus's son Ferdinand gives a lengthy account of this voyage in his biography of his father; but we possess no other proof of it than this. The controversy is still going on in our own day; the American historian C. E. Nowell[4] believes in the voyage, while the Spaniard Salvador de Madriaga[5] does not.

Unarguably, doubts do arise from the inaccuracies and historical errors that Ferdinand scatters through his account of his illustrious father's life. He has been blamed for committing a manifest absurdity when he claims that his father sailed his caravel more than three hundred miles north of Iceland without encountering the ice. As a result we hesitate to believe him when he tells of the admiral's

---

[2] Peary reached the North Pole on April 6, 1909; Amundsen reached the South Pole on December 14, 1911.

[3] Jean Amsler, *La Renaissance*.

[4] Charles E. Nowell, "The Columbus Question," *American Historical Review*, July 1939.

[5] Salvador de Madriaga y Rojo, *Christopher Columbus* (Madrid, 1940).

visit to Thule-Iceland, then to Jan Mayen Island, which he calls "the other Thule"; he even specifies that its latitude is 73 degrees, whereas the latitude of Jan Mayen is in fact 71 degrees. It is likely that much ink remains to be spilled over the Arctic aspect of the "Columbus question." [6]

At all events, we may allow ourselves to suppose that Columbus, as well as the Portuguese, considered it more worthwhile to sail for the Indies by way of the west. Against the gold and precious stones of the Indies, the meager resources of the north could scarcely hold their attention.

But the English, seeing that this way alone was open to them, hesitated no longer; they set out to attack the north, and in 1497 John Cabot's *Matthew* put out to sea with a crew of eighteen men and the blessings of his king. How much success was achieved by this voyage is not known, though it is known that Cabot later set out to sea with a flotilla of several vessels, one of which was to sink off the Iceland coast. It is thought that Cabot went down with her, and we do not know what he discovered. The beginnings of the English exploration of the Arctic were modest, as we can see, and they were to remain so until the great Willoughby-Chancellor adventure in 1553.

The first half of the sixteenth century, though it was a time when no major technical progress was made, still saw a certain number of European voyagers. The Portuguese made one further attempt in the north; the two Corterreal brothers, Gaspar and Miguel, the sons of Joâo, set out in 1500 with two caravels. They repeated their father's voyage, christened the lands they visited "Lands of Corterreal," then disappeared, in 1502.

At about the same time, Sebastian Cabot, the son of John, set off in his turn with three hundred men and provisions to last for two years; his return was mysterious; it is generally thought that he had an encounter with the northern fishermen and that they forced or persuaded him to give up his voyage.

Sebastian Cabot left England, and went into the service of Spain, in whose name he discovered Hudson Bay. He returned to England in 1548, and in 1551, he founded the Companie of the Mar-

---

[6] See Henry Vignaud. *Études critiques sur la vie de Colomb* and *Le Vrai Christophe Colomb.*

chants Adventurers for the Discoverie of Regions, Dominions, Islands and Places unknowen; he died in his bed in 1557.

Apart from Verrazano, this first half of the century may be regarded as the era of anonymous voyages: the Basques, the Portuguese, and the French traveled regularly to Newfoundland where they fished for cod, which they dried on the bare stones. As for Captain Thomas Aubert, of Dieppe, he brought back from Newfoundland in 1509 "seven savages with their weapons, boats and clothing." These savages used bearskins, sealskins, bark canoes, bow and arrows. Aubert worked for Jean Ango, who, at the request of a number of Lyons merchants, persuaded Francis I to finance an expedition to search for the "great passage." The king agreed to back the enterprise, and the Florentine Verrazano set sail for China, the land of silk, via the Arctic passage. He had four ships at his command, and it is believed certain that he rounded the North Cape (which he situated correctly at 72° N.) in 1523, ten years before Borough, its official discoverer; Verrazano, as can be seen, was seeking the Northeast Passage. The expedition lost two vessels before returning to port.

Verrazano set off again, in the *Dauphine*, and discovered the American continent: on March 7, 1524, after traveling eight hundred leagues west and four hundred north (in twenty-five days) Verrazano touched on the American coast, which he called "Francesca" in honor of King Francis. Going on northward by way of Cape Breton Island, he reached the polar circle. But as he was short of supplies, he returned to France. It is thought that he sailed once again to the Americas, and some say that a certain Jouan de Varassane managed to get himself killed in a battle with the American Indians.[7]

In order to continue his struggle against Charles V, Francis I decided to finance a new expedition to Cathay; in 1534, on the recommendation of Jean le Veneur, the abbot of Mont-Saint-Michel, he named Jacques Cartier as its leader. Cartier's expedition, which reached the mouth of the St. Lawrence in Canada is, of course, well known; if it is difficult to describe it strictly as a polar expedition, we must still recognize that it was of great importance to the Arctic voyages, for which it led the way. In fact, Cartier

---

[7] A. Hervé and F. de Lanoye, *Voyages dans les glaces du Pôle Arctique.*

made two voyages, the first in 1534 with two ships and six thousand pounds in financial backing, the second a year later with three ships and nine thousand pounds.

The three ships were the *Grande Hermine* of 110 tons' capacity, the *Petite Hermine* of 60 tons, and the *Emerillas* of 40 tons; they were difficult to equip, and an embargo had to be laid on the port of St. Mâlo in order to recruit sailors for them.

The French hunted the penguin;[8] they were familiar with maize, tobacco, and particularly with the native remedy for scurvy, which consisted of an infusion of Ameda-leaf.

Cartier, who had taken possession of Canada, and thus made France one of the great Arctic powers, died of the plague in 1557, a forgotten man.

But France was not yet ready to accept her polar vocation; she forgot the north almost entirely, despite the voyage made by the pilot Jehan Sauvage, of Dieppe, who rounded the North Cape in 1586 and who brought back from Archangel (which had just recently been founded), 250 enormous barges, loaded with salt, hides and grease.

By contrast, England had already affirmed her readiness to follow her own polar calling in 1530, in the famous letter written by the London merchant Robert Thorne to his king, Henry VIII. Impressed by Magellan's feat of circumnavigating the world by way of South America and Africa ten years earlier, Thorne drew up his own Declaration of the Indies in which he stated: "If the Arctic sea is navigable, it is certain that by sailing north as far as the pole, then sailing south again, we shall reach the spice islands by a shorter route."

(This was, we must point out, precisely the objective of the American submarine *Nautilus* which succeeded in accomplishing the feat in 1958.)

It was, however, only twenty-three years after Thorne's letter, during the reign of Edward VI, that a great expedition undertaken by Sebastian Cabot's "marchants adventurers" set sail for the north, on May 10, 1553.

It was commanded by Sir Hugh Willoughby and Richard Chancellor and, for the first time in history, its vessels were equipped

[8] The penguin is found only in the Arctic. Its cousin, the Emperor penguin (which is often wrongly called simply a penguin) lives only in the Antarctic.

specifically for the ice with all the devices that the state of technical progress allowed. In fact, this equipment consisted principally in the reinforcement of certain external parts of the ship and the insulation of the cabin section. The flagship, the *Bona Esperanza*, displaced 120 tons, carried a crew of 36, including a master gunner, a carpenter, two doctors and six merchants; Sir Hugh commanded it in person.

The second ship, the 160-ton *Edward Bonaventure*, was commanded by Richard Chancellor, the head pilot of the fleet, who was assisted by the two Borough[9] brothers, Stephen and William, as well as by Arthur Pet, all three of whom were to go down in glory in the annals of polar exploration. The expedition's third ship, the *Bona Confidentia*, displaced only 90 tons, and its twenty-eight crewmen were under the orders of Cornelius Durforth.

King Edward VI provided them with letters addressed to the potentates of the unknown lands through which they would be traveling; their mission was to find the Northeast Passage to China.

A violent storm in the Barents Sea separated Chancellor's ship, the *Bonaventure*, from the two others. As Willoughby and Durforth were unable to reach Novaya Zemlya, they attempted to spend the winter in Lapland, at the mouth of the small river Arzina. Two years later, Russian fisherman found sixty-four bodies along with Sir Hugh's journal, which ended in January 1554.

Richard Chancellor waited a week for his captain, then, as he saw no signs of his coming, he decided to carry out his mission. From Vardö, where he then was, he reached the White Sea and touched land at the mouth of the Dvina. He made a visit to the Czar, Ivan the Terrible, then called by the British the prince of Muscovy. He returned to England, having negotiated important commercial agreements, under which furs and seal oil would be purchased from the Russians, in exchange for English manufactured products. The elimination of German middlemen made the arrangement profitable for both countries.

After Chancellor's death, his former aide Borough, the commander of the *Searchthrift*, touched at Novaya Zemlya. But he pushed no further east, not wishing to risk his ship. The same waters were sailed by the Russians,[10] but their boats were more

[9] Also sometimes written Burrough.

[10] No one was to force the Northeast Passage before the Swede Nordenskjöld in 1878-80.

supple and faster than those of the English, thanks to their oakum joints.

Chancellor's voyage is notable in the history of the technical progress of navigation for the appearance of the arbalest (or more commonly, in English, the cross-staff). Chancellor used the cross-staff, an ancestor of the sextant, to measure the altitude of the sun above the horizon, and thus to determine latitudes; he preferred it to the astrolabe.

The arbalest (or Jacob's rod, astronomical stick, sailor's cross-bow, Golden Rod, Radiometer, Geometric Cross, Astronomical Ray, et cetera) consists of a graduated stem along which moves a disc or "target." The user places his eye at the end of the stem and slides the disc to the point where its lower edge forms a tangent with the horizon, while its upper edge is tangential with the heavenly body in question; a simple calculation gives the angle sought for.

The cross-staff's origin is obscure; the German cartographer and traveler Martin Behaim is thought to have adapted Ptolemy's "parallactic rules"; but we are now inclined to believe that Johann Mueller, called Regiomontanus, a German astronomer of the fifteenth century, is more likely to have been its real father. The cross-staff was to remain in use as a navigational instrument until the invention of the quadrant (or "English quarter," quarter of reflection, quadrant of ninety, shoehorn, et cetera) by the English astronomer Edmund Halley.

On the subject of navigation, it is worth noting that, during the course of his various voyages, William Borough made a large number of observations about the variation of the magnetized needle, and even systematized them in a *Discourse of the Compass and Magnetic Needle*, published in 1581.

It was some time after Chancellor's disappearance, in 1558, that an event occurred which was to cost England dear; this was the publication in Venice of the famous map of Antonio Zeno. Niccolò Zeno had discovered it, so he said, in the archives of his ancestor Antonio, who, with his brother Niccolò I was supposed to have carried out a great Arctic voyage in the fourteenth century. Zeno's map showed Greenland adjoining Norway, Iceland, a large island called Friezeland (between Iceland and Greenland), another Atlantic island called Icaria and sections of the American continent called Estotiland and Drogeo.

THE BEGINNINGS

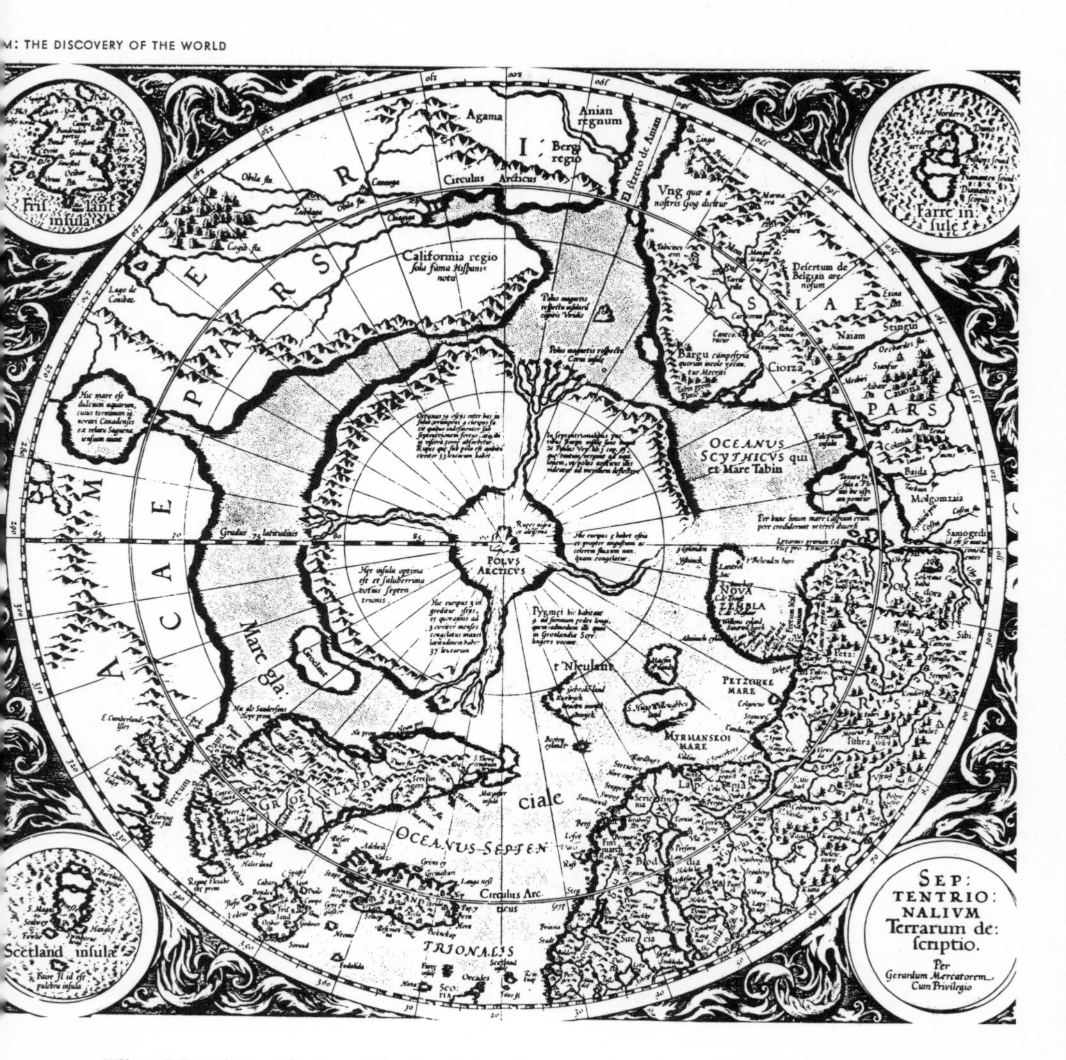

The Northern Polar Circle *(circulus arcticus)* as Gerhard Mercator (1512–94) imagined it.

Woodcut of a caravel, with explorers taking navigational measurements.

Sixteenth-century compass roses.

An early sextant.

uoir·treuuer

Maniere·de·treuer·Combien·

1583

An astrolabe.

A Viking ship.

(RIGHT) Barents and his companions, wintering in the Arctic.

FROM: THE DISCOVERY OF THE WORLD

Barents' hut, in which he spent the Arctic winter, 1596–97. It was dis

covered intact more than three centuries later by a Norwegian fisherman.

FROM: THE DISCOVERY OF THE WORLD

Eskimo's igloo. A shelter from the Arctic cold, unchanged over the centuries.

FROM: THE DISCOVERY OF THE WORLD

Cook's death.

FROM: THE DISCOVERY OF THE WORLD

(LEFT) John Ross and William Parry make contact with unknown "Arctic Highlanders" in Prince Regent's Bay, 1818.

The *Erebus* and the *Terror*.

(RIGHT) Dumont d'Urville's ship trapped in the Antarctic ice.

The *Astrolabe* and the *Zelée* (far left). This engraving of Dumont d'Urville's expedition shows his ships weathering a storm off the Powell Islands, January 27, 1838.

Men hauling a sledge across the ice.

Zeno was taken seriously, particularly by Mercator, the inventor of the system of projections which bears his name, in which the parallels and meridians cut one another at right angles. He was also taken at his word by English explorers for more than a century; as late as 1631, Luke Fox was to carry with him maps on which the imaginary Friezeland was to be found. In 1731, Hans Egede himself was to attempt to find the passage between Friezeland and Greenland, as Frobisher, relying on Zeno, had dreamed of doing; fortunately, this was to be the last error due to what certain historians have called the "Zeno forgery." [11]

Had it not been for the intelligence and the prudence of the first real Arctic pioneer, Martin Frobisher, his voyages of discovery in search of the famous "great passage" indicated on Zeno's map would have turned into a catastrophe. In fact, we owe Frobisher the credit for having explored part of southern Greenland, and for having been the first man to describe at length the Eskimos' way of life and the details of contact between ships and ice masses.

As a very young man, Martin Frobisher, who was already being described as a youth of great spirit and bold courage, dreamed of finding a northern route to the ocean that Magellan had discovered by sailing south; he had the polar calling. He allowed himself no rest until he succeeded in setting up an expedition; with the agreement of Queen Elizabeth (acting on the advice of the Earl of Warwick) and the financial support of the Muscovy Company represented by Michael Lock, Frobisher set off with his little fleet on June 17, 1576.

It consisted of two astonishingly small ships, the 25-ton *Michael*, and the 20-ton *Gabriel*, as well as a 7-ton pinnace to be used for soundings and short-range exploration.

Preparations were made down to the smallest detail; frequent conferences were held by Frobisher and his collaborators on the subject of the maps and charts they ought to take with them. Stephen Borough and Sir Humphrey Gilbert contributed the fruits of their experience, while one Dr. Dee taught the *Gabriel*'s commander, Christopher Hall, the art of navigation. The expedition's provisions were chosen with special care: biscuits, salt beef, butter, cheese, oatmeal, rice, raisins, almonds and licorice. The

---

[11] Markham, *The Lands of Silence*.

daily ration per man was one pound of food (before cooking) and a gallon of beer.[12] The stores also contained coal, wood and charcoal.

When the little convoy sailed out of Greenwich Palace harbor, firing its cannon, Queen Elizabeth, standing in a window, graciously returned the salute with her gloved hand.

The voyage began badly; the pinnace went down in a gale with four men aboard, and the *Michael* returned to port to announce wrongly that the *Gabriel* had sunk. Frobisher continued on his way nevertheless, still seeking for Zeno's Friezeland and Estotiland. In a storm, he had the gift of inspiring his crew by his own courage and his skill as a sailor. But it was not long before he ran into icebergs and ice floes. To protect himself from them, Frobisher invented a system which consisted of using the base of an iceberg for shelter, by anchoring to it or by carving a dock out of it. (This system was to be used later by many other polar navigators.) Frobisher describes at length the "fearful spectacle" of the ice smashing into the sides of the ship. "We felt our hearts fail at each blow," he writes.

Rounding Greenland, Frobisher thought he had discovered a strait that cut through it; he christened it with his own name, but he did not realize that it was nothing more than a deep bay cutting into Baffin Island. He gave names, moreover, to all his discoveries, calling them after his benefactors and collaborators; we need do no more than glance at the map to find in this region the names of Queen Elizabeth, Hall, Lock, Warwick and many of their contemporaries. Frobisher was to christen thirty different points in this way in the course of his three successive voyages, and set an example for future explorers, whose ambition was henceforward to be the inscription of their names on the unknown lands of the world.

During his voyage, Frobisher had frequent and friendly contacts with the Eskimos, on whose way of life he wrote at considerable length. Having noted that their homes were "very strange and beastly," he had his crew build a "cottage," which he decorated stylishly in order to show the savages what an English house was like. This house, intact and decorated with "all sorts of knick-knacks," was to be found nearly three centuries later, in 1860, when

[12] Beer was wrongly thought to be an effective preventive against scurvy.

the American Charles Francis Hall came upon it in the course of his search for the English explorer John Franklin.

"These savages are strange infidels whose like was never seen, read nor heard of before," Frobisher tells us. "They have long black hair, broad faces and flat noses and are tawny in color, wearing sealskins; the women are marked in the face with blue streaks down the cheeks and round about the eyes; their boats are all made of sealskin with a keel of wood within the hull."

Frobisher's men brought grasses and flowers on board as well as a few samples of a strange black rock.

Relations with the natives took a bad turn; a small boat with five men aboard disappeared. Furious, Frobisher succeeded in capturing a savage with his kayak; it is said that he managed this by attracting him with an ordinary hand bell, the strange sounds of which seduced and disarmed him. Frobisher took the Eskimo back to England, which he reached on October 9, 1576.

He and his men were given a delirious welcome by the Londoners, who, because of the false report of the *Michael*, had believed them lost. Michael Lock was extremely interested in the black stone that his friend had brought home; two scientists analyzed it and declared that it was nothing more than iron pyrites, but an Italian alchemist named Aquello succeeded in extracting from it—or so he claimed—a particle of gold.

Frenzy broke out. A new company, the Cathay Company, was immediately formed to exploit the rich deposits of "gold marcasite" in Frobisher Strait. A new expedition was organized. A 200-ton royal vessel, the *Aid*, joined the *Michael* and the *Gabriel*, and Frobisher weighed anchor for the second time on May 26, 1577. Having tried in vain to find the five men he had lost on the previous voyage, he abandoned his search and settled for bringing two hundred tons of the famous black rock back to London.

Immediately, a third expedition was set up, composed of a fleet of fifteen ships crowded with volunteers and professional miners. A prefabricated wooden house was even carried aboard one ship.

The expedition set sail on May 31, 1578.

Coming in sight of Greenland, which he still took for Zeno's Friezeland, he decided to land. With a sloop and a handful of men, he forced his way through the ice pack and went inland to visit an Eskimo camp; he thus rediscovered the Greenland which had been forgotten since the disappearance of the Viking colony.

He then headed for his "strait," which he found blocked by the ice floes; taking the lead in his flagship, with his other ships in Indian file behind, he tried to break the ice. He lost forty men in the adventure. Commander Christopher Hall mutinied. Frobisher, driven as he was by the demon of discovery, finally realized that his strait was only a bay, but succeeded all the same in entering Hudson Strait. Having to sail home with his cargo of black stones, he could not carry on his exploration. He filled his holds, and, as winter was approaching, gave up his original idea of founding a colony on the spot. He returned to England to learn that the black stone was valueless. He was a ruined man; there was nothing more for him to do but unload his cargo on the Dartford piers, where it has only recently been rediscovered.

Queen Elizabeth, who held a high opinion of Frobisher and called him her "loving friend," came to his assistance, promoted him to admiral and even knighted him. When he died at the siege of Crozon, near Brest, on November 22, 1594, the Queen was deeply saddened; she named no other admiral in his place.

"Among the Elizabethan worthies," Sir Clements Markham writes in *The Lands of Silence*, "Sir Martin Frobisher justly takes his place in the first rank. He was one of our great Arctic heroes."

5

THE FIRST ARCTIC WINTER

DESPITE THE RELATIVE failure of Frobisher's expeditions, accounts of them inflamed the popular imagination. The Nordic countries began to consider the possibilities of the polar lands, and this was particularly true of the merchants. Certainly the failure of the Cathay Company had for a time discouraged the English from organizing new expeditions: down to the end of the sixteenth century, the only explorers who dared to set out were Arthur Pet (1580), Sir Humphrey Gilbert (1583), and John Davis (in 1585, '86, and '87).

Arthur Pet and Charles Jackman attacked the Northeast Passage; their two ships, the *George* and the *William*, displaced forty and twenty tons respectively and carried crews of ten and six men. This was a very modest expedition indeed. Its results were modest too; the explorers discovered the strait that separates the island Vaygach from the Continent, south of Novaya Zemlya, and then their two ships were stopped by the ice. Only Captain Pet's *George* managed to return to London; he brought with him a series of soundings made off the Novaya Zemlya coast.[1]

Sir Humphrey Gilbert's attempt was catastrophic. His project was to found an English colony in the new northern territories; thus, he was following the Viking pattern. Queen Elizabeth granted him all the lands he might discover in return for one fifth of their riches. After two fruitless attempts,[2] Sir Humphrey succeeded in setting sail with five ships and 260 men. He lost three ships, and of the two that remained, small vessels of ten and forty tons, he was able to bring back to London only one.

The English merchant adventurers were not to be put off by these failures, and they organized three voyages, one after the other, under the command of a remarkable and intelligent sailor named John Davis. Davis had been fascinated by his reading of the *Discourse of a Discoverie for a New Passage to Cathaia,* written by his friend, the unfortunate Sir Humphrey Gilbert. With the help of Sir Walter Raleigh, who introduced him to his various silent partners, Davis was able to realize his dream and set out for the north.

He commanded the *Sunshine* (50 tons) and the *Moonshine* (35 tons). The latter's crew consisted of a gunner, a carpenter, eleven sailors and a cabin boy. Relying on Frobisher's assertion that these countries were inhabited by "sensitive" savages, he chose four sailors who were able to play music with which to charm them. Thus, the violin became, thanks to an imaginative and psychology-oriented man, a technical tool for the conquest of the poles. Davis personally oversaw the loading of provisions: salt beef, cod, biscuits, cheese, butter, beer and peas.

Davis's voyage was methodical; he ceaselessly wrote out minute descriptions of the regions he visited, complete with every specification that could be of interest in navigation. He visited the

---

[1] Novaya Zemlya, in Russian, means New Land.

[2] On the second try, Sir Humphrey was joined by his half-brother, Sir Walter Raleigh. A storm put an end to their attempt.

south and west of Greenland and called it the "Land of Desolation," because of "the irksome view of the ice."

He made a stop at Godthaab, which he named Gilbert Sound. Then he made contact with the Eskimos; the music won them to him, and he was able to buy leather suits and kayaks. He passed through the strait that bears his name, as far as Mount Raleigh, and explored Cumberland Bay, which he at first took for another strait. He returned to England, bringing with him an ample collection of observations on seals, whales and bears (of which he had killed five).

The account of his voyage inspired a great deal of confidence; he was able to set off again the following year, this time with four vessels chartered by the merchants of Devonshire; the *Sunshine* and the *Moonshine* were joined by the 120-ton *Mermaid* and a 10-ton sloop, the *North Star*. He was to explore the fjords and the coastal islands with a sloop which he had brought in unassembled pieces in his hold.

Rounding the southern tip of Greenland, which he christened Cape Farewell, in a violent storm, he stopped to visit with his old friends the Eskimos of Davis Strait, who greeted him enthusiastically. His friendship with the natives was so real that Davis's men organized jumping contests and even soccer matches. Having gathered a great deal of information on their way of life (he emphasized the "thievish" side of their nature) and their language, Davis went on his way with new volunteers aboard the *Moonshine*. He explored the eastern part of Baffin Island, and went as far as Labrador, where he got into a serious skirmish with the Indians; he then returned to London.

Having observed cod banks of considerable size (to which he had been led by sea birds), he immediately organized a third expedition; he obtained three ships (the *Elizabeth*, the *Ellen*, and the *Sunshine*) accompanied by two collapsible sloops, on the understanding that he would pay his expenses out of profits on his fishing.

Davis arrived in Gilbert Strait in June 1587. He sent the *Elizabeth* and the *Sunshine* on to take care of the codfishing and took command himself of the minuscule (20-ton) *Ellen*, which he sailed as far as latitude 72° 12′ N. in Davis Strait. He almost became icebound and had to beat a retreat. He later explored the lands discovered by Frobisher and found the entrance to the Hudson Strait. He returned to England with his holds full of fish, which easily paid the expenses of the expedition.

In spite of his desire to set off again, Davis was unable to do so, for the struggle against the Armada required the services of all Her Majesty's sailors; he died in 1605, in Malacca, at the hands of Malay pirates. He had made a magnificent record as a discoverer, leaving behind him fourteen new names on the map of the North.

From the point of view of the strictly technical aspect of navigation, we owe him credit not only for his inestimably worthwhile documents and maps but also for the development of a new instrument for measuring the altitude of heavenly bodies—which in turn serve to determine latitude—the precursor of the quadrant, and an obvious improvement over the cross-staff: the Davis "quarter," built on a sufficiently large scale to compensate for errors in graduation.

From the commercial point of view, we owe him credit for establishing the great codfisheries of Newfoundland and the fruitful industry of whaling. The account of his continual encounters with whales, coming before those of Barents and Hudson, set off a veritable whale rush at the beginning of the seventeenth century.

This century was also remarkable for the rapid rise of Dutch power, which was to result in their carving a great empire at the expense of the Portuguese. From the end of the sixteenth century, the Dutch sought a northeast passage to Cathay; the English invasion of their own trading center at Archangel forced them to seek new commercial openings. This was all the more true as they were the inventors of a new process for preserving fish: "sauring." At the top of the stove, which was a kind of stone oven, they hung fillets of fish; they then burned wood and ferns in the oven; the procedure depended principally on making the fire smoke as much as possible by using humid wood covered with a thin layer of earth.[3] "Sauring" allowed fish to be stored easily, and hence favored their exportation.

The need to find new markets for Holland, which had been independent since 1579, did not escape the attention of the immi-

---

[3] The expression "sour herring" derives from the name of this process; in England, it is generally known as kippered herring.

grant shipowner Balthazar Moucheron (originally a Frenchman) who persuaded the Dutch government to organize an expedition to this end; he would pay one third of the expenses himself.

The Dutch government offered a prize of 25,000 florins to anyone who found the passage, and it granted its blessing to Moucheron, who organized three expeditions; it was understood that if he were successful, he would be guaranteed the exclusive privilege of exploiting the new route for eight years.

On June 4, 1594, three vessels sailed from Texel Island under the command of Cornelis Nai,[4] on board the *Swan*. The second ship was the *Merkur;* the third, also named the *Merkur*, but now rechristened the *Gesandte*, had as its captain William Barents,[5] whose name was to go down forever in the history of the conquest of the poles, as having been the first man to have spent a winter in the Arctic.

Barents was a remarkable navigator, an accomplished pilot and a clever seaman. He carried with him the logbook of Arthur Pet, who, fourteen years earlier, had been stopped at the entry of the terrible Kara Sea. Parting company with the two other ships, Barents sailed alone, and ran into the Novaya Zemlya ice barrier at latitude 78° N. He beat a retreat and joined the two other ships, which had succeeded in entering the Kara Sea by Pet Strait and believed that they had discovered the passage to China.

They then returned to Holland, where a second expedition was organized by the Estates General; seven ships under the command of Cornelis Nai set out once again to sea. Barents was only head pilot, but in fact, he directed operations. This second expedition was also halted by the impassable ice floes and had to return to Holland; the only results obtained were soundings and the observation of a large number of whales.

These paltry results began to weary the Dutch government, which refused to finance a third expedition. Thus, Moucheron and his friends had to charter it on their own; it consisted of two ships commanded by Jacob van Heemskerck and Jan Cornelius Rijp. William Barents was again head pilot.

In 1596, the two ships discovered the small Bear Island, set between Norway and Spitsbergen, which they left to make an ex-

---

[4] Or Nay, or Naij.

[5] Or Barentz.

cursion to Spitsbergen, at latitude 79° 49′ N. After killing a bear and observing the variations of their compass, they returned to Bear Island, convinced that they had just explored a part of Greenland, which they named Spitsbergen ("pointed mountain").

After a few days' rest on this rocky and dangerous island, where there lived a large number of polar bears—which was the reason for its name, *Björnöya* (from *Björn*, bear, and *öya*, island)—Barents and his men set sail for Novaya Zemlya: Rijp, who did not agree with Barents's view of things and had had frequent arguments with him, decided to return to Holland.

Shortly after rounding Nassau Cape, Barents's ship was caught by the ice floes, which all but smashed the vessel. Impressed by the "terrifying spectacle of the ice pack moving with the sound of thunder," and seeing their ship badly damaged, the Dutch decided to take shelter. It was thus that on August 26, 1596, "in terrifying cold, in the blackest of misery," they came to understand that they would have to be the first men in history to spend the winter in the Arctic. They were seventeen men, and they were at that point on the northeast coast of Novaya Zemlya, in a bay which they named Ice Haven.

We owe a debt to the Dutch chronicler Gerrit de Veer, who accompanied Barents, for his detailed account of this first winter.

The first task of these unwilling winterers, after they had abandoned their ship, which was by then nearly destroyed by the ice pack, was to build a cabin. They managed this, thanks to the abundance of driftwood available, to which they added planks and ribs borrowed from the ship's forecastle. The hut was 33 feet long and 19 wide. They piled into it every object that seemed precious to them: provisions, weapons and tools.

A chimney set in the center of the building gave the roof something strangely like the aspect of a village bell tower; a fire was kept permanently alight. The sailors slept on wood cots arranged in a row along the back wall. A clock and an hourglass told the hours of the watch.

On the advice of the doctor, who was also the dentist, surgeon and barber, a Turkish bath was built out of a large wine keg.

An oil lamp, burning bear grease, hung from the ceiling. There were, all the same, times when this grease was lacking; we can imagine that handful of men, shivering in spite of the hot stones that they held pressed against their feet, terrified by the polar night, which "turns men mad," that interminable, treacherous and depressing night, which the human imagination had believed to hold certain death.

Fear must surely have been the dominating emotion in these men, who, for the first time, and in spite of themselves made the "great experiment" which Stefansson was to make in the twentieth century "for pleasure."

Barents did all he could to keep up the morale of his flock. By the flickering bear-oil lamp he read them Mendoza's *History and Description of the Great Chinese Empire*. Seated in a circle around the smoking fire, their backs frozen, the men listened to their chief, the "scholar" who would one day get them out of the spot they were in.

They trapped foxes, ate the flesh and made clothes out of the skins. They killed bears with a harquebus, cleaned them with a hatchet and saved the skins. They were even forced to fight walruses which attacked them. The ration of bear, walrus, and fox meat was supplemented with biscuits, lard and wine.

They had a small arsenal of various tools at their disposal. On September 7, 1871, the Norwegian Elling Carlsen,[6] in command of the *Solid*, was to discover Barents's winter quarters and was to find this little arsenal still intact, preserved for three centuries in the ruins of the cabin, which had been maltreated by the bears in the meantime. He found the famous iron clock, cauldrons, halberds, vases, pewter candlesticks, a bronze bell, leather galoshes which had belonged to the poor little cabin boy, cooking utensils, a tripod over which food was cooked, and a pile of miscellaneous objects.[7]

They also found navigational instruments (including a cross-staff), three books[8] and the Dutch translation of Pet's and Jackman's logbook. They were surprised to discover in a chest various edifying religious images with which it was doubtless intended to redeem the pagan souls of Cathay.

The cold became terrifying; the little cabin boy died of it. Barents himself was very ill, as was a sailor called Adrianszoon, who very nearly died. Scurvy began to have its effect. But the winter-

---

[6] Another Norwegian voyager, Gundersen, was to visit Ice Haven in 1875.

[7] These relics are now to be found partly in the National Museum in Amsterdam and in the Naval Museum at the Hague.

[8] A translation of a Spanish work on navigation by Medina, a Dutch chronicle and Mendoza's *History of China*.

ers held desperately on to existence. Thanks to their leader's discipline, organization and lucidity, these men conquered the Arctic winter for the first time in history.

Toward the end of January the Arctic winter's grasp began to loosen; spring was approaching, chasing away the wild animals, bringing a bit of light back with it, and little by little freeing certain sections of the sea. On January 13, 1597, so as to avoid all risk of having to spend another winter, the party decided to abandon their damaged ship, which had become unusable. They set off in the ship's boats.

Before going, Barents left a message, the first of its kind, giving an account of their story so far and of their intentions; this message was placed in the chimney of the hut.

The men piled their provisions into the two longboats. The two sick men, Barents and the seaman Claas Adrianszoon were each put in a separate boat. They entrusted themselves, as Barents wrote, "to the mercy of God."

When they rounded the northernmost part of Novaya Zemlya, Barents asked to be held up so that he could look at "that damned spot one more time." That day Barents asked his friend de Veer, the chronicler, to give him something to drink. He drank and breathed his last, followed shortly by the sick seaman.

On July 19, the sea was ice-free. Nine days later, the escapees met two Russian ships which gave them provisions. After a period of battling scurvy by chewing what little grass they found along the coast, they finally met the Dutch vessel commanded by Rijp; their sufferings were at an end.

The arrival in a bewildered Amsterdam of these ghosts dressed in bearskins with white fox caps, the heroes of the first great Arctic epic, marked the beginnings of Dutch power in the seventeenth century.

Queen Elizabeth was deeply impressed by the accounts of their exploit. No one had a healthier mistrust for the Dutch spirit of enterprise than did the English; and rightly so, for by the middle of the seventeenth century they were to see more than two thousand fishing boats flying the colors of the Low Countries.

And so the British merchants redoubled their efforts and multiplied the number of their commercial expeditions. The promoters included associations of London merchants (the Weymouth expedition in 1603); Sir Francis Cherrie (Stephen Bennet in 1603, who was to rediscover Bear Island which he named Cherrie Island in honor of his shipowner); and the Muscovy Company (Knight in 1606 and Henry Hudson, 1607; Poole, 1610, who was seeking a direct passage to the Pole, but had to satisfy himself with hunting walrus; Button, in 1612).

After Davis and Barents, Henry Hudson was the first man to leave his name permanently on the map.

Hudson had first distinguished himself by reaching, in 1607 while he was in the service of the Muscovy Company, latitude 80° 23′ N., in the region of Spitsbergen, a record which was not soon to be beaten. Returning from this voyage, he discovered an island which he named "Hudson's Tutches," and which was to become Jan Mayen Island when it was discovered for the second time by the Dutchman Jan May.[9]

Then in 1607, Hudson set out in his turn to attack the famous Northeast Passage. He too failed.

In 1609, in the service of the Dutch, he set out in search of the Northwest Passage. It was during the course of this voyage that he sailed up the river which now bears his name and that he founded the colony of New Amsterdam, which was later to become New York. Irritated by all this, the English took him back into their service, so that it was under the British colors that he discovered the famous bay that bears his name. His ship was a good and handsome sailing vessel, the *Discovery*, the first of its name in a long series of polar ships.

Hudson and his crew had suffered a very harsh winter; their privations led his men to mutiny, and Hudson, for all his gentleness of character, could not manage to dissuade them. His crew's revolt cost him his life; in 1611 the mutineers set him adrift in a longboat with five sailors who had remained loyal and his son John, unarmed, without provisions; and he disappeared.

Some of the guilty men met with immediate punishment; five of them were massacred by the Indians. In order to feed themselves, the others had to kill sea birds, out of whose bones they manu-

[9] Marthe Emmanuel cites an ancient naval chart of fairly great precision made by the adventurer Jean Vrolicq who haunted the Spitsbergen region between 1618 and 1634. On it, Spitsbergen is called "Arctic France" and Jan Mayen Island is called "Richelieu's Island" or "Bluff Island." Vrolicq claims to have been the first discoverer of this island, in 1612.

factured a kind of paste to use for tallow. The *Discovery* nevertheless made its way back to London and was ready to set off again the following year (with, of course, another crew) along with Sir Thomas Button's *Resolution* in an abortive attempt to find Hudson and his companions.

In 1615, the same *Discovery* set sail with another very great explorer aboard; this was William Baffin, who made more progress on the Northwest Passage question than anyone before him. Having reached the conclusion that Hudson Bay would not lead him far, he decided to conduct his research farther to the north, beyond Davis Strait.

With the small but valiant *Discovery*—which had a capacity of only fifty tons—he reached the point on the Greenland coast where, in 1910, Rasmussen was to found Thule (which has since become an enormous American air base). He then discovered Smith Sound. He was halted by the ice at latitude 78° north. It was there that he made note of the greatest variation—56 degrees—in the magnetized needle; without knowing it, Baffin had passed very close to the North Magnetic Pole.

Baffin's achievement was not to be bettered until the first half of the nineteenth century. His observations were numerous and varied. They dealt with magnetism, as we have seen, and with the ice floes; he even measured an iceberg 230 feet high. He studied the patterns of the tides and currents of the Arctic seas, as well as the life and customs of the natives he encountered.

Above all, Baffin was the first man to determine longitude by the "lunar distances" procedure; this achievement alone is sufficient for Markham to speak of "his genius as an inventive observer." To determine the longitude of any point by this procedure, one first measures the angular distance between the center of the moon and a particular planet or star at a given moment, establishing the time, by Greenwich Observatory, to which, according to certain tables, this distance corresponds.

These tables are contained in publications known as nautical almanacs; they indicate the angular distances at three-hour intervals for every day of the year. If the value of the angle obtained coincides precisely with one of those in the table, one simply notes the hour inscribed opposite the appropriate angle. The calculation of the longitude is an easy matter, as it comes down to a simple measurement of times; one need only compare the exact local time with the time at Greenwich meridian. This method was first outlined by the Nuremberg scholar Johannes Werner, in 1514.

Baffin had available to him the astronomical tables of John Searle, which provided lunar distances for the meridian of London, as well as those of David Origenus with the same figures for the meridian of Wittenberg. Moreover, they both included a list of particular points with their latitude and longitude in time, as well as a conversion table from degrees and minutes into time.[10]

On June 22, 1615, Baffin, who then lay opposite Salisbury Island in Hudson Strait, saw the sun and the moon both in the sky at the same time; he immediately took his bearings and read off the angular distance between the two bodies; since his instruments were not large enough, he was unable to measure the angle of 104 degrees between them, but he deduced this angle from the difference in azimuths.[11]

The exactitude of this result was to remain an object of admiration to all the navigators who followed him in these regions. To do homage to him, Sir William Edward Parry christened a nearby island with the name Baffin in 1821.

As we can see, the equipment of the navigator was becoming quite extensive. The azimuth compass with a movable arm (or alidade) was in use, although the marine compass was still a precarious instrument, liable to be influenced by the iron in the ship. The telescope was in existence; it had four lenses and a large number of diaphragms. At night it was replaced by the two-lensed Galilean glass. The rudimentary barometer enabled the sailor to foresee storms. Finally, the navigational arsenal included the quadrant, along with navigational charts and documents, though these last were still in their infancy.

Striking improvements were made in the ships themselves during the seventeenth century; this was the period of the great sailing ships, with superstructures that took the traveler's comfort more seriously into account than ever before. More care was lavished on their construction, and they were more solidly built, than in

---

[10] Longitude is measured either in degrees—as latitude is—or in time; one hour equals 15 degrees of longitude.

[11] The azimuth is the arc of the heavens extending from the zenith to the horizon, which it cuts at right angles.

the period of the caravels. It was the Dutch who boasted the best fleet in the world, and the most famous shipyards.

Various models were in use;[12] the yacht, a veritable nutshell, was the smallest, and the ship-of-the-line the largest. The frigate was a miniature man-of-war, and the store ship was specially designed for transport. The ship preferred by the explorers was to be a vessel of between 200 and 300 tons, drawing very little water; it was armed with a few guns and could be handled by a crew of twenty-five.

The English and the French were to begin by imitating the Dutch; they would end, however, by outdoing them in the delicacy and minute accuracy of their shipbuilding.

It is worth pointing out that it was during Baffin's time, in 1620, that the merchantman *Mayflower* made her celebrated Atlantic crossing. This was also the era of the *Sovereign of the Seas* (1637), the first great English three-decker, and of the revolutionary French ship, the *Couronne* (1638), which was 205 feet long, with a mainmast 189 feet high. It was a remarkably fine sailer; with its 72 guns, it was to remain for two centuries the image of the ideal sailing ship.

The ship's rigging (the whole system of ropes supporting the masts and used for handling the sails) in use at the beginning of the seventeenth century would hardly change at all over the next 150 years. Only the bowsprit and the mizzenmast would be slightly modified, the mainmast and the foremast remaining unchanged till the final disappearance of sailing ships altogether.

The whaler, finally, was one of the most widely used ships in the seventeenth century; she was a highly functional craft, designed exclusively for the task of hunting the earth's largest mammal, whose favorite waters have always been the coldest seas. In man's conquest of the poles, whaling was to be one of the great motivating forces and was to form one of the most important steps along the way to that conquest.

---

[12] Pierre Charliat, *Trois siècles d'économie maritime.*

6

THE FIRST SEXTANT

It seems that, during the whole of the Great Century (the seventeenth) and during the first half of the eighteenth, no progress was made in polar exploration. Between Baffin (in 1615) and Bering (1740)—nearly a century and a half—there is a remarkable absence of great names.

Of course, the efforts of Munk, Foxe and Egede are not in the least negligible, but we have to wait till 1778 to see, in Captain James Cook, the first great explorer after Hudson and Baffin. For more than a century little was achieved.

It almost seems as if the explorers were waiting for new, more precise, more certain and more extensive technical means before setting out again. When, at the beginning of the nineteenth century, these became available, the real "assault," as Gustave Lambert called it, was to begin, and it was to end only when Commodore Peary planted his starry banner at the "roof of the world" in 1909; men were then to turn their attention toward the south and were to carry on, down to our own day, the methodical conquest of those terrifying and fascinating regions. Of the Antarctic nothing was known before Cook.

In 1701, Sir Edmund Halley, the celebrated astronomer, carried out a scientific mission in the Southern Hemisphere without ever suspecting the existence of the Antarctic continent. In 1708, William Dampier, who was known as "the great freebooter," sailed to latitude 60° 58′ S. but pressed on no further. On the other hand, the French mathematician and geometrician Frézier deserves the credit for first guessing the existence of an Antarctic continent; in 1712, his ship encountered floating ice, and Frézier deduced that this could only derive from a nearby land mass. In 1721, the Dutchman Roggeveen passed very close to the continent; in fact a storm pushed him to latitude 62° 30′ S. He saw the South Shetland Islands without drawing any general conclusions from them. This is an indication of the world's ignorance of the Antarctic continent before Cook's voyages.

To the north, the poverty of means of investigation, the mediocrity of the instruments available and the lack of methods of exploration put a stop to all progress. The merchants preferred to turn their attention to the Indies, while the whalers and the herring and cod fishermen were satisfied to exploit the regions that were already known.

But one day in 1665, an apple fell from a tree in an English garden; this event formed the point of departure for Isaac Newton's genius and for the upsetting of many previously held human concepts. Slowly, discretely, progress was carrying out a series of dress rehearsals; people were searching, experimenting, trying, improving. General ideas were growing more precise; there was an abundance of apparently small finds. Such-and-such a new instrument would appear, as the chance events of some voyage or other might have it, to add its contribution to the march of progress.

It was, for example, during the course of a voyage made by

Luke Foxe[1] in 1631 that we see the log line used for the first time. Certainly, some people have held the belief, based on an obscure passage in Antonio Pigafetta,[2] that Magellan used the log before him. But the first definite mention of its use occurs in Foxe's account.

Invented in England, possibly in 1576 by a certain Humphrey Cole (who was the manufacturer of Frobisher's navigational instruments), the log line provided a great improvement in the sailor's ability to judge his own velocity, since it enabled him to measure the distance traveled by a ship in a given amount of time, from which he could deduce its speed.

The log consists of three parts: the ship (or chip), the line and the reel. The ship is a piece of wood about eight inches long, in the shape of an isosceles triangle. It floats with two thirds of its length underwater and is held upright by a lead weight. The line is a thin hemp cord rolled on the reel and attached by three bridles to the three top corners of the log ship.

The so-called log ship is thrown into the sea, where it rides practically motionless in the water. The length of the rope unwound over a given time indicates the distance traveled by the vessel during that time.

The line is measured out by knots into a certain number of divisions; the knots occur every 50′ 8″ (1/120 of a nautical mile). Time was measured with a 30-second hourglass. If then, for example, the line unrolled eight knots in 30 seconds, it was said that the vessel was "making eight knots" which was equivalent to saying that it was traveling at eight nautical miles per hour (a little better than nine land miles).

The log obviously left room for a good deal of error, since its use was based on the assumption that the chip would ride absolutely motionless. It was inconvenient and scarcely accurate, but it was nonetheless of considerable assistance to sailors; dead reckonings became more nearly exact. The navigator who had till then judged his speed by eye, taking into account the winds and his ship's sailing trim, now at last had a real measuring instrument at his disposal. The buoy log was to remain in service till the nineteenth century, when it would be replaced by the patent log.

---

[1] Or Fox.

[2] Markham, *The Lands of Silence.*

The problem of astronomic reckoning (the astrolabe, the Jacob's rod and the Davis quadrant were hardly precise instruments) would have to wait for the appearance of the octant, which was then to give way to the sextant, whose use would become general in the second half of the eighteenth century. It would attain a precision of within one sixtieth of a degree.

To measure the altitude of a heavenly body above the horizon, in other words, the angle between that body and the horizon, the only rational way to proceed is to sight them both simultaneously, while bringing their images in line with one another by some device or other. After several timid tries by Davis and especially by Hooke, it was Newton who brought this device into being, by utilizing double reflection on mirrors.

The principle of the octant (the eighth part of a circle), which was to remain in fashion for half a century, is contained in this elementary theorem: If one observes an object reflected by two mirrors perpendicular to the same plane, the angular distance between the object and its image is equal to double the inclination of the two mirrors.

When one wishes to observe the angular distance between two heavenly bodies with the aid of a sextant, one sights the first directly through the transparent part of the small mirror. Then one holds the instrument in the plane of the two bodies, while moving the alidade (the arm of the instrument) which pulls the large mirror along with it. When the image of the other body is superimposed (by a double reflection) on the body sighted directly, one reads off the distance indicated along the rim. The real angular distance is double the distance indicated by the instrument.

If one wishes to obtain the altitude of a body, all that is required is to make the image of the body in question coincide with the horizon line.

Newton had found the principle, but it was the astronomer Halley (famed for the discovery of the comet which bears his name) who, in 1731, produced the model of the first instrument built on the principle of double reflection; it was still the same instrument, in its conception, which was to be used by Peary to make certain that he had reached the North Pole in 1909. Henceforward, the sailor would have a simple instrument available to him with which to calculate latitude.

The determination of longitude remained a precarious business and was to find a satisfactory solution only with the introduction of the chronometer, which, as we shall see, Captain Cook carried with him in 1772.

These advances, it must be made clear, were slow and far from spectacular. The tally of polar explorations over this period reflects this. They consisted—for the whole period down to Parry in 1818—of ships making summer forays beyond the polar circle. When the bad weather approached, the explorers beat a retreat, terrified at the prospect of wintering in the interminable night.

For nearly two centuries, every winter spent in the Arctic was an involuntary accident. The accounts of these adventures demonstrate to the full the horror felt by the unfortunate icebound voyagers. *God's Power and Providence*—runs the title of one of these accounts—*shewed in the Miraculous Preservation and Deliverance of eight Englishmen, left by mischance in Greenland Anno 1630 nine moneths and twelve dayes*. Other pamphlets published in Amsterdam at about the same time bear such titles as: *A journal kept by seven sailors on St. Maurice Island in Greenland in 1633, 1634, where they passed the winter and where all of them died*. Or: *The journal of seven sailors who wintered in Spitsbergen in 1633, 1634, with an account of their adventures, sufferings, and struggles against bears and whales, amid terrible cold and fearsome storms. They died in 1635*. Or yet again: *The true and brief story of 42 persons who perished in Spitsbergen in 1646*. None of these journals or tragic accounts was likely to reassure the public—or any future explorer, for that matter.

On this subject, we must point out a slight failing in the polar explorers: they did not hesitate, in their accounts, to depict good-naturedly their anguish and their sufferings, which were sure to give them something of the look of heroes and which often moved those who had sent them to raise their salaries. This cult of heroism has been long kept up by the explorers, and by some of the greatest.

And, even if it has now been proved, for over a half century, that it is possible to live in the polar regions as well as anywhere else in the world, provided that one knows how to adapt to the altered conditions of life, still the "polar halo" is, even in our own day, deeply etched in the public mind.

This is true to such an extent that, when Byrd flew over the

South Pole aboard a comfortable airplane in January 1956—after numerous airborne crews from the American expedition of the International Geophysical Year had done the same thing many times over during the course of the preceding months, and at a time when a station was under construction at the same point—the newspapers of the entire world announced this flight as a "unique exploit," while all that was really involved was a routine flight.

Fortunately, the modern explorer no longer has any psychological problem—or hardly any. He goes because it pleases him to work in the polar regions rather than elsewhere. He does not feel that he will become a hero simply for this reason. He does not expect to suffer, and, as a result, he usually doesn't.

But during the period that we call heroic—which, in many ways, it was—it was in certain men's interest to be taken for heroes and to preserve the hellish reputation of the polar regions; men with the call turned up all the more rarely, and the fishermen as well as the fur traders could get on with their business in the midst of the ice floes. This is how they managed to sell "unicorn horns" to the gullible, which were in fact the teeth of the narwhal.

Moreover, anonymous explorations were to continue through the seventeenth and eighteenth centuries, with the same intensity as before, despite the lack of official exploration. This was all the more the case as, at the beginning of the seventeenth century, the major official explorations got off to a bad start with the catastrophic winter camp of Eriksen Munk [3] in 1619.

With two boats flying the colors of King Christian IV of Denmark, the *Lamprenen* (Lamprey) and the *Een-Hiorningen* (Unicorn), Munk entered Hudson Bay, where he became icebound and decided to winter at Port Churchill. He worked out the longitude of this point, by the way, with remarkable accuracy. As it happened, an eclipse occurred on December 20, 1619 at 8 P.M. The same eclipse was observed in Paris at about 3 A.M. Munk concluded that Port Churchill and Paris were seven hours apart:

"If we assign the value of 15° to the hour," he wrote in his account, "it appears that the meridian of our point lies 105° from that of Paris."

During his winter stay, Munk lost the greater part of his men, killed by scurvy and cold. Munk and three other survivors suc-

---

[3] Or Munck.

ceeded in returning to Bergen on September 25, 1620. This tragic adventure did nothing to increase the number of Arctic vocations, particularly as the general picture included, as a final detail, the death of James Hall in 1610, at the hands of an Eskimo.

Thus, it required a good dose of courage for Luke Foxe ten years later to undertake a voyage in the old 70-ton gunboat *Charles* with a crew of twenty-three and provisions for eighteen months. Foxe was a student of Henry Briggs, the mathematician to whom we owe the perfecting of the logarithmic system (invented by Napier), which he accomplished by giving it a decimal base. Foxe, then, had a solid scientific background. He set sail on May 5, 1631.

A second expedition left England at the same time; it was under the command of Thomas James. The navigational instruments Captain James took with him included: a quadrant with a semidiameter of four feet, an equilateral triangle with a radius of five feet, a quadrant two feet in semidiameter, two staffs (one of seven feet, the other of six feet), a Gunter's cross-staff [4] (also called the logarithmic rule or slide rule), various instruments for reading angular altitudes which had been used by Davis, meridian compasses, numerous magnetic needles, a loadstone to "refresh" the needles, a clock 5½ inches in diameter, a smaller clock, several small hourglasses, the geographical documents of Hakluyt and Samuel Purchas, as well as all the most recent mathematical books.

Foxe and James dined together, and each set off in his own direction. Foxe discovered several islands and capes (Foxe Basin is to be found still on the map) and returned to England, without daring to spend the winter, but without having "lost one man, nor boy nor any manner of jackling." He published an account of his voyage, which many consider an authentic masterpiece of Arctic literature.

James, whose wish it had been to take on board neither married men nor any man who had already seen the ice floes, wintered at Charlton Island and experienced "terrible suffering." It was only with great difficulty that he was able to repair his ship. The crew forced James to return home.

The results of these voyages were extremely modest, but they

---

[4] Edmund Gunter, the English mathematician (1581-1626) was the inventor of the slide rule; the year 1631 marks the first appearance of a slide rule as part of a navigator's equipment.

deserve credit for having created an Arctic tradition within the Royal Navy.

The merchants, for their part, had not given up the battle, and they gave striking proof of this by founding the Hudson's Bay Company in 1668; a charter guaranteed the company sovereign rights over the Bay and over Hudson Strait, where trading posts were soon founded.

We might point out that this exclusive English presence in the Bay was due at least in part to a Frenchman, Groseilliers, who, having had his own plans for colonization rejected by France, offered his services to the English. He had wintered on the banks of the Rupert River in 1667 and built Fort Charles, the first English establishment in that area.

The Hudson's Bay Company was an undeniable success. It held full trading rights from the Crown until 1869, after which it engaged only in the fur trade.

The Northwest Passage, blocked as it was, turned out to be more fruitful for commerce than the Northeast Passage, where John Wood failed once again, in 1676, to make his way; his new frigate, the *Speedwell*, ran up on a reef. The crew took refuge on a spit of land off Novaya Zemlya "surrounded by bears." The expedition's second ship managed to save them and brought the whole party back to London.

During this period, technical progress was slow. Ships, especially those used in war, underwent certain improvements. The hull became sharper-bottomed; the forecastle was cut down; the rigging was perfected, and construction became sturdier. The Dutch flute (from 150 to 300 tons), a ship designed for commerce on the high seas, was the acknowledged champion of fast sailers.

Freebooting and pirate raids interested men more than polar exploration. Indeed, the voyage to Lapland made by Jean François Regnard in 1681 went entirely unnoticed; Regnard wrote a lengthy description of the Lapps' way of life; he was astonished to meet with sleds more than ninety miles beyond the Arctic Circle.

This was the period of Voltaire's *Micromegas*, the book in which he makes such witty fun of Maupertuis and La Condamine, two scientists who were later to measure the meridian in Lapland and in Peru (in 1736). Geophysics, which was to grow to such an extraordinary extent in our own day, was born.

In the same period, a young Swedish scientist, Karl von Linné,[5] was becoming interested in polar vegetation, and was beginning to work out a system of classification based on the appearance of the sexual organs of these plants; botanists were finally provided with a universal language. Linné, or Linnaeus, had a number of disciples, among whom were Hans Egede and his son, who deserve the credit for returning Greenland to Europe, in 1717. Egede, who was an Evangelical missionary, wandered over Greenland in search of any trace of Eric the Red's colonists. He found only Eskimos, whose friend he became. The Egedes, in their *Description of Greenland,*[6] proved themselves to be excellent ethnologists and naturalists; this book was for a long time the "breviary" of polar explorers, as Pierre Charliat called it.[7]

Another explorer set out to sea at nearly the same time as Egede; his name was Vitus Bering, and his voyage was to mark the start of the Russian rush to the Far North.

There are in the North Pacific Ocean, not far from the Arctic Circle, two little islands, three miles apart. When it is noon today on the smaller, it is noon "yesterday" on the larger. But these two islands—the Diomedes—are separated by more than the international dateline; one of them is American and the other Russian. A more formidable barrier than the sea or the ice separates them: the border between two continents, the frontier between two different worlds. These two islands are the farthest outposts separating two giants which never cease to observe one another.

---

[5] His true name was Carl Nilsson Ingemarsson, but he affected a Latin name —as was fashionable at the time—Linnaeus, which in its turn has been Gallicized into Linné. The *Larousse* Dictionary even speaks of Charles de Linné.

[6] In fact the *Description of Greenland* is the work of Hans Egede alone. Povel, his son, is the author of a sequel to this work: the untranslated *Relationere betreffende den Groenslanske Mission, Tilstand og Beskeffenhed* (Copenhagen, 1741).

[7] Charliat, *Trois siècles d'économie maritime,* p. 134.

7

THE FIRST RUSSIAN

We need do no more than glance at the map in order to understand the interest taken by America and Russia in the polar regions, in the past as in the present.

The Americans became conscious of the importance of the Arctic only as a result of the development of modern aviation; their polar vocation is quite recent. The Russian case is not quite the same; in 1948, they celebrated the tercentenary of the discoveries of the Cossack Semeon Ivanov Dezhnev, who was the first man to sail through Bering Strait, eighty years before Bering himself.

Since 1930, following a single-minded plan, the Russians have colonized their vast northern territories, the Krainyi Sever. This empire of snow and ice has as its frontier half the gigantic circle that rings the earth. It is guarded by two gates, Spitsbergen and Bering Strait. A colossal technical effort has converted this underdeveloped region into one of the richest and most important in the world.

As far back as 1926, the dirigible *Norge*, which had twice flown over the North Pole with Amundsen, Ellsworth and Nobile, had brought back photographs of the giant industrial centers the Russians were building there.

Today there are fisheries, canneries, hydroelectric and atomic power stations, scientific installations, mines of all sorts—fertilizer, copper and nickel; rare metals such as Cerium, Titanium and Uranium; and precious metals as well. (The Russian gold mines produce more than those of South Africa; a figure of 550 tons of gold has been quoted for 1947.) Various sorts of farming, animal breeding, hunting and forestry have also been developed in the Russian Arctic.

Large cities like Murmansk (with a population of 200,000) have sprung up in these territories and have been linked by modern means of transportation and communication. It would obviously be superfluous to give a specific account of the strategic importance of this part of the globe, so lately realized by the Western powers, though so long familiar to the Russians. "More than any other country," we read in the report submitted to the Russian Minister of Finance in 1902 by the great chemist Mendeleyev,[1] "Russia is called to seek the real conquest of the polar ice."

Peter the Great understood this perfectly well, when, on his deathbed, he ordered that an expedition be organized to explore the northern frontiers of his empire, more than a third of which lay beyond the polar circle.

The first Russians had appeared on the shores of the White Sea in about the ninth or tenth century; the *Pomoryets* (trappers and fishermen) are thought to have discovered Novaya Zemlya and Spitsbergen in the same period.

In 1601, the Russians founded the town of Mangazeia in the estuary of the Taz; archaeological discoveries made in 1940 prove

---

[1] Dmitri Ivanovich Mendeleyev (1834-1907) to whom we owe the periodic classification of the elements.

that these hardy sailors had already rounded Cape Chelyuskin by 1617.

This was the era of the Cossack colonization of Siberia. The Cossacks were familiar with metallurgy and with the harnessing of horses for transport. They knew how to build sleds, carriages and sailing ships. It was one of them, Semeon Dezhnev, who, accompanied by Feodor Alexeyevitch Popov and a crew of trusty men, set out from the mouth of the Kolyma with six *kotches:* the *kotches* were quite small, light boats designed for navigation in the great estuaries and the coastal waters of the Siberian seas.

Dezhnev lost three *kotches,* but succeeded in sailing round the extreme tip of Siberia, which today bears his name; emerging into the Pacific Ocean, he discovered the solution to the problem of the continuity between the two continents.

This voyage has been much and often discussed; the naturalist Buffon found it "extremely suspect." But Buffon also gave the opinion elsewhere that no man "could ever go to the North Pole."

In any event, this exploit was still unknown,[2] in December 1724, when Peter the Great called on one of his best navigators, the Dane Vitus Bering, to survey and draw up a map of Siberia.

After having a ship built, Bering, with his thirty men and his two junior officers, was to follow the east coast until he met a "European establishment." Peter the Great had believed in the Northeast Passage ever since he had been shown harpoons found in two whales caught off the coast of Kamchatka; these harpoons had been manufactured in Holland.[3]

Bering understood; Danish by birth, he was, at forty-four, a calm man accustomed to taking authority and initiative. He chose his compatriot Martin Spanberg and the Russian Alexey Chirikov as his supporting officers. The Czar died, but the senate reconfirmed his orders, and Bering was thus able to set off for Okhotsk, via Yakutsk, where he arrived in the middle of 1726.

For he had to cross the whole of Siberia, more than five thousand miles, by land with all the equipment necessary for the construction of a ship—guns, iron fittings, navigational instruments,

---

[2] It was not till 1736 that the historian Gerhard Muller, Bering's collaborator, was to discover the documents connected with this voyage in the archives of the town of Yakutsk.

[3] Cornelia Goodhue, *Journey in the Fog.*

sails, rigging, ropes, as well as provisions and miscellaneous other equipment.

This journey was already an exploit in itself; across the immense expanses of snow, the swamps, the rivers, the steppes, the mountains, tons of equipment were transported, on men's backs, in chariots, by horse (more than six hundred horses were requisitioned for this purpose) and in sledges. The sledges were very much in favor in the far Siberian north under the name of *narti* and were used by the Russian officers of this period to explore the territories they had discovered.

These sledges generally had runners 5 feet 10 inches long and 21 inches wide. They were made of birch, with the upper surface of the sledge woven willow shoots. The whole was "sewn" together with leather thongs. Before being used, the sledge was turned over and its runners sprinkled with water; the water froze and formed a thin crust of ice, which is the best possible surface for gliding on the snow. In good weather, these birch runners were replaced with whalebone. The sledges required a team of twelve dogs, which could pull as much as 1260 pounds' weight in summer, but could hardly manage 360 pounds in winter.[4]

Bering reached the Kamchatka peninsula with the aid of a bark, the *Fortune*, and another, smaller vessel; he settled on the east coast and started construction on a galiot which he christened the *San Gabriel.* He set sail for the north in the spring of 1728 with forty men and a year's provisions.

He discovered St. Lawrence Island (which today belongs to America), then the Diomedes Islets. Against Chirikov's advice, Bering refused to venture any farther north, and having recognized—despite the fog—that a strait separated the two continents, he turned back home. He had reached latitude 67° 18′ N. He had even made his way through the strait without seeing it, having met only one or two boatloads of "savages."

Fifty years later, Captain Cook was to follow the same route, thanks to Bering's logbook; he was to have the good fortune to see the mists rise and to be able to contemplate the two points of land.

After an attempt in the direction of the west coast of America, an attempt which failed as a result of storms, Bering returned to St.

---

[4] Markham, *The Lands of Silence.*

Petersburg in 1730 to make his report to the Empress and the senate. The senate examined his report for two years without making any decision, then, noticing that Bering had not accomplished his mission, which had been to "sail until he met a European establishment," it refused to pay him his salary. The Academy of Sciences, for its part, held that the proofs—of the existence of the strait—were not conclusive.

Bering defended his position by pointing out that the inadequacy of his vessel had prevented him from going any farther; he was given the answer that his own report mentioned that the natives traveled every year to the "Americas" in *baidors,* small sealskin boats with whalebone ribs and keels.

But the French professor, Joseph Nicolas Delisle, who was a geographer like his brother Guillaume, came to Bering's aid, and presented the Empress Anne a *mémoire,* advising her to pursue the discoveries. It was at this point that the "Great Expedition to the North" was decided upon; the command was to remain in the hands of Vitus Bering, assisted by the faithful Spanberg and Chirikov.

This was a colossal operation in which a large number of scientists participated. As in 1725, an enormous amount of equipment was transported across Siberia, and no less than six years were required for Bering and a thousand men to arrive at Okhotsk, a boom town where technicians, scientists and sailors elbowed among government officials, trappers, traders and colonists.

The means at Bering's disposal were considerable; credits of 360,000 rubles had been voted him, all the garrisons had been alerted, and a veritable mobilization of the Russian colonists in Siberia had been decreed to transport, convoy, build and prepare. Academicians, astronomers and cartographers went through all the archives in Siberia; maps were drawn up by triangulation, and a *Flora Sibirica* was undertaken, while four ships were being constructed. Quadrants, thermometers, astrolabes and slide rules were studied and built by specialized workers. A mass of assistants were prepared for their tasks, among them interpreters speaking Greek and Chaldean. A vast library had been selected; *Gulliver's Travels* and *Robinson Crusoe* were both in it.

During the winter of 1736, the historian Gerhard Muller made an important discovery: a document mentioning the voyage of Semeon Dezhnev, the first Russian to pass through the strait, in

1648. The document was written in Dezhnev's own clumsy hand and began: "In the year 1648, on the twentieth day of June, I, Semeon . . ."

After a great many administrative problems had been overcome and the formidable work of preparation completed, Bering gave the signal to depart. His orders were grandiose: to discover a quarter of the Northern Hemisphere, a task which was, in fact, to take his successors more than a century of exploration.

Finally, along with several relatively minor land expeditions, two naval convoys departed from Petropavlovsk [5] on June 4, 1741. As for the two smaller vessels, the *Hope* and the *Archangel Michael*, which had been finished in 1739, they had set off for Japan with Spanberg.

Bering on board the *St. Peter* and Chirikov on board the *St. Paul* set sail for America two years later. They first realized that a certain "Gama Land" which appeared on Delisle's map did not exist; the search for this imaginary land was, moreover, the source of all the misfortunes suffered by Bering, for whom this was to be the last voyage. In fact, during the course of a storm, the two ships lost sight of one another. They were never to see each other again.

Chirikov reached American soil in July, lost several of his men on land and returned to Kamchatka exhausted, suffering from scurvy and tuberculosis; he never regained his powers.

For his part, Bering made an immense voyage and arrived at the American coast near Mount St. Elias, which he named. The land he had discovered was explored in several hours by Georg Wilhelm Steller, a German naturalist on Bering's staff; he found buried huts containing copper tools, smoked fish and even a tinderbox.

Exhausted by scurvy, his enthusiasm extinguished, Bering set out once more on the high seas. After sailing the length of the Aleutians, the *St. Peter*, its crew entirely drained of strength and its sails in tatters, ran aground in the cove of a small island "infested with bears," Bering Island. There, on the eighth of December, Vitus Bering died.

The rest of the crew then built a dinghy in which they managed

---

[5] Named in honor of the two principal ships of the expedition, the *St. Peter* and the *St. Paul* (today a very important Soviet naval base).

to make their way back to Petropavlovsk. In 1743, the *Gazette de France* was to dispose of the whole event in a few lines:

"Captain Bering, who had set out to see whether it was possible to sail to America by the North Pacific, shipwrecked on the rock-bound coast of a deserted island, where he perished along with the greater part of his crew. . . ."

The results of Bering's expedition were important nonetheless. To it we owe the first accurate map of the great Russian north-east, and also the first scientific approach to Arctic nature. The map which had been drawn up by Delisle was to remain usable in the main for many long years to come. Steller wrote an account of *The Animals of the Sea;* it was a great success at the time and set off a rush to the north, the paradise of furs.

Bering had given the Russians a taste for the Arctic; Muraviev and Pavlov (1735), Malygin and Skuratov (1736), Pronchishchev and his wife (who reached 77° 29′ N. in 1739), Chelyuskin (who traveled by sled in 1742 to the cape that bears his name), as well as the great scientist Lomonosov (who studied the central polar basin in 1765) were only a few of these pioneers.

After Bering, the exploration and the exploitation—the conquest, as we should say—of the Arctic regions by the Russians was to go on at an accelerated rate and was to result in the present industrial and strategic mastery of the Soviets.

This conquest is such an evident fact that it already has its legends. The story[6] is told, of a radio operator on duty at the Thule base (in Greenland) who recently picked up a message sent from a Russian transmitter at the other end of the Arctic Ocean: "*Respectfully point out that you have forgotten to put out the searchlights on your runway.*"

---

[6] Édouard Calic, *L'Univers polaire.*

8

THE FIRST MAN IN THE SOUTH

THE PLANET VENUS will not pass over the sun again until the year 2004, and it is a great pity. For the observation of this natural phenomenon enables us to determine the distance between the earth and the sun. Of course, in our day that distance is known. But we must never deprive our men of science of the slightest pleasure—like that of demonstrating once again the fact that they have not made a mistake.

The distance from the earth to the sun was accurately determined for the first time in 1769; the occasion was, as it happened, the transit of the planet Venus across the face of the sun. It might seem that this observation was out of place here, were it not for the fact that it helped to contribute one of the greatest names to polar exploration—that of James Cook.

The method, recommended by the learned Scottish astronomer James Gregory, a contemporary of Newton's, consisted in observing, from various (naturally, distant) points on the terrestrial globe, Venus's "entry" into and "departure" from the solar disc, as well as the chord described on this disc—great care, of course, being taken in noting the time required.

From the comparison of these various observations, each giving the curve described by Venus on the disc of the sun as seen from a different point on the earth, it was possible to deduce the sun's horizontal parallax; the parallax is the angle at which an observer placed at the center of the sun would see the earth's light.

Venus's passages across the disc of the sun are rare; they last occurred in 1761 and 1769, 1874 and 1882.

In 1769, observations were made in Tahiti, in Wardehuus, Norway, in Cajaneburg and Kola, Lapland, in St. Petersburg, in Paris, in California, in Hudson Bay; they gave a result of 8.5776″ for the value of the parallax.

Every astronomer was mobilized. The Empress Catherine II called the French-German Professor Peter Simon Pallas to her in Russia, while Jean Chappe d'Autoroche journeyed to California. Louis Antoine de Bougainville sent Véron to the Moluccas to wait for the day of passage, June 3, 1769. The "poor apprentice" died of fever there.

In England, the Royal Geographical Society called on the Treasury and the Admiralty for aid in organizing a scientific expedition to Tahiti, which was felt to be the best-situated point from which to observe the phenomenon.

The Scottish scientist Sir Alexander Dalrymple[1] was suggested for commander. But the adventures of the astronomer Halley, who seventy years earlier had proved that it is possible to be both a great scientist and a wretched captain, led the British Admiralty to refuse to entrust a ship to a civilian. Instead, the First Lord named a young naval officer who had already distinguished himself

---

[1] Sir Alexander Dalrymple (1737-1808) published numerous naval maps and a *Historical Collection of the Several Voyages and Discoveries in the South Pacific Ocean.*

by his abilities both as sailor and as scientific observer, principally in Newfoundland. His name was James Cook. He was forty years old and possessed a reputation as an "excellent mathematician." From a modest background (he was the son of a farm servant), Cook was self-educated. But he had a cool head, a lucid brain constantly on the alert, a sense of duty and authority; he was the ideal man for the job.

His mission was simple—to set up a scientific post at Tahiti, where an observatory was to be built, and to make scientific observations (botanical, physical, et cetera) all through the voyage. But Cook was also carrying secret orders: the Admiralty wanted him to push on and explore "to the south." These instructions were to revolutionize the state of geography and of human knowledge in general.

Having a methodical mind, Cook carried out the preparations for his voyage with the greatest and most minute care. He may be considered as a precursor to the modern science of equipment and supply, generally referred to now as "logistics."

Cook first picked out a corvette, the 370-ton *Endeavour*. This choice provoked a good deal of astonishment; for the vessel in question was normally used for the transport of coal in the north of England. But the *Endeavour* was easy to beach, and she possessed a large number of holds in which Cook stored his scientific equipment; this equipment included butterfly nets as well as fishhooks. A special glass "by which, put into the water, you can see at a great depth" was on the list, and the ship's library would have made many a scientist turn pale with envy.

Cook took into account the conclusions arrived at by Dr. James Lind in his *Treatise on Scurvy*, published in 1753, in selecting his provisions. With regard to navigation, Cook took advantage of two new improvements: in the compass, the telescope replaced the alidade, and the sextant took over from the octant. Moreover, the sextant became a more accurate instrument itself thanks to the invention of the graduator (in 1765), which enabled the divisions of the scale to be established with great precision; the era of the artisan who engraved the divisions by eye was over.

The only lacuna in this first voyage of Cook's was that of an accurate method for determining longitude; this gap was to be filled by the time of his second departure.

For everything happened as though this first voyage were nothing more than a dress rehearsal for the second—the great voyage which was to bring Cook his glory.

Having set off on August 26, 1768, with the naturalist Joseph Banks,[2] the astronomer Charles Green, and the draftsman Alexander Buchan on board, Cook visited Tierra del Fuego and then landed on Tahiti. After visiting the Society Islands (so named for the Royal Society in London, which was behind him), Cook steered a course toward New Zealand and Australia, then returned to England.

In his journal, he expressed the conviction that the Antarctic continent, if it indeed existed, could lie only in the farthest latitudes. "Therefore," he summed up in his report, "to make new discoveries, the navigator must circumnavigate the globe in a higher parallel than has hitherto been done." This famous continent, this "great object," as Cook called it, was beginning to attract the attention of the principal powers.

Dalrymple stirred up public opinion to convince the English government to organize a great expedition, while, in France, Charles de Brosses proclaimed his conviction that there must exist a southern continent placed there in order that, "the symmetry between the two hemispheres be maintained."

In 1738, the Frenchman J. B. C. Bouvet de Lozier, of the Compagnie des Indes, had already been sent off "in search of southern lands." He did not find any, but he did discover the hostile and unapproachable island that bears his name. Then, at 48° 50′ S., he saw the first great tabular icebergs with their fauna (penguins and seals) and described them.

Returning from his famous voyage to Tahiti (1768), which he made on the *Boudeuse*, and which was rich in scientific results, Bougainville presented, in 1772, a precise and detailed plan for an expedition to the north,[3] going so far as to specify the modifications that ought to be made in the ships to make them resistant to the ice. This project was rejected by the French Minister of the Navy, on account of "lack of funds."

---

[2] Sir Joseph Banks (1743-1820), Swedish by origin, born in London, devoted his fortune to research. During the Napoleonic wars, he succeeded in restoring to the Museum of Paris whole collections taken by the English. He left behind him a great amount of work in the natural sciences.

[3] Emmanuel, *La France et l'exploration polaire*.

Authorization to set out was, nevertheless, granted to Yves Joseph de Kerguélen-Trémarec, who, with the *Fortune* and the *Gros Ventre*—"a charming little barge or flute"—traveled to the Southern Hemisphere, where he discovered Desolation Island, which is known today as Kerguelen Island, at latitude 49° 40′ S.

Kerguélen was already known for his voyage to Greenland, where he had rectified the errors on certain maps of the regions he visited. His voyage to the south must have confirmed his reputation, in spite of certain annoyances that he had to undergo in his dealings with the Admiralty; against all the rules, he had carried a woman on board. Kerguélen asserted that he had discovered "Australian France"; but what was involved was nothing more than a small island halfway between Australia and the Cape of Good Hope.

When Captain James Cook decided to organize his second expedition, there was very little information available to him on the Antarctic regions.

When he had to choose two ships (he felt that to set out with a single ship would involve too many risks for an expedition), Cook did not hesitate at all; he took two coalers, just like the *Endeavour*, which had proved itself to be sturdy and manageable. The *Resolution* and the *Adventure* were corvettes (462 tons with a crew of 112, and 366 tons with a crew of 91, respectively); each of them carried cannon and a large ship's launch.

Making use of the experience he had acquired during the first voyage, Cook gave the greatest care to his preparations for the second. All that science had created in the way of new equipment was taken aboard—a device for distilling sea water, a theodolite, a surveyor's chain and plumb line, and a depth thermometer. But, most important of all, Cook took with him the instrument which was going to revolutionize navigation: the chronometer. Its use finally offered the possibility of calculating longitude with the greatest accuracy; the science of geography was to be reshaped by it.

Up till then, the observation of lunar distances remained the only practical means of determining longitude; this astronomical solution was neither convenient nor precise.

The only rational method of determining longitude, as described by Newton, involved the use of the clock. In the course of a sidereal day, the earth brings all the meridians beneath the same star. Now, as this rotation is uniform, it follows that each point on the globe describes a full circle of 360 degrees every 24 hours, or an arc of 15 degrees per hour, an arc of 15 minutes per minute of time, and an arc of 15 seconds per second of time.

If, for example, at a given moment, it is 7:35 A.M. at point A and 9:36 A.M. at point B, it is clear that point B lies 30 degrees 15 minutes of longitude away from point A.

We can see that the determination of longitude comes down to a simple measurement of time. All we need is to have available an accurate chronometer which has been set according to the precise time at our point of departure, a point whose longitude is known. (If we choose the meridian of Greenwich as our point of departure, its longitude is taken as 0.)

As a result, when we wish to determine the longitude of the point where we now stand, we take the exact time at that point (to do this we must determine the precise moment at which a given star, or the sun, passes over the meridian of that point) and compare it with the time at point of departure, in order to find the longitude.

All this presupposes that the chronometer available to us operates with perfect exactitude. But before 1760, the technical means available were not adequate to guarantee the operation of such an instrument.

The development of a perfect chronometer seemed so important a task that the British Parliament had promised an enormous reward to the watchmaker who would succeed in creating it, while the French Academy of Sciences and Naval Academy did the same. An English watchmaker named Sully, working at Versailles, spent thirty years working at the problem without success, though he brought to it all the great improvements that had been made in the watch trade up to that time.

Between 1726 and 1761, the English horologist John Harrison developed a huge traveling clock, which was insensitive to variations in temperature. He received half the Parliamentary prize for this effort, though his instrument was still difficult to copy, and also to adjust.

Elsewhere, a competition was going on between Julien Leroy of Tours and the Swiss Ferdinand Berthoud and it was Leroy who won the Academy of Sciences prize.

In October 1772, the frigate *La Flore,* which had just completed a year's cruise, with the purpose of experimenting on the two models, fired all its guns on both sides; the salvo did not affect the operation of the two clocks. It set off the era of the chronometer.

Henceforward, one could navigate with certainty and begin to make accurate maps, since it was easy to determine longitude, a thing which Champlain had not even hoped for, when, a century earlier, he had asserted in his *Traité de la Marine* that "God did not allow man to find the longitude."

For his second voyage, Cook carried with him four chronometers, including a replica of Harrison's prototype. He also had available to him a considerable scientific staff, including naturalists and astronomers, as well as an assortment of seeds, plants and animals to be used in acclimatization experiments in the Pacific.

Cook (who had just got his captain's commission) was in command of the expedition and sailed on the *Resolution*. The *Adventure* was commanded by Furneaux. They weighed anchor on July 13, 1772. At the Cape, Cook learned of Kerguélen's discoveries and of the departure of the Frenchmen Marion-Dufresne and Crozet for the Antarctic. Cook felt no bitterness toward them; he continued south in obedience to the orders he had been given.

He ran into ice, passed through six waterspouts, traveled 3,660 leagues (7,900 nautical miles) without sighting land, lost the *Adventure* and, having reached 67° 15′ S., decided to put in at New Zealand. Having recovered the *Adventure*, he made a series of accurate maps of New Zealand. Then, having lost the *Adventure* once again, he set sail for the south. (The *Adventure* was to return to England.)

Rounding the Great Ice Barrier, he reached 71° 10′ S. "Attempting to get farther to the south would have been a dangerous and rash enterprise. . . . It was *my* opinion that the ice extended quite to the pole." He based this judgment on the existence of tabular icebergs, which could not have been formed, so he thought, anywhere except on a continent.

As his crew was threatened with illness, Cook returned north and dropped anchor before Easter Island, where he admired the Maori statues and tombs. Passing the Marquesas Islands, he ascertained their longitude with his chronometers, then sailed on to Tahiti and the New Hebrides (so named by Cook himself). Then, still with only a single ship, he returned south to run into the ice barrier once again. On July 30, 1775, Cook sailed into Plymouth with an impressive collection of new knowledge. For the first time, the Antarctic had been approached and circumscribed, its polar circle crossed (twice), its frontiers explored. Having circumnavigated the globe in its most southerly latitudes, Cook was in a position finally to demolish previous speculation on the famous continent.

His journal—one of the most valuable in polar literature—places that continent within its true borders: "Although I had proved that there was no continent but what must lie far to the south, there remained, nevertheless, room for very large islands in places wholly unexamined; and many of those which were formerly discovered are but imperfectly explored, and their situation as imperfectly known. I was, besides, of opinion that my remaining in this sea some time longer would be productive of improvements in navigation and geography as well as the other sciences."

Down to the beginning of the nineteenth century, the world was to regard the question as settled.

Cook himself was to return to the south after an attempt to find the "great passage" in the north. Captain Constantine John Phipps—later Baron Mulgrave—had attempted to find the same eastern passage in 1773, following Bougainville's notes; he had been unable to get beyond a point 80° 48′ N. and 20° E., in the vicinity of Spitsbergen. Phipps had had two bomb vessels, the *Racehorse* and the *Carcass*, both enormous, capable of withstanding the explosion of mortars. They had each been reinforced with a beak with which to break the ice pack; the principle of the icebreaker was already in operation.

During the course of the voyage, one of the *Racehorse*'s launches was attacked by a band of walruses and was saved only by the intervention of another launch from the *Carcass*, under the command of a young and fiery midshipman, Horatio Nelson; it was during this voyage that the future viscount and admiral killed a polar bear with one masterful musket shot.

In 1776, Pagès, on board a Dutch whaler, reached 82° N., "162 leagues from the North Pole." "If my Dutchmen," he wrote in his journal, "had had the same wishes as I did, those winds and currents which drove them north would have filled their hearts with joy, in the hopes of breaking through to a place that had always been believed inaccessible. . . . I do not regard a voyage to the pole as impossible."

It was on July 12, 1776, that Captain Cook sailed from Plymouth on his third and last voyage; the *Resolution* was accompanied by the *Discovery* under the command of Charles Clarke. On board was a naval officer named William Bligh, who was to distinguish himself some years later as commander of the *Bounty*.

For this voyage, Cook limited the number of scientists to be taken along—they had in the past caused a great deal of annoyance—and chose professional officers who were also capable of taking care of the scientific tasks.

Cook visited the land that Kerguelen had discovered. It was he who christened it with the name of the French navigator. Then he headed north, following Bering's course. On August 17, 1777, Cook's two ships entered the "blink," the area on the outskirts of the ice barrier where the sky at the horizon is filled with a milky luminosity caused by the reflection of light from the enormous mass of ice. Several hours later, they were halted by the ice barrier itself at 71° N. Cook had had the time to verify Bering's remarkable observations and had had the luck to see the veil of mist separate, thus discovering the famous strait.

Cook then returned to Hawaii, after sailing along the Alaskan coast. Following an incident with the inhabitants, the man whom Buffon calls "the greatest of all the navigators" died, knifed in the back by a native.

Cook's three voyages were the prelude to the most brilliant period in the conquest of the poles. In the north this period begins with John Ross and William Edward Parry in 1818, and in the south, with John Davis's landing on the Antarctic continent on February 7, 1821.

The handsomest tribute paid to this exceptional man comes from a Frenchman, the great Dumont d'Urville, a man who cannot be accused of having had too great a feeling of sympathy for him: "He was," he said, "a sailor in the fullest sense of the word."

9

THE FIRST HARPOON GUN

After Cook, the man who can be immodest, the man who, forced to travel a thousand paces in his footsteps, then takes five or six on his own and afterward thinks himself his equal is a madman who will never add a jot to his nation's glory. . . . No one will ever again be the equal of that immortal navigator. . . ."

Without ever being quite as glorious as Cook, the author of these lines was oddly enough to suffer the same fate as the "immortal navigator." His name was Jean-François Galaup de La Pérouse.

He had set out, accompanied by two hundred picked men, with the ambition to complete the map of the world begun by Cook.

Like Cook, he met his death in the South Seas. The two men possessed the same temperament. The same mixture of bravado and humanity was to be found in each of them.

Cook's generosity to the "savages" of New Zealand in 1777 was mirrored by that of La Pérouse, who, having been ordered in 1782 to destroy the English establishment in Hudson Bay, tried to perform this task in the most "humane" way possible. From the point of view of navigation, it was Cook and La Pérouse who together won the battle of longitude with the first chronometers.

It was natural then that it should be La Pérouse who was given the task of completing the work of his illustrious predecessor, when King Louis XVI decided to launch a great expedition around the world. The program for this expedition, drawn up by the king himself, was extensive. It dealt with the Arctic as well as the Antarctic and was to send La Pérouse beyond Bering Strait and the islands of the South Seas.

His mission dealt with commerce, astronomy, geography, physics and natural history. He was to make observations on the declination of the magnetic needle, on the air, on atmospheric pressure, on the variation of weights and on the tides. He was to use little aerostatic balloons to study air currents at various altitudes. He was to study whales and storms as well as the formation of icebergs. As if to point up the similarity in their destinies, England transmitted Cook's two dipping needles to La Pérouse; she remembered the order given by the king of France to "allow M. Cook and his vessels to pass" in spite of the war then going on between England and France.

It was on August 1, 1785 that La Pérouse sailed from Brest with the *Boussole* and the *Astrolabe*, two barges, or cargo ships, a little too easily rebaptized frigates, but remarkably well fitted out;[1] Cook might have dreamed of their sumptuous chart rooms, their laboratories and their twelve-hundred-volume library. The technical arsenal was extremely sophisticated for the period. It included, among other things, three sextants, a portable observatory, five of Berthoud's marine clocks and an English chronometer.

La Pérouse was not, in the same sense as Cook was, a polar

---

[1] Had La Pérouse accepted the candidacy of a young pupil at the military academy of Paris, named Napoleon Bonaparte, the fate of the world would probably have turned out differently.

explorer; he nevertheless deserves the credit for having confirmed the great English navigator's conclusions with regard to several of the old geographical myths, like the famous intercontinental canal crossing America via Hudson Bay. He was also the first real explorer of the coast of Alaska and of northwest America; George Vancouver—a former midshipman of Cook's—and Alexander MacKenzie were to explore this region some years later.

The journey of MacKenzie, who gave his name to a great river spilling into the Arctic Ocean, brings us back to the Far North; we are not far from the beginning of the most important phase in its conquest. And, as it is true that the period of the great polar offensive of the Rosses, Parry and Franklin is about to commence, it is necessary to emphasize how much of their success these men owed to such extraordinary figures as the Scoresbys, father and son, and to the whaling trade in general.

The areas in which whaling is carried on are marked out by the presence of a small shrimp of the genus *Euphansia superba*, more popularly known as the "krill," which is consumed by the whale in enormous numbers. The "krill" is generally to be found in the fronts between different waters—at the confines of the Atlantic and the Baltic, for instance, or in the polar waters, where the ice pack plays the role of a front as a result of the difference in salt content which is produced around it.

In spring, the whales customarily head for the polar and subpolar zones which are at that period extremely rich in macroplankton; it is there that for centuries men have journeyed, in spite of danger, ice and storm, to seek them out.

For a whale is worth a fortune. Not one ounce of the 150 tons that a blue whale is likely to weigh is lost; there is, above all, the oil, which, after being treated in various ways, gives lubricants, glycerine, soap, margarine, beauty creams, paints, varnishes, cosmetics and a whole range of industrial and consumer products. Candles can be made from it as well as linoleum.

From the liver, the pharmaceutical industry extracts medicines rich in vitamins and hormones, while the bones become fertilizer and intestines meal for cattle. With the value of whale oil standing at ninety pounds sterling a ton in 1947, it is easy to understand the relentlessness with which men have pursued it.

It is also easy to understand why the whalers were the first and the boldest of the polar explorers; to navigate in the glacial waters in hunt of the largest animal in the world was a necessity for them. Long before anyone else, the whalers were frequenting Spitsbergen, Greenland and Smith Strait. But they took great care not to reveal their geographical knowledge, in order to avoid competition.

Little by little, the whaling men began to accept the responsibility to co-operate with the geographers and the explorers; their contributions to polar discovery then became extremely important. Often, moreover, the accounts of explorers like Davis, who declared that he had seen whales continually would set off a whale rush; this was the case with Sir James Clark Ross in the Antarctic and with Hudson in the waters around Spitsbergen.

The first whaling men were the Basques; they were skillful harpooners, but their place was rapidly taken by the English, Dutch and Norwegians.

Down to 1860 and the appearance of petroleum, it was fish oil that lighted the world and that made whaling an exceptionally lucrative industry. This fact explains why the whalers were willing to endure such great suffering and privation before the invention of the harpoon gun by the Norwegian Svend Foyn in 1872.

We can get an idea of these by imagining the enormous disproportion that existed in the struggle between man and beast as it was immortalized by Herman Melville in *Moby Dick*.

"A blue whale," writes Georges Blond,[2] "is as long as four trolley cars. By climbing on its back, you could enter the second story of a house. Its tongue weighs as much as an adult elephant. Its skeleton weighs 22 tons, its meat 50, its blubber 25. The whale's total weight can go as high as 330,000 pounds. If it were possible to set this animal on one side of a scale built to accommodate him, you would have to place 36 elephants or the population of a town of 2,500 inhabitants on the other half to balance him."

The whale is a mammal of the cetacean order, with lungs and warm blood. All the cetaceans have horizontal tails. Some have teeth (the sperm whale, the orc or grampus, the narwhal, the dolphins, and the porpoises); the rest have baleen or whalebone[3]

---

[2] Georges Blond, *La Grande Aventure des baleines*.

[3] An elastic horny substance which grows in a series of thin parallel plates in the upper jaw in place of teeth.

—whales with creased bellies (the finner, or rorqual, the piked whale); and whales with smooth bellies (the right whales).

It is by the "blow" that the fisherman has always been able to recognize the whale; for six to eight seconds it expels several cubic yards of hot air from its lungs; this air is loaded with humidity which expands on contact with the atmosphere and then falls back in the form of fine droplets; thus, the whale does not spout water, as sailors believed for centuries.

When the watch had given the traditional cry: "There she blows!" the whaling ship would put off two or three small boats carrying the harpooners.

Against this monster, the greatest of all the animals that have ever existed, measuring as much as 113 feet in length, man's only weapon was a simple harpoon attached to a long cable. Soundlessly the longboat approached the whale. The harpooner hurled his weapon at a spot above and behind the eye. The boat pulled away to avoid the waves the animal would make in "sounding," or plunging down to the depths.

The right whale hardly ever goes deeper than 600 or 650 feet, while the sperm whale,[4] or cachalot, may go as deep as 3,200 feet; the cachalot descends to these fantastic depths, withstanding the incredible pressures working on him, to hunt the octopus, of whose taste he is inordinately fond. (In 1932, an American cable ship extracted a cable from a depth of 3,237 feet and found a sperm whale caught on it.) The hunters pursuing a harpooned whale had to wait till the wounded animal returned to the surface to breathe, and they took advantage of this moment to finish him off with pikes. When the whale "blew" its own blood, it was beaten.

The enormous profit represented by a single whale explains the risks that were run and explains even better the tenacity with which the whalers significantly reduced the world's supply of whales, some species of which have almost disappeared. Between 1863 and 1904, when an international agreement interrupted the process, it is estimated that the number of whales caught in the Arctic alone was of the order of 18,000. When the blue whale—the largest of all—had been almost totally annihilated, the whalers turned their attention to the common rorqual and the cachalot, animals which bring a smaller return and which are capable of fleeing much faster.

[4] Moby Dick was a sperm whale.

In 1872, Svend Foyn, a seal hunter, had the idea for a harpoon gun; the harpoon was furnished with a grenade which exploded inside the monster and killed him.[5] As for the small oared launch, Foyn replaced it with a steam launch; out of an archaic and hazardous enterprise, Foyn made an industry; this was the prelude to the modern era of vast floating factories.

To prevent the whale's total extinction, an international conference in 1944 drew up a code of whaling regulations; the number of whales caught by the world whaling fleet is not to exceed 16,000 blue-whale "units" per season; no floating factory may use more than ten boats, and each factory ship must carry two inspectors. It is forbidden to kill a cow whale accompanied by her calf. A time limit was put on the hunting season, and the whale was protected altogether south of 40° S.

In 1952, there were sixteen factory ships employing ninety boats. The modern floating factories run from 13,000 to 18,000 tons and have 8,000-horsepower engines. The top deck of the floating factory is specially fitted out for the dismembering of whales, which are brought aboard through an opening in the stern. The boilers designed to extract the oil can handle eight blue whales a day, or a daily production of 800 to 900 barrels (a barrel is equal to about 375 pounds; therefore, the production runs from 300,000 to 337,500 pounds).

The floating factory is equipped with all the improvements wrought by modern technology: radar, laboratories, hospitals; the Norwegian *Kosmos II* even carries X-ray and diathermy machines. Several hundred men work on board these ships during the six-month season. Each floating factory has its own boats, which are about one fiftieth the size of the mother-ship, are driven by 1000-horsepower engines, and have a 75-millimeter harpoon gun in the prow.

In the time of the Scoresbys, who made seventeen voyages to Spitsbergen between 1803 and 1822, the floating factories did not yet exist. They hunted in whaling ships of between 300 and 400 tons, with iron-reinforced bows. A permanent watch in the rigorous cold was kept by a lookout stationed in the crows'-nest specially designed by the elder William Scoresby in 1807. The lookout,

---

[5] In 1952, the explosive grenade was replaced by an electric discharge, which kills the whale instantly.

seated in this cask fixed to the top of the main-mast, scanned the horizon. He had a telescope and various other navigational instruments to hand.

Every whaler carried six or seven deal launches, 26 feet long and 6 feet wide; the keel, the gunwale, the bow and the stern were all made of oak. The hemp harpoon line was about 4,200 feet long. The harpoon was 39 inches long and the picks or lances about twice that. Each boat carried two harpoons and six lances, as well as a flag with which to announce that the whale had been taken.

The crew had a pecuniary interest in the catch, since they shared in the season's profits.

William Scoresby was the son of a farmer who rose to the position of whaling captain. His son, who was a pupil of Joseph Banks, Cook's companion, went to sea with his father at the age of seventeen, to make observations on the ocean and the ice in the intervals between whale catches.

The elder Scoresby deserves credit for a large number of improvements in the technique of navigation in the ice floes, a form of navigation with which he was remarkably well acquainted. The younger Scoresby discovered certain points on the Greenland coast, as well as Liverpool Island. He made an astonishing series of observations on ice formation, as the director of more than thirty scientific missions.

The Scoresbys' name was to remain of great importance in polar history. Thanks to the report they submitted to the British Admiralty drawing its attention to the inexplicable breaking-up of drift ice in 1817, it was they who gave the signal for the great departure for the conquest of the poles.

And if John Ross, Edward Parry, David Buchan and John Franklin took to the sea in 1818 to become immortal, we have the Scoresbys, whaling men, men of science and men of good will, to thank for it.

10

PARRY AND FRANKLIN

Sitting in the aircraft plowing its way toward the Pole and enjoying a cup of hot coffee from the thermos jug, I could not refrain from thinking of the pioneers who struggled across the ice to the Pole. Only those who have tried to blaze their trail on foot through the jumble of heavy polar pack ice can fully appreciate the efforts and spirit of those determined men who toiled across the floes floating on the deep Polar Sea. Day after day, carrying heavy loads, they pressed toward the unknown, in front of exhausted dogs, pulling the sledges over the interminable chaos of ice, climbing over hummocks which blocked their advance, wading through snowdrifts and slush ice up to their knees. . . .

And then the heart-breaking discovery that, after they had walked all day, the current, while they slept at night, had brought them back to where they started."

These lines, by the Norwegian physician Kaare Rodahl, who participated in the establishment of the T3 floating station in 1952, give us a perfect notion of the state of mind of the polar explorers at the start of the nineteenth century, even though they were written 150 years after that time.

Up till then, the intrepid navigator had always been halted by the ice barrier, and man had been prevented, by that uncrossable frontier, from knowing what lay in the regions between 70° N. and the North Pole. It was not known whether there existed an open sea, or perhaps an icebound one, or a vast Arctic continent; the roof of the globe appeared on maps in white.

Never, however, had man felt a greater need for knowledge; the formidable technological revolution of the nineteenth century was on the way. Taking advantage of it, the explorers were to set off for the north in increasing numbers, and were to go on chipping away at the latitude minute by minute until that day in 1909 when Peary was to plant the American flag at the summit of the planet, thus cheating England of the crowning glory of her long labors.

For it is clear that in this conquest, England's role was considerable, even predominant. More propitious conditions for polar exploration had never presented themselves than those which existed after the battle of Waterloo, which made Great Britain the supreme world power and opened the period of *Pax Britannica*.

The first stage of the polar offensive could have been carried out only by sailors, and England possessed the pick of the world; for more than a half century, the great pioneers on the ice were all naval captains.

To drive northward, to confront the ice barrier, to try to master it and to find the Northwest Passage: this was the ambition of all young British naval officers of the period; it had a romantic appeal for them, it was a tradition that had been bequeathed them by their elders.

The British naval officer had become more than a mere navigator; he had scientific ambitions. Indeed, scientific research had the freedom of the ship on His Majesty's vessels; it was not a rare sight to see guns dismounted to be replaced by new "instruments."

Immense horizons opened up before the boldest spirits; lively discussions were going on in naval circles over Fulton's experiments; in 1802, he had navigated a small boat equipped with an eight-horsepower engine on the Seine (though this feat failed to impress Napoleon).

When, in 1807, this same Fulton sailed valiantly up the Hudson in the second of his steamers, the *Clermont*, there came a notable increase in the number of enthusiasts for the "steam-horses" who, as Tristan Bernard wrote, "at a signal from the engineer, would rush among the cylinders in little troops of ever-increasing size." The first crossing of the English Channel, in eighteen hours in 1816 by the *Elise*, and of the Atlantic, in eighteen days in 1819 by the *Savannah* (a 389-ton, three-masted bark-rigged schooner with a steam-operated paddle wheel), ended by arousing widespread interest among the pioneers; ten years later, in 1829, Sir John Ross, a Royal Navy captain, was the first man to attack the ice in a steam-driven paddle-wheeler.

All the new ideas and original technical methods were immediately assimilated, experimented on and adapted. At the same time, human knowledge was undergoing a period of classification, a rationalization and hierarchization marked by the birth of such institutions as the geographical societies (that of Paris in 1821; of Berlin in 1829; of London in 1831).

There was surely no lack of illogicality in the behavior of the pioneers of this ebullient period. On the one hand, they were trying out the steam engine on the ice barrier; on the other hand, they entirely neglected to adapt their clothing to the cold; their handsome uniforms were better suited to London society than to the Pole. On board, they suffered from scurvy and hunger; but they would not admit the possibility of eating their rations off anything but the massive china of the period. This must have been as moving a sight as that of the St. Cyr cadets going into battle in their white gloves and plumed shakos in 1914.

The term "assault" as applied to the poles is by no means too strong; the year 1817 marks the opening of a veritable war—a hundred years' war—between man and the cold.

Everyone knows how it began: with a *débâcle*.[1]

The whaling captain William Scoresby, Jr., noted the existence,

[1] The technical term—in English and French—for a breaking-up of the ice.

in the year 1818, of exceptionally mild climatic conditions; the ice which was broken up and churned about had left free a great stretch of sea and allowed him to land on the eastern coast of Greenland between 72° N. and 74° N., latitudes which were normally closed to navigation.

He wrote a report on his experience and sent it to his former teacher, Sir Joseph Banks, pointing out that he had observed about two thousand square leagues between 74° N. and 80° N. perfectly void of ice. Banks immediately alerted Sir John Barlow, the secretary of the Admiralty, who was later to be called "the father of English polar exploration."

Barrow transmitted the report to Lord Melville, the First Lord of the Admiralty, at the same time advising him that it would be "somewhat mortifying if a naval power but of yesterday [Russia] were to complete a discovery in the nineteenth century which was so happily commenced by Englishmen in the sixteenth." A plan was immediately worked out, then approved; two British expeditions were to be sent north, while Parliament offered a 5,000-pound reward to the first navigator to reach latitude 89° N. or longitude 110° W.; it would have been difficult to offer a greater inducement to the explorers for the discovery of the Northwest Passage.

The first expedition, under the command of David Buchan, was to seek the passage via Spitsbergen; the second, under Captain John Ross, was to try to break through via Baffin Bay. The two expeditions raised anchor in the Thames in April 1818. The Admiralty had neglected no detail of their technical equipment.

Captain Buchan was in command of the *Dorothea* (370 tons), and his second-in-command, Lieutenant John Franklin, had the *Trent* (250 tons), while John Ross sailed on the *Isabella* (385 tons) and his second, Edward Parry, on the *Alexander* (252 tons); the four ships were all whalers, specially reinforced for the polar regions. To this end, they had been given a second, exterior lining of oak, three inches thick, and their interior ribs had been propped with stout wooden beams set athwartship and designed to withstand the pressure of the ice. Their prows had been plated with thick iron armor.

The gentlemen of the Admiralty devoted infinite solicitude to the problem of the crews' health and physical well-being. The inconvenient hammock was replaced by a soft, warm bed, while numerous stoves fitted with long heating pipes made between-decks a sailor's paradise.

A complete assortment of fur-lined clothing and boots was provided, as well as a set of tarpaulin tents. The provisions—for three years—included a large amount of dried vegetables, preserves, cordials and all kinds of remedies for scurvy. Everything was provided for a long winter to be spent in the polar regions.

For, with Buchan, Franklin, Ross and, particularly, Parry, the second great period in polar exploration was beginning; that of the Arctic winter and the transference of European techniques to the Arctic regions. The first period, as defined by Stefansson, had been that of the summer excursion by sea, coupled with the refusal to spend the winter; this stage ended with Parry.

The Buchan-Franklin expedition (the *Dorothea* and the *Trent*) was, nevertheless, a total failure. Halted by the ice pack to the north of Spitsbergen, despite the efforts of the haulers towing the ships from the edge of the ice, Buchan and Franklin narrowly escaped a final catastrophe among the icebergs; all the same, they reached 80° 34′ N. The *Dorothea* and the *Trent* (which had developed a leak) returned to England, bringing with them nothing but a meager map of the west of the Spitsbergen archipelago and an admirable account of the journey by one Lieutenant Frederick William Beechey.

The second expedition, under the command of Ross and Parry, was scarcely more successful, but it was more picturesque. Among the ninety-four volunteers, we should note the presence of the commander's nephew, James C. Ross (who was to become famous in his own right); Captain Sabine, in charge of magnetic observations; and an Eskimo interpreter named John Sacheuse, or Sackouse, who had been forced to travel far from his native Greenland as the result of an unfortunate love affair, and who had been dropped by a whaling ship in London. Sackouse agreed to accompany Ross on condition that he be returned to England. He proved very useful in the many dealings the expedition had with the Eskimos. Ross got a dog sledge with its full equipment in exchange for a smooth-bore rifle and provided unexpected treats for the natives, thanks to a Scottish musician who was a member of the crew.

But the expedition had its much more dramatic moments among

the ice floes; they had to tack and tack about again from moment to moment; they had to warp and tow the boats. "We even," Ross reported, "had to cut a path through the ice which closed up around us immediately." One day, the terrible pressure of the ice smashed the two ships up against each other with such violence that a launch was shattered to bits between them; ordinary ships could not have withstood the shock.

On August 30, with the expedition at 74° 19′ N. in Baffin Bay and in sight of Lancaster Sound, the decision was made to enter the strait with all sails spread; this amid the hurrahs of the crew, who were already dreaming of the reward promised to the discoverers of the great passage. But Ross himself did not share this enthusiasm. Having noted that there was neither a northwest current nor any driftwood coming from that direction, he abruptly ordered the ships to tack about, to the surprise of everyone and against the advice of his second-in-command, Edward Parry.

His return to England was greeted with disappointment, although the scientific results of the expedition were far from negligible; he brought back useful and accurate cartographic information and important observations on the fauna of the ocean depths. To make these observations, he had invented an ingenious device which he called a "deep-sea clam"; with it, moreover, he succeeded in capturing a jellyfish from six thousand feet below sea level.

Ross had also discovered the Arctic Highlander Eskimos and had trained his whole crew for further polar navigation; he had also found several new whaling areas and given names to a number of new territories (Melville Bay, Cape Isabella and Cape Alexander). He had, finally, succeeded in solving the mystery of "red snow," a phenomenon produced by the multiplication of a kind of algae, the *Protococcus nivalis*. Nevertheless, in private the geographers passed a harsh judgment on Ross, whom they accused of cowardliness, stupidity and incompetence.

His second-in-command, Edward Parry, seemed so disappointed by his superior's "renunciation" and so enthusiastic about the idea of setting off again that Sir John Barrow did not hesitate to offer him the command of a new expedition, while he put John Franklin in charge of a coastal expedition in search of the passage.

These two impetuous officers made no secret of their disagreements with Buchan and Ross; indeed Lord Melville, the First Lord of the Admiralty, is reported to have said to them: "You claim you can do better? Go ahead."

"Without an equal as an organizer and administrator," Markham wrote of Parry, "unsurpassed as a leader of men, he was an accomplished officer and a bold and resolute navigator, knowing when to take risks and when to avoid them. He was the ideal of an Arctic officer."

His success has a miraculous side to it, nevertheless, not only because of the geographic discoveries he made, but still more because, in the course of his three voyages, he singlehandedly set out the techniques for systematically wintering in the Arctic, an enterprise never deliberately undertaken by anyone before him.

When he became commander of the expedition of 1819, Parry was only twenty-nine, but he had already amassed considerable experience; for his knowledge of naval matters and his scientific contributions he had already been elected a member of the Royal Society. It was through a book he had written on nautical astronomy that he had won Sir John Barrow's favor.

When, the following year, he was named head of the new expedition, he took care to choose from among the many volunteers, a crew entirely made of young men; the eldest officer, Sabine, was not yet thirty, while the age of the men ranged from seventeen to nineteen (these volunteers received double pay).

For his ships, he chose the 375-ton bomb vessel *Hecla* and the 130-ton brig *Griper,* the deck of which was raised six feet to increase storage space. Command of the *Griper* was given to Lieutenant Liddon. The stem and the keel were given maximum reinforcement in order to withstand the ice. As he was perfectly aware of the sensitivity of his compasses, he made certain that there was no piece of iron, however small, in their vicinity; he went so far as to replace the iron guns at the stern with bronze ones.

He gave particular attention to the provisions, which were intended to last three years: preserved meat and soups, essence of malt hops and spruce; lemon juice, vinegar, pickles, and herbs to be used as preventives against scurvy. Coal in the holds served as ballast. The men had warm clothing and wolfskin blankets.

Having left England in May 1819, the *Hecla* and the *Griper* reached the entry into Lancaster Sound on July 28; they had counted eighty-eight icebergs along their way. An as yet un-dreamed-of navigational problem came up in the sound; the artillery officer Sabine, in charge of magnetic operations, found that the inclination of the compass had increased to 88° 26′ and concluded that the needle, deranged by the proximity of the Magnetic Pole, could no longer be counted on to give bearings; he relegated the compass to the carpenter's workshop.

"On the 10th," Parry wrote, "the weather was very thick with snow, which was afterwards succeeded by rain and fog. The compass being useless and the sun obscured, we had no means of knowing the direction in which we were going except that we knew the wind had been southward before the fog came on." Having finally taken his bearings, thanks to a rift in the fog, Parry proceeded on into Prince Regent Inlet, after verifying the existence of the Croker Mountains, which Ross thought he had seen.

Halted by the ice, he returned westward and reached Melville Island via Barrow Strait; he had passed longitude 110° W., thereby assuring his crews of winning the 5,000 pounds prize money offered by Parliament.

Icebound in Port Winter, the expedition passed the winter without serious incident; seven men who set out from the *Griper* to hunt musk ox on Melville Island were lost. Parry hung lanterns from the mainmast of the *Hecla*, fired his guns and set off rockets in the air; the seven men made their way back to the ships three days later, unharmed except for a few frozen fingers. To commemorate his joy, Parry called the spot Cape Providence.

He then settled down to organizing his nine months' winter camp, a thing unprecedented in the annals of the British Navy. The masts were dismantled down to the most insignificant topgallant and then used to support a wooden roof, insulated with woolen flock over the maindeck; this remarkably airtight and watertight shelter served the men as a promenade area during bad weather. Belowdecks, a system of ducts distributed the heat produced by the stoves and established an even, bearable temperature; the sleeping quarters were equipped with a false ceiling to improve the insulation.

The men were divided into small groups, each commanded by an officer who was responsible for their good behavior and cleanliness; once a week the sailors' legs and gums were inspected by the doctors, and every day the men had to take their ration of lemon juice under the eyes of an officer. Water cress was cultivated in hothouse frames, and the hunters were often able to furnish fresh meat. Concentrated broth and vegetables preserved in vinegar were regularly distributed, while hard liquor was forbidden and its place taken by wine and beer.

But the most dangerous adversary was boredom; Parry had foreseen this. He founded a theatrical troupe, which was directed by Lieutenant Beechey. The repertory was restricted to a small number of plays, but, for Christmas, Parry himself composed a musical comedy, whose theme was his own expedition; *The Northwest Passage* was enthusiastically played and received, while the temperature outside was 31 degrees below zero.

Every Monday, from November 1, 1819, to March 20, 1820, there appeared the *North Georgia Gazette and Winter Chronicle*, whose editor-in-chief was Captain Sabine. It included various humorous chronicles, as, for example, the following:

ARCTIC MISERIES
by Old Comical

Going out in a winter morning for the purpose of taking a walk, and before you have proceeded ten yards from the ship, getting a cold bath in the cook's steep hole [a hole in the ice for steeping salt meat, etc.].

When on a hunting excursion, and being close to a fine deer, after several attempts to fire, discovering that your piece is neither primed nor loaded, while the animal's four legs are employed in carrying away the body.

Setting out with a piece of new bread in your pocket on a shooting party, and when you feel inclined to eat it, having occasion to observe that it is so frozen that your teeth will not penetrate it.

Returning on board your ship after an evening visit in a contemplative humour and being roused from a pleasing reverie by the close embrace of a bear.

But, as only two of the men knew how to read and write, Parry organized evening classes for the illiterate.

Parry was remarkably successful in distracting his men and in dispelling their fears of the polar night, which lasted eighty-four days, and during which the temperature varied between 4 and 50 degrees below zero. Few serious incidents occurred. One observation hut caught fire, and one man had to have his frozen fingers amputated. Only one sailor died.

In the spring, Parry made numerous sorties on Melville Island; he encountered musk oxen, reindeer, white hare, geese, golden plover, ptarmigan, wolves and foxes. In sheltered corners, he found patches of grass, moss, saxifrage and poppies. He also discovered traces of Eskimo encampments.

It was with the aid of a sort of improvised wagon drawn by four men that Parry managed to cross Melville Island, a unique exploit which marked the beginning of Arctic exploration on land. In his account of it, Parry only very rarely betrays the feeling that this was an exceptional sort of effort; thirty-five years later, however, Sir Francis Leopold McClintock was to find the tracks left by the wagon still visible in the snow.

By opening the period of Arctic exploration by land, Parry forced technology headlong into dealing with new problems that no one had ever thought of before and which were not raised by life on board ship. Appropriate clothing had to be devised to permit the necessary physical action and to provide protection against the cold and the wind. It also became clear that the provisions to be carried must be as light as possible, while still answering to the body's requirements. These provisions had, moreover, to be cooked or reheated; fire, fuel and suitable containers had to be thought of. Studies had to be made of facilities for lodging and sleeping. Finally, it was necessary to find an efficient means of transporting, over the snow and the ice and the "rivers" which cut through the ice pack, all the equipment that was indispensable for human survival.

The idea never entered anyone's mind that for thousands of years there had been men who had solved all these problems in perfectly satisfactory ways. It took the greatest specialists, the most intelligent and astute explorers, more than a century to understand that all that was required to solve these problems was to adopt Eskimo techniques.

It seems inconceivable now that for scores and scores of years the polar explorers, some of whom established immortal reputations, should have been forced to rediscover on their own—and at the price of terrible, often fatal, difficulties—techniques as old as the world of ice. And even after some (but not all!) of these techniques, such as the dog sledge, had finally been adopted, there were still some great men who contemptuously regarded them as unsporting.

One of the greatest, Robert Scott, wrote before his last expedition: "No journey ever made with dogs can approach the height of that fine conception which is realized when a party of men go forth to face hardships, dangers and difficulties by their own unaided efforts." This stoical sentiment was to cost him both the conquest of the Pole and his life; Roald Amundsen reached the South Pole a month ahead of him, seated on a dog sledge. And after planting the Norwegian flag, he even allowed himself the luxury of a cigar.

Scott's technique of 1911, the "man-hauled sledge," was a practically unchanged version of the one in existence on that day in June 1820 when Parry set out with eleven men to cross Melville Island.

Into his snow chariot—which was built of wooden planks and the wheels of a field gun—Parry piled tents (blankets held in place with ropes and pegs), provisions for three weeks (a pound of biscuits, fourteen ounces of bully beef, one ounce of sugar and a gill of rum per man per day—nearly nine hundred pounds in all), warm clothing and firewood. Each man carried his own sleeping bag (twenty-two pounds) on his back and took his turn at hauling the wagon.

When the vehicle broke down, the eleven explorers had to trudge back, with each man carrying ninety pounds of equipment.

Scott was to calculate his rations more scientifically, was to invent studs for the men's boots, was to use a more advanced method of harnessing and more modern sledges, but the principle, as we shall see, was to remain constant. It is for this reason that Parry's first journey belongs to polar history.

His ships were got free on the first of August, and, faced with the impossibility of making any westward progress beyond Cape Dundas (113° 47′ W.), they set sail and returned home after sighting and naming Banks Land. Parry arrived in London toward the end of October, convinced now that the search for the Northwest Passage ought to be carried on more to the south; it was to carry on this search that he decided to set sail again the following spring.

Lieutenant Franklin, who had been commissioned to head the exploration by land complementing Parry's voyage along the

American coastline, was not to return to England till two years later, in 1822. With Dr. Richardson and the officers Back and Hood, he landed at Fort York, to the west of Hudson Bay, on August 30, 1819, after three months of difficult and dangerous sailing.

His first stop was at Fort Chipewyan, where he was to complete the organizing stage of the expedition. The English made their way across the 750 miles of country separating them from the fort, but only at the price of unheard of difficulties, using snowshoes, plagued by the "inconvenience of marching with a weight of between two and three pounds constantly attached to galled feet and swelling ankles."

Franklin was all but drowned in a torrent. He reached Fort Chipewyan only to find that there was not more than 500 pounds of dried buffalo meat there. He then called on the Copper Indians; after they had smoked the peace pipe and drunk rum together, the chief, Akaitcho, asked whether Franklin had had any news of Captain Parry's ships, of which he had heard reports, and finally agreed to accompany Franklin to the polar coast with nine of his men (two guides and seven hunters). They reached the coast in 1821, after an exhausting journey and two very harsh winters.

Having got to the sea, Parry rectified the co-ordinates of the mouth of the Coppermine River, which had been calculated fifty years earlier by Hearne, the first explorer to visit the region. He set out eastward, marking out the coast of Coronation Gulf as far as Hood River, for Parry's eventual use; he then turned toward Fort Enterprise.

Game became scarce, then lichen (a mucilaginous substance, called *tripe de roche*) as well; the boats were broken up to make canoes, then the canoes to make firewood. An Indian went out of his head and killed, first, two French Canadians who had joined Franklin, then Lieutenant Hood. "Our sufferings," wrote Franklin, "caused by the weather and a cold of 4 degrees below zero, sheltered by a poor cloth tent, can easily be imagined, but they remain, nevertheless, well below those brought us by hunger."

The retreat to Fort Chipewyan began. The men lived off the rare lichen that was to be found and off the carcasses of dead deer, which had already been devoured by the wolves; a foul broth could be made from the putrid bones, seasoned with fragments of hide or old shoes; on this diet, the journey was tantamount to a slaughter.

On arrival at Fort Enterprise—which was nothing more than a simple hut—there were only five survivors remaining from the twenty-three who had begun the journey. They would all have died had Ensign Back not succeeded, heroically, in locating Akaitcho's Indians.

By the time he returned to Fort York in July 1822, Franklin had traveled over and surveyed—at the price of inhuman suffering—more than five thousand miles.

The Far North had let its prey escape this time. It was to lie in wait for him for more than twenty years; it was in 1847 that Sir John Franklin met his death in "the Arctic hell."

11

THE FIRST ASSAULT

THE YEAR 1819 marked the opening of the rush to the north. It also was the year in which the Antarctic continent was sighted for the first time.

Up till then Captain Cook had set the tone: summer sorties, and, in the autumn, a return to more bearable latitudes. The frightful atmospheric conditions around the edges of the Antarctic continent made its approach a considerable exploit. This approach was unquestionably accomplished by American and British whaling men and seal hunters, who were ceaselessly on the lookout for new hunting grounds.

Nevertheless, it was a captain in the Royal Navy, William Smith, aboard the *Williams*, who was the first man to land on King George Island (62° S., 58° W.), in the group which he named the South Shetlands, on October 16, 1819. Several sealers had already hastened there by January 1820; in the summer of 1820-21, forty-four of them had arrived, and a year later, there were ninety-one.

Smith, accompanying Lieutenant Edward Bransfield, returned to the neighborhood, and, on January 30, 1820, discovered the northwest coast of Graham Land.[1] Bransfield was thus the first man to see and to map the Antarctic continent, and his expedition was the first scientific Antarctic exploration.

But it is to the Baltic Baron Gottlieb von Bellingshausen, then at the head of a Russian expedition, that we must assign the credit for having circumnavigated the Antarctic along a more southerly latitude than that followed by Cook. With two corvettes, the *Vostok* and the *Mirny*, he discovered Peter I Island, the first land discovered below the polar circle, and then, Alexander I Land; he reached latitude 69° S. before returning to Kronstadt; on his way he had crossed paths with the American sea captain Nat Palmer, who on November 17, 1820, sighted Graham Land, which he named Palmer Land. So it is that the Antarctic peninsula is called Graham on English maps and Palmer on American maps.

During this slightly confused period of the approach to the Antarctic by the sealers, we may note several achievements:

That of the first American sealer to visit the area, the *Hersilia* under the command of James P. Sheffield (1819-20);

That of the first vessel to bring back sealskins, in 1819, the Argentine *San Juan Nepomuceno*, commanded by Carlos Timblon; it returned to Buenos Aires on February 22, 1820, with 14,600 skins;

That of the English Captain Clark and his ten seal hunters aboard the *Lord Melville*, who were the first human beings to winter in the Antarctic, in the South Shetlands, on King George Island in 1819-20.

That of the first man to set foot on the ice of the Antarctic continent, the American Captain John Davis, on February 7, 1821. It was the Yale cartographer, Alexander O. Vietor, who discovered the logbook of Davis's sealer, the *Huron*, in which this "landing" was recorded. Searching for seals, Davis arrived at noon, February 7, 1820, before the mouth of a wide bay situated at 64° 01′S. "Land

---

[1] In honor of Sir James Graham, First Lord of the Admiralty at the time.

high," he noted, "and covered intirely with Snow. The wind comming around to the North'd and Eastward with thick weather." The weather became very bad. Davis decided to stay in the bay (Hughes Bay). He wrote, "I think this Southern Land to be a continent." The lack of precision of the *Huron*'s logbook prevents us from assigning the discovery of Antarctica unqualifiedly to Davis.

And finally, that of the famous Scottish sealer James Weddell, who beat Captain Cook's record for latitude, reaching 74° 15′ S., in the sea that bears his name, on February 20, 1823; he was only 940 miles from the South Pole. It was to take almost a century for those few miles to be conquered. Weddell found the sea miraculously free of ice and did not wish to go farther because of the nearness of winter.

He was in command of the 160-ton sealer *Jane* (with a 22-man crew); her consort the *Beaufoy* (65 tons, 13 men) was under the orders of Captain Matthew Brisbane. The provisions were planned to last two years. Weddell carried no scientific equipment, but he did possess a full arsenal of navigational instruments. His aim was fishing, but this did not prevent him from bringing back to London unique specimens of the sea leopard, which were of considerable value to the scientists. It was also the demon of curiosity that forced him to press on southward; for this fisherman had the soul of an explorer. He was, in any case, a remarkable navigator; his calculations of longitude (he had brought with him four of the best chronometers obtainable) were of astounding accuracy. He never left off noting, every day, the temperatures of the air and the water, and the variations of the compass.

Before deciding to return, Weddell had a double ration of rum distributed to the men, noted the depth of the water (1,476 feet) and threw a bottle containing a message into the sea; it was never recovered. On the way home, in South Georgia, having dropped anchor in Adventure Bay and having scaled a peak on the island, he was surprised to observe that the mercury in his artificial horizon was trembling so much that he could no longer use it; volcanic quavers had transformed it into a seismoscope.

Weddell died on October 9, 1834, in London, at the age of forty-seven. His name is inseparable from the map of Antarctica, and his record was to be beaten only in 1842, by Sir James Clark Ross, who was to make his way to latitude 78° 09′ S. Moreover, Ross was to set off only after having made sure to take Weddell's logbook along with him in his cabin.

None of these attempts in the south, as we can see, was particularly decisive; we shall have to wait for Biscoe, Dumont d'Urville, Balleny, Wilkes, and especially Ross, to find real progress being made in the discovery of the Antarctic, during the course of the nineteenth century; its conquest really began only with the nascent twentieth century.

The north was much the more fascinating subject in the eyes of the public in Weddell's time.

Parry, who had already come to resemble a legendary figure, headed three expeditions to the north, one after the other; he succeeded in approaching within 8 degrees of the Pole, after a fantastic march over the drift ice.

Hardly had Parry returned from his first expedition, when he decided to set out again to search for the "passage" by way of Hudson Strait. He kept the *Hecla*, but the *Fury* (377 tons) replaced the *Griper*, which had proved too small; he had chosen two exactly identical ships, so that he could interchange parts without difficulty, a point which gives us some indication of Parry's organizing capacities. His own flag flew from the *Fury;* the *Hecla* was commanded by Captain G. F. Lyon; young James Clark Ross, Sir John's nephew, was a midshipman attached to the expedition.

Several technical innovations marked this voyage: a new system of heating, invented by a Mr. Sylvester, was successfully adopted; a receptacle for melting snow was set above the galley fire, while the provisions now included a good proportion of flour as well as hardtack.

In May 1821, the two ships set sail for Hudson Bay, where they were icebound for several days. The men took advantage of their free time to kill a 1,600-pound polar bear, a creature of such vitality that "the heart continued to beat on being taken out, although the animal had been three hours dead."

They made contact with the Eskimos, who offered them whale oil, seal and reindeer skins, walrus tusks, and even weapons, in return for iron, "an inestimable treasure in their eyes." They would accept an ordinary nail in exchange for a spear with an ivory head! In this way, the Englishmen sold them everything down to old barrel rims; "no sooner had they received an article than it was applied to the tongue and licked several times." Some of them offered their children—naked—or even their wives' favors in payment.

Finally, free of the ice, the ships were able to enter Foxe Channel on their way to Repulse Bay. On an excursion inland, Captain Lyon discovered an entire whale's skeleton in a ravine situated more than a hundred feet above sea level; the layer of humus covering the bones attested to its antiquity, though it gave no explanation of its presence.

By sawing a channel for themselves, the *Hecla* and the *Fury* reached Winter Island (on the polar circle) where they settled down to spend the winter. The experiment begun on Melville Island was successfully continued, with the hunt providing certain improvements in the daily fare; the meat fell to the community as a whole, while the hunter had a right to the head, the feet, the heart and the liver of his kill. This time costumes and bits of stage sets had been brought along, and the "actresses" were forced to sacrifice their beards and mustaches. A generous English lady had even made Parry the gift of a complete set of lantern slides.

Between one aurora borealis and the next, Eskimos came to visit the winterers; Parry was astonished to see their six snow huts, containing sixty people and their dogs, built only a few yards from the ships without any of the Englishmen having noticed. Parry had an organ concert given for them (he had thought to bring an organ along) and spent a long time studying their tattoos, which were made with a piece of whalebone and soot mixed with saliva and oil. He also tried to teach them to wash themselves, but they were too eager to swallow the soap, as they had done earlier with the candles. He also observed their method of fishing for seals, stretched flat on their bellies before holes in the ice with a harpoon ready in their hand.

On July 2, 1822, the ships were ice-free, and they set sail to the north, discovering a strait which was named for the *Fury* and the *Hecla*, then settling at Igloolik for another winter. New Eskimos came to visit them. Parry bought two teams of dogs from them, and he used these to draw launches, masts, anchors, etcetera from one ship to the other. Captain Lyon noted that one day his team of nine dogs covered just over a mile in nine minutes with a sledge carrying a 1,760-pound weight, and formed the opinion—without drawing any practical conclusions from it—that these dogs could accomplish similar performances for seven or eight hours every day.

The winter of 1823 was very hard. By the end of July, the two ships were still icebound. They succeeded in disengaging themselves at a time when scurvy was beginning to appear. Having given up the possibility of going on farther, Parry set out on his return voyage after christening the Melville Peninsula.

Concerning this voyage, we should take particular note of the following points: the exploration of Fury and Hecla strait by a midshipman with four men at his command, ten days' provisions, a tent, and two large planks with which to get across the crevasses; the use of dogs by the English (it was to take more than sixty years nonetheless before the dog sled became a regular technique in polar exploration); and finally the difficulty in finding the famous Northwest Passage.

The following year, moreover, in 1824, Parry set off again with the same ships and tried to force a way through Prince Regent Strait; the *Fury*, dismantled by the storms, was lost, and the *Hecla*, halted by the ice, had to return to England.

At the same time as Parry's, two other expeditions had been organized; Franklin resumed his "continental" exploration, while Beechey was given orders to sail the *Blossom* to Bering Strait, rounding the Americas by Tierra del Fuego.

With his old friends, Dr. Richardson and Lieutenant Back, John Franklin returned to Fort Chipewyan before wintering at Fort Franklin on Great Bear Lake. Setting off again on June 28, 1826, he made his way down the Mackenzie River to the Arctic Ocean. The expedition divided to reconnoiter the coast, then met again at Fort Franklin for a second winter's stay. This period, for which careful preparations had been made, went off without incident, despite the cold (which went as low as 51 degrees below zero).

Franklin returned unhindered to England in the autumn of 1827, bringing back an ample scientific harvest, gathered thanks to the "man-hauling" technique—that is, to human traction.

Parry's former lieutenant, Beechey, arrived at about the same time on the northwest coast of America, on board the war frigate *Blossom*. Having fitted out a longboat, armed by ten men, he made his way to Kotzebue Bay, beyond Bering Strait. Studying the natives' way of life and exploring the coasts as far as Beechey Point, Beechey found he was unable to make contact with Franklin and returned to England only to learn that the indefatigable Parry was preparing to set off again.

This time the hero of the English throng had decided to throw himself quite simply into an assault on the Pole.

But the ingenious explorer had dreamed up a revolutionary new technique: the system of amphibious sledges. Parry's plan was simple; starting from the most northerly point that was then known, Spitsbergen, his "Ultima Thule," he counted on reaching the Pole by crossing the icepack.

Parry did not know what condition the icepack was in; he supposed that it was sufficiently smooth to be crossed by men hauling sledges. But, suspecting that it might be cut by watercourses at certain points, he decided to use longboats as well as sledges; the combined use of the two sorts of transport would, theoretically, enable him to go all the way to the Pole. On the advice of William Scoresby, the whaler—who had by this time become a priest—he took reindeer with him; but as early tests with them proved fruitless, he never used them.

He left England in April 1827, aboard the *Hecla.* His two lieutenants were James Clark Ross and Crozier. Leaving his ship north of Spitsbergen, Parry set out northward with two longboats, four light sledges and provisions for seventy-one days. The boats, christened the *Enterprise* and the *Endeavour,* both had flat bottoms and measured 20 feet long and 6 feet wide at their widest point. "On each side of the keel," writes Sir Clements Markham, "there was a strong runner shod with metal, on which the boat rested when on the ice. A hide span across the fore part of the runners had two drag-ropes attached to it. The boats had two thwarts, a locker at each end, and a light framework along the sides for provisions and spare clothing; they carried a bamboo mast and tanned duck sails, fourteen paddles and a steering oar. The daily allowance for each man was about ten ounces of biscuit, nine ounces of pemmican,[2] one ounce of cocoa and a gill of rum." There was no lemon juice.

Parry organized the march with careful attention to the proper use of time. To avoid snow blindness he decided to travel by night, as Peary did later, though the line between day and night was indistinct. The team, who slept in the long boats sheltered by an

---

[2] Dried meat pounded into a paste with melted fat and dried fruit, pressed into cakes, originally an Indian preparation.

awning made from the sails, was wakened by a bugle call. The men said their prayers, took their meal and marched, pulling the sledges behind them, for five hours. After an hour's halt for lunch, they set off for another five hours' march; then another meal, prayers again, and to bed in raccoon-lined clothing.

It was a terrible journey; ceaselessly loading and unloading, hauling the sledges, setting the boats afloat, struggling against turbulent ice floes and raging elements (torrents of rain fell), Parry's men went on advancing northward at the price of awful suffering.

But Parry, who was endlessly checking and rechecking his position, perceived with despair that they were not advancing at all; the ice pack drifting southward as they slept robbed them of the distance they had conquered during the day's march. Discouraged, Parry decided to give up on July 26, 1827, at 82° 45′ N., 437 miles from the Pole. "Sincerely as we regret," he wrote, "not having been able to hoist the British flag in the highest latitude to which we had aspired, we shall perhaps be excused in having been the bearers of it to a parallel considerably beyond that registered in any other well-authenticated record."

Parry's record was to be beaten only forty-eight years later, by the British officer Albert Markham, of the Nares expedition (1875-76), who made his way boldly to 83° 20′ N.

In his fantastic northward march, Parry had covered almost 700 miles on the drifting ice pack, but had, in fact, advanced only 173 miles; this exploit terminates the polar career of William Edward Parry, who was honored, on April 29, 1829, with the title "Sir." Parry, who had married the daughter of Lord Stanley of Alderley in 1826, now entered private industry and contributed in large measure to the adoption of the propeller on English steamships.

With the steamship, a new era was about to begin in the history of the conquest of the poles, and it was two years after Parry's record that the old and stubborn John Ross set it going.

12

THE FIRST ARCTIC STEAMSHIP

It was partly thanks to the virtues of whisky that the North Magnetic Pole was first discovered. Not that the hold of the *Victory*, the first Arctic steamship, was ballasted with it; but if John Ross and his nephew James Clark Ross got the opportunity to perform this exploit in this boat, it was thanks to the silent partnership of Felix Booth, Sheriff of the City of London and a distillery magnate.

The English government, discouraged by the lack of positive results achieved by recent explorations, had refused to organize any more. It had even withdrawn the prize offered to the conqueror of the Pole. But John Ross, who had been violently criticized, who had run up against the more or less justified enmity of Sir John Barrow, and who was unable to look on without bitterness as his former second-in-command, Parry, and the young Franklin covered themselves with glory, was not halted by such trivialities and went on seeking a patron who would agree to finance his expedition (for 18,000 pounds).

Moreover, he was not in the least upset at having to do without the Admiralty's support, for their prudence would no doubt have prevented him from following through on his idea of using a steamship. The satisfaction that Ross was able to get out of this new source of energy was extremely slight; in fact, the *Victory*'s adventure was a misfortune, and the first steam engine to attack the ice floes was defeated by them.

The *Victory* was a small sailing ship displacing scarcely 85 tons, equipped with a steam engine driving paddle-wheels; it had been doing ferry service between Dover and Calais before Ross acquired it. The enormous engine took up a considerable amount of space on board ship. It never stopped leaking, in spite of the patches that were continually applied to it.

Ross persuaded his nephew James Clark, then twenty-nine years old, to accompany him. This young and brilliant officer, a specialist in terrestrial magnetism, who had already, as we have seen, participated in his uncle's and in Parry's expeditions, was now a commander in the Royal Navy.

His plan being to search for the Northwest Passage via Prince Regent Strait, where Parry had been stopped, Ross rounded Cape Farewell at the south of Greenland on July 5, 1829, with one thousand days' provisions in his hold.

It immediately became clear that the boat was carrying a monster; the infernal steam engine was soon up to its old tricks. As it would not make the *Victory* do more than three knots, Ross ordered that the sails be spread; and that was how it arrived at Somerset Island, where Ross discovered the remains of Parry's *Fury*.

They found a tent very nearly intact in spite of the visitation of the bears, and they were surprised to note the perfect state of preservation of the meat and vegetables, sealed up hermetically, it is true, in metal cases according to the process devised by the Englishman Bryan Donkin. The wine, the liqueurs, the bread, sugar, flour and chocolate were also intact. The sails were dry. But they sought in vain for the ship, which doubtless had been shattered by the ice and had sunk.

Having taken aboard all that he could of the *Fury*'s provisions, Ross set off again, using the steam engine once more; but again it proved such a source of worry and fatigue that he decided to dismantle and unload it as soon as winter came and the ship was icebound; this occurred on October 8 in Felix Harbor, at 69° 59′ N., on Boothia Peninsula (named in honor of the financier Booth).

"The prison door was shut upon us for the first time," wrote Ross. "It was impossible to repel the intrusion of those thoughts which, if they follow disappointment, press on us ever more heavily. Should we have done better had the engine not disappointed us, had we been here, as we ought to have been, a month or six weeks sooner? Was it the badness of our vessel which had prevented us from completing the outline of America, from ascertaining the 'northwest passage' in a single season?"

The *Victory* remained icebound in Felix Harbor for two winters. Ross took advantage of the time to study the Eskimos' way of life (but without ever neglecting to have prayers said and tea served at five o'clock). He made the acquaintance of a woman named Tiriksiu, who sketched a map of the entire region from memory, a map that gave more details than the one Ross had with him. He also met a one-legged man named Tulluahui, for whom Ross had a wooden leg made. The Eskimo's joy was uncontainable: "All the surgery of this case," Ross wrote, "lay indeed with the carpenter; but I doubt if any effort of surgery ever gave more satisfaction."

James Clark Ross continued, however, to be preoccupied with the problems of magnetism. Having succeeded in calculating the approximate position of the Magnetic Pole, he set off on an expedition along the southwest coast of Boothia Felix. By May 31, 1831, he had reached the North Magnetic Pole, at 70° 05′ 17″ N., 96° 46′ W.

"The chief object of our present expedition having thus been accomplished," he later declared, "in a manner even more satisfactory than we could have expected, I became desirous to extend our knowledge of the country as much further to the northward as the state of our time and our provisions would admit." He set up a cairn, crowned it with the British flag, and then returned to the ship after having explored King William Land.

In the month of April 1832, despite all their efforts, Ross's men were unable to get the *Victory* free from the ice; they had either to winter for a third time or abandon her. The commander chose the latter alternative. Boats, provisions, sledges set out on the long, slow, tribulation-filled journey over the shifting ice. On the first of July, they reached the point where they had discovered the *Fury* and where they were to spend a third Arctic winter. Fortunately, the provisions were still intact, except for a few crates of candles that had been broken into by foxes.

The month of August came around for the third time. Ross decided to set out in his ship's boats. Finally, on August 15, 1833, he reached Lancaster Sound. On the twenty-sixth at 4 A.M., they were sighted by a passing ship.

"What is the name of your vessel?" Ross asked the ship's officer.

"The *Isabella* of Hull, once commanded by Captain Ross."

"I am Captain Ross."

The officer had some difficulty in believing him, for Ross had been officially declared dead two years earlier. But when this misunderstanding was cleared up, delirium broke out. The crew of the *Isabella* gave the polar heroes a triumphant welcome.

Ross was knighted on October 19, named rear admiral, and—along with his crew—received a 5,000-pound reward from Parliament, which also reimbursed Felix Booth and promoted James Clark Ross to the rank of captain. Sir John Ross had had his revenge and had re-established his reputation as an officer and a gentleman.

But, loaded down with honors as he was, he still dreamed often of his poor *Victory*, his "friend" buried somewhere in the Far North, of the first steam engine in the history of polar exploration smashed to bits on the ice pack; it had had the honor of leading to the discovery of the North Magnetic Pole, the first great step in man's conquest of the four poles.

13

THE LAST GREAT SAILING VOYAGE

James Clark Ross was thirty-nine in 1839, he was a captain in the Royal Navy and had spent fourteen years of his life in the Arctic, including eight winters. He was also the discoverer of the North Magnetic Pole. Though he might well have been satisfied with all this, he dreamed of only one thing: of going and planting the (original) flag from the North Magnetic Pole at the South Magnetic Pole.

This obsession with magnetic phenomena was understandable; in a period when enormous technical advances were being made in naval matters (iron construction, steam and the propeller), navigation required that thorough knowledge of the problem of terrestrial magnetism be achieved.

We were, of course, to have to wait till the International Geophysical Year in 1957 before a map of polar magnetism was finally drawn up; even then, all its laws were not yet to be formulated.

The I.G.Y.'s success in this area was certainly a result of the fact that all the various observations bearing on it could be coordinated together. But Ross was only a single, isolated traveler, with no chance at an over-all view of the phenomenon. He guessed—and proved—that the magnetic poles do not coincide with the geographic poles.

The isoclinal lines,[1] as well as the magnetic equator are undulating, not regular, lines. The intensity of the terrestrial magnetic field varies in the ratio of 2.5 at the Pole to 1 at the equator. There also exist centers of maximum intensity which do not coincide with the poles; it is easy to imagine how much groping, how many individual observations were necessary before this over-all view could be obtained. We ought to add, to give an even better notion of the difficulty involved, that the two magnetic poles are not fixed.

Ross had found the North Magnetic Pole at 70° 05′ N. and 96° 46′ W. In 1904, Amundsen's observations located it at 70° 30′ N. and 95° 30′ W. In 1945, the British officer MacLure, flying an airplane, the *Ares,* found it two hundred miles farther north, while in 1947, a Canadian scientific expedition spotted it north of Prince of Wales Island, at 73° N. and 100° W.

Thus, the Pole appears to have shifted more than two hundred miles in half a century, at a rate of about four to five miles per year; this movement is thought to follow an ellipsis running south to north and to occur between noon and midnight, while a movement in the reverse direction occurs during the other twelve hours. On the other hand, it is thought that the Pole may shift relatively each day, in the normal course of its general movement, within a radius of twenty-two miles in normal weather, and forty-four miles in a magnetic storm or during the aurora borealis.

In the Southern Hemisphere, the Pole was not to be discovered till 1909, by T. W. Edgeworth (later Sir Edgeworth) David, of

---

[1] Lines connecting points on the earth's surface at which the magnetic inclination, or dip, is the same.

the Shackleton expedition, at 72° 25′ S. and 115° 16′ E., on Victoria Land; it was located at 68° 07′ S. and 148° E. by the geophysicists of the French polar expedition on Adélie Coast in 1952; its shift is thus more rapid than that of the North Magnetic Pole.

In light of this inconstancy in terrestrial magnetism, the great German physicist Karl Friedrich Gauss deserves all the more credit for having announced, at about this time, that the South Magnetic Pole would surely be found at 66° S., 146° E.; the beguiling precision of this prediction was still another reason for Ross to set out in search of that "mysterious power which seems to baffle all our attempts at discovery," of that "extraordinary phenomenon," as it was called by the German naturalist Humboldt.

England took a long time about making up her mind to attempt her first great adventure in the south. When she did come to a decision, in 1839, Ross, who was to command the expedition, had already been preceded by two other great navigators: the Frenchman Jules Sébastien César Dumont d'Urville and the American Charles Wilkes.

Dumont d'Urville, who discovered the famous Venus de Milo and who, during the course of his career, sailed every sea of the globe aboard the *Astrolabe*, a simple sailing ship somewhat pompously called a corvette, was not originally regarded as a polar explorer. It was during his fourth cruise in the South Seas that he became one. His ambition was to follow the course of Weddell's voyages and to give France the glory of having come closer to the Pole than any other nation had yet come.

At the same time, the United States was eager to share some of the polar glory, and Congress had given command of six ships to a forty-year-old officer, Lieutenant Charles Wilkes, with orders to outdo Captain Cook's exploits.

These were the two official expeditions; they in turn were preceded by private parties hunting sea elephants and the fur-bearing seals whose hides fetched five dollars apiece in China. The brothers Enderby of London had financed the following: Captain John Biscoe (in 1830; he discovered Enderby Land, Adelaide Land and sighted Graham Land); Captain Rae (in 1833; one of his ships was dashed to pieces at 60° S.); Captain Kemp (in 1834; he discovered the land that bears his name at 60° W.); and especially, John Balleny (in 1839), who discovered his archipelago and who was the first to suspect the existence of the land later named for him.

Dumont d'Urville left Toulon in January 1838, on board the *Astrolabe* (formerly the *Coquille*) accompanied by the *Zelée* (under the command of Jacquinot). These two corvettes were old ships, both under 300 tons, each having to transport about a hundred men. Neither was equipped for the ice. They stood up to it nevertheless, twice in 1839, and again in 1840, when Dumont d'Urville returned to the Antarctic to search for the South Magnetic Pole between the meridians of 120° and 160° where it had been situated by Gauss.

To this desolate and grandiose coast, beaten by terrifying winds, he gave the romantic name of his wife, Adélie. Then he landed his men on a small island off the coast; in their enthusiasm, the French flag was hoisted and a bottle of wine was drunk in honor of the king of France.

Sailing on, they were surprised to see an American warship, the *Porpoise*, from Wilkes's fleet, looming up on the horizon. Arrogantly, the two ships spread full sail and passed without even saluting; the haughty Dumont d'Urville and the quarrelsome American behaved like two spoiled brats.

Wilkes had left America on August 18, 1838, at the head of his squadron: The *Vincennes* (a 780-ton cutter-rigged coasting vessel); the *Peacock* (a 650-ton sloop); the *Porpoise* (a 230-ton brig); the *Seagull* (an old, 110-ton pilot boat from the port of New York); the *Flying Fish* (a 96-ton pilot boat); and the *Relief* (a very slow cargo boat, which was sent home during the course of the voyage).

Wilkes, like d'Urville, wanted to discover the magnetic pole. It was after sailing along more than 1500 miles of coast that he met the Frenchman on January 30, 1840. Seeing two ships approach, Lieutenant Ringgold believed they must be two of Ross's, and he prepared to "cheer the discoverer of the North Magnetic Pole." But when he saw the French colors appear, and when he realized that this must be Dumont d'Urville who was now piling on more sail, he decided that he was being offered an "insult," and, striking his own colors, he proceeded on his way.

The incident between Wilkes (who approved of his lieutenant's actions) and Dumont d'Urville flared up again when it had to be decided which of the two of them had "discovered" Adélie

Land; France spent a century making up her mind, for it was only in 1926, at the instigation of Jean Baptiste Charcot, that she asserted her claim to that sector. On January 20, 1950, 110 years to the day after Dumont d'Urville's landing, the members of the French polar expedition, aboard the polar dispatch boat *Commandant Charcot*, set foot on Adélie Land, where they were to install a base and begin a series of expeditions which have gone on almost uninterruptedly year after year since that time.

It was considered proper that the French base of the International Geophysical Year should be called the "Dumont d'Urville Base," to the glory of the great navigator to whom his own century had been so cool—to such a point that on his tomb in the Montparnasse Cemetery,[2] the Geographical Society had the following inscription engraved.

POINT DE DEUIL
UN PEU DE CENDRE
UN PEU DE TERRE
BEAUCOUP DE BRUIT[3]

These wounding words were, fortunately, erased. It is a consolation to think that time as well would have worn them away.

On January 30, 1840, the American Lieutenant Ringgold, seeing the Frenchman appear, had believed that he was James Clark Ross. But the English commander did not arrive before Possession Island, quite close to the continent, until January 11, 1841, almost a year later.

Having learned at Hobart (in Tasmania) of Dumont d'Urville's and Wilkes's first discoveries, he decided to modify his plan and to carry out his attack farther to the east. He enjoyed a double advantage over his two predecessors: first, his great polar experience; and second, his two ships, the *Erebus* and the *Terror*, which were later to participate in a glorious tragedy under Franklin.

---

[2] He died in the Versailles train wreck of May 8, 1842.

[3] No mourning
A bit of ash
A bit of earth
A great deal of noise

They were both relatively small signal-barges (370 and 340 tons), but extremely sturdy. Rigged like three-masted barks, they were made entirely of wood which had been specially reinforced for the ice. The capacities of their holds were considerable. A small crew (64 men) was sufficient to run them. Iron was replaced wherever possible by copper to avoid interference with the magnetic compass. The decks were reinforced with two strong thicknesses of planks separated by a layer of waterproof cloth. Every part of the superstructure that could possibly come in contact with the ice had been carefully reinforced.

Organizer that he was, James Clark Ross, Parry's pupil, had taken particular pains with the provisions. The base of the diet was concentrated soup and preserved meat. Enormous quantities of vegetables (including five tons of carrots and four tons of pickles) were piled into the holds. The sailors (all volunteers receiving double pay) had warm clothing of excellent quality at their disposal. Each ship carried, besides the captain, three lieutenants, a surgeon, a purser, three executive officers, and an assistant surgeon in charge of zoological and geological observations. The usual navigational instruments of the period were to be found on board, but everything dealing with magnetism was particularly elaborate and sophisticated.

On September 30, 1839, the *Erebus*, with Commander James Ross aboard, and the *Terror*, under Crozier's command, sailed out of the Thames. After exploring Kerguelen Island, Ross paid a visit to Sir John Franklin, who was at that time governor of Tasmania. On November 13, 1840, Ross set sail for the south.

He ran into the ice pack at about 66° 32′ S., and, to his surprise, succeeded in getting across it. The *Erebus* and the *Terror* were thus assured of the glory of having been the first ships to force the ice.

Finding the sea free once again at 69° 15′ S., he halted on January 11, 1841, at Possession Island, which he dedicated to the young Queen Victoria. On January 24, he reached an island on which stood two volcanoes, one of them active, to which he gave the names of his two ships (Ross Island: 78° S., 168° E.). The crew received a double ration of rum for having beaten Weddell's record. There Ross was stopped by an immense wall of glass, the Ross Barrier, along the edge of which he sailed to the east.

Pressed by the approaching winter, he was unable to explore

the barrier till the following year. In it, he discovered the Bay of Whales.[4] In the course of a violent storm among the icebergs, collision between the two ships very nearly resulted in catastrophe. They succeeded in separating, and, battered by the elements, set sail for the north.

Ross (who was knighted by Queen Victoria in 1844) had not discovered the South Magnetic Pole. But the contribution he made to the discovery of the Antarctic was still considerable; he opened a way into the heart of the continent for Scott, Schackleton and Amundsen. He had, also, with two minuscule boats, just completed the last of the great polar sailing voyages.

---

[4] Where Amundsen set up his Framheim Base in 1910 and Byrd built his successive Little Americas.

14

THE NORTHWEST PASSAGE

In 1829, the German scientist Georg Adolf Erman discovered, on the New Siberian and Lyakhov Islands, an extraordinary accumulation of elephant, rhinoceros and buffalo bones. Jules de Blesseville, who had set out in 1833 aboard the *Lilloise* to explore the Greenland coast, went down, as Charcot was to do a century later. In 1838, the Frenchman Gaimard observed Spitsbergen with the aid of the first captive balloon.

It was then, in 1845, that the slow agony of the two most glorious ships in polar history, the *Erebus* and the *Terror*, began. These were the ships which Ross had commanded so triumphantly in the south. Sir John Franklin, the veteran of the Arctic (he was fifty-nine), was given command of them in order to attempt once again to find the Northwest Passage. Parry had turned down the same offer in favor of the former governor of Tasmania, whom he considered "the most capable man in England."

The *Erebus* and the *Terror* set sail for the north in late spring, 1845; they were never to return; this was, in Stefansson's term—around which he wrote a book—the first of the "great unsolved mysteries of the Arctic." [1]

Never had a voyage been better prepared for. The *Erebus* and the *Terror* were equipped with all the latest and most highly perfected technological devices. The hulls were reinforced with thick iron plates, and central heating (an ingenious system of heating the cabins with hot water) was installed on board. Each of the two ships had a 50-horsepower auxiliary engine, which had first been used on locomotives. The engines were to function only in case it became impossible to advance otherwise—which gives an indication of the sailor's traditional mistrust of steam; each of the boats, moreover, carried only a ten days' supply of coal.

There was one great improvement, however, over John Ross's *Victory;* the paddle wheel was replaced by a propeller, which, thanks to an ingenious device, could be withdrawn in the ice. This was a recent invention; the Frenchmen Delisle (1823) and Sauvage (1832) had suggested the use of an Archimedean screw at the stern. But it was the Englishman Smith and the Swede Ericsson who, in 1836, constructed the first propeller-driven ship. In 1840, the paddle wheel was consigned to the naval museums, and the *Victory* herself became one of the first propeller-driven ships in history.

Provisions for four years were taken aboard; the tableware was porcelain, the glasses crystal and the forks silver. The library of each ship boasted twelve hundred volumes and a complete file of *Punch*. A barrel organ, an ancestor of the jukebox which was to be found on board the American submarine *Nautilus* in 1959, offered more than fifty selections, ranging from the Scottish reel to religious cantatas. Paradoxically, the clothing provided was of stout blue regulation fabric, which shows how far the Eskimo techniques still were from being assimilated by the English.

The crew included 138 men with experience in polar navigation.

---

[1] Vilhjalmur Stefansson, *Unsolved Mysteries of the Arctic*.

The commander, Franklin, was aboard the *Erebus*, while Francis Crozier was in charge of the *Terror*. The two ships both had black hulls, white masts and yellow superstructures. "We desire"—so ran Article Five of Sir John's Instructions, drawn up in twenty-three paragraphs by the Admiralty—"that every effort be used to endeavour to penetrate toward Bering Strait. . . ."

On July 27, Franklin reached the mouth of the strait, where he met two whaling ships; this was the last time he was seen. A grave error had been committed by the expedition's planners; they had neglected to specify a meeting place for each summer, where the expedition could transmit news of itself to the outside world.

By 1847, the absence of news was beginning to arouse uneasiness in England. Aware of the faultiness of the over-all plan, the Admiralty organized three rescue expeditions, one each from the east, west and south; the Royal Navy's search was beginning; it would cost twenty million pounds and forty expeditions.

Step by step the rescue parties were to retrace the agonizing journey of Franklin and his companions. For nearly thirty years they were to scour the north in search of the truth. This fantastic combing, this gigantic inquest was to have at least one result; science and geographic discovery were to turn it to account. In 1878, at the time of the Frederick Schwatka expedition, which was to close the thirty-year search, the whole North Canadian system was almost entirely explored and mapped. The "great passage," which had cost so much in effort, sacrifice and human life, was at last discovered.

Nevertheless, during this period of the search for Franklin we find very little real technical progress. It is a sort of time of truce in the conquest of the poles. Everything that was going on gave the impression that men were polishing up their weapons, trying out their resources, perfecting their tools and their state of knowledge before the great assault.

Old John Ross, for example, who set off in search of Franklin (in 1848-49), with his two lieutenants Francis Leopold McClintock and Robert John McClure, made no new contribution to polar exploration. He distinguished himself, however, by the efforts he made to try to transmit information to the missing commander. He set afloat kegs containing messages, fired off gunshots, captured foxes which he later released wearing engraved collars, built cairns, and set off rockets—all for nothing.

The only important example of technical progress occurred in the search to the east: the use by Kennedy and Bellot of Eskimo methods (the igloo, dogs and hunting techniques) which marked the opening of a crucial period in the conquest of the poles.

At the instigation of the Admiralty, which offered 20,000 pounds to anyone who might find Sir John, and of Lady Franklin, who devoted all her efforts and all her fortune tirelessly to the same end, the expeditions followed one after another from 1850 forward. The whaler William Penny found the first traces in that year. Captain Horatio Austin, in 1851, set out with four ships, but could gather no new information.

It was then that, thanks to a public subscription, the *Prince Albert* set out to sea on June 3, 1851; she had a capacity of only 80 tons and a crew of only eighteen men. But she was commanded by two exceptional men: Captain Kennedy and the French Lieutenant Joseph René Bellot, whom Lady Franklin looked upon as she would her own son.

Kennedy was an old whaling man, tough as nails, who spoke French Canadian, wanted to retranslate the Bible, and dreamed of settling in Baffin Land to teach the Gospel to the Eskimos. Young, but already a brilliant officer, Bellot had, for his part, obtained the French Navy's permission to participate in the search, thereby maintaining a French link in that great chain of solidarity.

"Take care of yourself," Lady Franklin said to him over her sobs as he boarded the ship.

The *Prince Albert* spent the winter of 1851-52 in Batty Bay at 73° N. Setting out from the ship at the beginning of March 1852, with five men equipped in the Eskimo fashion, Kennedy and Bellot explored (via Bellot Strait) an immense amount of territory, stretching beyond Prince of Wales Island to Cape Walker, a point at which Franklin must have touched.

They used dog sleds, built igloos, and dressed in fur clothing. However, they did not go all the way with the Eskimo method; they lived on pemmican and tea. They suffered terribly from scurvy.

As Kennedy had refused to bring along any scientific instruments, Bellot had to take readings as best he could. But the commander was so impressed with his second-in-command in the long run that, in 1853, he was prepared to set out again under his orders. Bellot refused, out of tact, and signed on as an ordinary lieutenant on board the *Phoenix;* he met his death on May 10, 1853, in a crevasse at the far end of Lancaster Sound.

Lady Franklin wept for him as for a son, and promised to have a memorial plaque put up to him beside her own husband's monument on Beechey Island. In him, France lost a great polar explorer who, had he not died at twenty-nine, would certainly have become the equal of Dumont d'Urville and Charcot.

It was Captain McClintock, of the steamship *Intrepid,* a member of Sir Edward Belcher's expedition of 1852-53 composed of three sailing ships and two steamers, who participated directly in the discovery of the Northwest Passage. In September 1853, one of the detachments from his ship found a message left on Melville Island by McClure, who had sailed from Bering Strait. The junction was made.

Robert McClure had left England on January 31, 1850, on the *Investigator,* along with Richard Collinson, the commander of the expedition, on the *Enterprise.* The two ships separated; Collinson was able to gather a few relics of Franklin from the Eskimos, reaching a point—without suspecting it—only a few miles from where the *Erebus* and the *Terror* had wintered in 1846-47.

McClure, an independent and obstinate Irishman, tried his luck on his own, feeling that the best way to find Franklin would be to search, as he had been doing, for the Northwest Passage. He sailed up the length of Banks Island and approached Melville Island; if he succeeded in reaching it and passing through Barrow Strait, his goal would be attained.

But he was blocked by the ice on September 9, at 73° 10′ N., about thirty nautical miles from Melville Sound. The ship's hull suffered from the enormous pressure of the ice pack; with huge blocks of ice threatening to cave her in, McClure had the provisions piled up on the deck. On September 30, the *Investigator* became completely immobilized; the ice held her prisoner.

In order to explore Barrow Strait, the other neck of the "passage," McClure organized an expedition. From the summit of a hill which he had reached in the course of a scouting trip, he sighted the tip of Banks Island. He set up a cairn, left a message and returned to camp to prepare his sortie.

On October 26, 1850, two sleds left the ship; they carried pemmican, chocolate, water, oatmeal, and sleeping bags. They were drawn by the men. After five days of hell, they arrived at the tip of Banks Island. The sailors let McClure climb the last hill alone; the view was hidden in the darkness, but it would not be long before the sun appeared—for a few minutes—before plunging back into the polar winter.

With the map stretched out before him, McClure watched the view loom up slowly out of the darkness; the strait and Melville Island were before them; the passage was discovered. Enthusiasm broke out. McClure thanked God aloud, the sailors began to dance, and a victory fire was made out of one of the sleds as night fell.

When the sun reappeared in February (1851), the *Investigator* was still icebound. But as the ice was opening up behind him, McClure decided to retreat and skirt the island to the west. "When the ice barrier blocks his path, he mines it, blows it up; it vibrates, trembles, cracks; it dissolves; the *Investigator* gains a few miles; but even gunpowder is powerless against centuries of cold." [2]

The ship found itself—miraculously—icebound again in Mercy Bay and spent her second winter there. In the spring of 1852, the passage was still frozen; McClure decided to make his way across it by sled. The message he had left on Melville Island was found by McClintock's men.

But, having wintered a third time, McClure realized that he would have to abandon his ship. He was preparing to leave her when, on April 6, 1852, he saw a man with his face smeared with soot[3] approaching him; this was Lieutenant Pim of the *Resolute* who had come out in search of him. McClure and his men joined the squadron coming from the east. Its commander, Sir Edward Belcher, decided to abandon the most damaged ships, and it was on the *North Star*, accompanied by the rescue ships *Phoenix* and *Talbot*, that the expedition returned to London.

Belcher appeared before a court martial—as was customary in such cases—for having abandoned certain of his ships, but he was acquitted with honor. McClure's crew received the 10,000 pounds' reward. Even if Franklin had not been found, the Northwest Passage was now known and a great stretch of new territory mapped.

But for those who are interested in the history of polar tech-

---

[2] Robert de la Croix, *Les Disparus du Pôle*.

[3] For protection against sunburn.

niques, very special mention ought to be made of the work and personality of McClintock, who is considered today as having been one of the most able organizers of all times of sorties by sled.

He was the inventor of the system of depots and relays which has been employed by everyone since his time. Markham who has analyzed at length the performance of the Irishman McClintock, "the founder of sledge traveling," feels no hesitation about declaring that there is "nothing to be compared, in magnitude and efficiency" with his work, nor about describing him as a "genius."

It was during the Austin expedition (of 1850-51) that McClintock worked out his system. Austin, who was wintering to the southwest of Cornwall, sent out groups in all directions in search of Franklin; McClintock went west and beat Parry's record (of 1819) in eighty days of traveling.

The sledges used by McClintock were made of Canadian elm with ash crossbars. A three-inch, slightly convex iron rim was fixed to the runners. A ten-man sledge was about thirteen feet long, a six-man sledge nine feet.

McClintock took four 8-foot-high tents, sleeping bags and spirit lamps (capacity 1½ gills) for cooking. The rations per man per day were: ½ ounce of lime juice; 1 pound of pemmican; 10½ ounces of biscuits; 5 ounces of boiled pork; ½ gill of rum; 1 ounce of biscuit dust; ¾ ounce of tea-and-sugar; ¾ ounce of chocolate-and-sugar; ½ ounce of tobacco; salt, pepper, curry and onion powder. About a pint of spirits was required to cook this amount of food.

McClintock's plan was to provide each sledging party with an auxiliary sledge fifty miles from the ship. Every long-range sledge was to have a second provision sledge 100 miles farther along. At an average speed of ten miles per day, this would allow the exploring parties a range of 350 miles from the ship; they would find depots awaiting them on their return journey.

McClintock had given careful thought to clothing: flannel undershirts and drawers, woolen socks, duck boots, moccasins, shirts and trousers lined with chamois, fur caps, and a water bottle worn next to the skin. Each sledge had a name, a motto and a flag as well as a captain; the motto of McClintock's sledge was: *Usque ad Finem Perseverare*—"All the way!"

His journey set a new record: forty-four days out and thirty-six days back, 800 miles covered, with a maximum of 300 miles from the ship, at an average speed of better than ten miles a day in 22 degree-below-zero weather. It was during this journey that the Irishman discovered the tracks of Parry's snow-wagon preserved in the ice for more than thirty years.

On his second journey, with Sir Edward Belcher, McClintock perfected his method; he organized depots on a very extensive scale in the autumn for his spring expedition. It was also on this second journey that he learned to use dogs to haul his sledges.

With one assistant and twelve dogs, he did the distance between his own ship, the *Resolute*, and the *North Star* in five days, then pushed on to the *Assistance* in forty-eight hours: a round trip of 470 miles in fifteen days at an average of 31 miles per day. He discovered that two dogs required the same weight of food as one man, but that "a dog could draw a man's load for a distance about one-quarter greater than a man would." He concluded, a little hastily, that man was superior to the dog over long distances.

This did not in the least prevent him from using dogs on his third journey, in 1857, when he succeeded in lifting the veil that hung over the fate of Sir John Franklin and his companions.

In 1854, a Dr. John Rae of the Hudson's Bay Company had found some silverware engraved with Franklin's crest among the Eskimos on Back River; certain stories told by these Eskimos suggested that one of the two ships had sunk off the coast of King William Island. The Admiralty had, nevertheless, given up the search and had crossed the names of the missing men off its books.

But Lady Franklin would not admit defeat; supported by private subscribers, she put McClintock in charge of a further expedition. The 177-ton steam yacht *Fox*, which had been rapidly put into condition for the ice, was fitted with heavy iron armor, which turned out later to be most beneficial. With twenty-eight months' provisions, the *Fox* sailed down the Thames on July 1, 1857.

McClintock called first at Upernavik in Greenland, where he took aboard thirty-two dogs and two Eskimo guides, then dropped anchor on August 11 at Beechey Island, where he set up a monument in Franklin's memory, just beside the Bellot monument.

It was there that the crew became panic-stricken at the unaccustomed sight of a paraselene, a bright spot on the lunar halo resembling a second moon. The captain put everyone's mind to rest and then set off for King William Island. In Bellot Strait, his steam engine blew up; icebound, the ship wintered at Port Kennedy. McClintock took advantage of this time to undertake reconnaissance missions by sledge; he even touched at King William Island and thus, after ten years, found proof of the shipwreck of one of Franklin's ships.

On April 5, he set out with two sledges hauled by eight men in breast-harness and one sledge with six dogs. He learned from the Eskimos of the shipwreck of the second ship and of the men's death during their return march. He found an unidentifiable skeleton, while his lieutenant, Hobson, discovered a document describing Franklin's death on June 11, 1847, and the breakdown of the crews after the abandonment of the *Erebus* and the *Terror*.

On May 25, McClintock's dogs came to an abrupt halt, scratched at the ground and refused to go further. In front of them, they discovered the corpse of one of Franklin's officers, Des Voeux; this incident substantiated the account given by one of the Eskimo women: "They fell and died as they walked. . . ." On May 30, a boat was found buried in the snow; it contained two corpses and various pieces of equipment. Realizing that there was nothing more he could do, McClintock returned to the *Fox* during the month of June; on September 23, he returned to London with relics and proofs of the fate of the missing men.

In 1904, Amundsen was to find the graves of several sailors from the *Erebus* and the *Terror;* in 1930, Burwash was to collect some of their meteorological notes; Gigson and Skinner, in 1931, were to identify several decapitated and burned bodies, and a group of Canadian airmen, in 1952, were to bring to light several depots of provisions—and that is all.

A large number of questions remain unanswered.

Why should men who were too exausted to load themselves with tools have carried silver spoons with them? Why should so many officers have died, when experience indicates that, in case of a polar catastrophe, it is usually they who hold out longest because of their higher morale? How can we explain the almost total absence of documents when other explorers faced with death (like De Long and Scott) have shown themselves so verbose on the subject? Could it be that McClintock uncovered much more evidence but that he was advised to suppress it?

Franklin's death remains to this day one of the great unsolved mysteries of the Arctic.

15

THE NORTHEAST PASSAGE

FRANKLIN'S GREAT EXPEDITION was a failure, but a glorious failure; it is unarguable that Sir John was on the point of discovering the Northwest Passage via Peel Sound. The expedition also forced a consciousness of the Arctic on the masses. At the time of the disappearance of the *Erebus* and the *Terror,* the sale of books of adventure and books on polar exploration increased tenfold; shopwindows took Voyages to the Far North as their theme, and the most incredible rumors went around. This feverish excitement decreased after McClintock's return.

The great, almost exclusively British, period in the exploration of the north was over. Henceforward, we shall see the emergence of numerous other nations in the chronology of the conquest of the poles, and most particularly that of Sweden, Norway and the United States.

The American Elisha Kent Kane was the first man to explore the immense Humboldt Glacier in Greenland, in 1853. The following year was that of the strange journey of a butler by the name of Morton, who, with one Eskimo, and a number of dog sleds, reached a point beyond 81° N., then proceeded to hoist a flag covered with Masonic emblems on Cape Constitution opposite Hall Basin, which he took for the "free polar sea."

A more decisive event occurred in 1867; on March 31, Russia ceded the immense territory of Alaska to the United States for $7,200,000. The importance of this transaction is obvious today; at the time, the New York *Herald* could find no better explanation for it than that the United States government was using it as a means of drawing attention away from its own internal difficulties.

It was also at this period that certain events occurred which were in the long run to set off a steady process of evolution in polar technique: the development of the construction of iron hulls (the first ironclad was the *Great Britain*, launched in 1843; it was 320 feet long and could carry 260 passengers as well as 1,200 tons of freight); and the discovery of petroleum, in about 1860.

The steam engine itself was improving noticeably; the proof of this is to be found in the southward journey of Sir George Strong Nares, whose *Challenger*, a corvette of more than 2,000 tons, was the first steamship to cross the Antarctic Circle, in 1874.

To give some notion of the progress being made in this area, we need do no more than cite the example of a French ship, the *Napoléon*, put in service in 1852. Planned and built by the great French engineer Dupuy de Lôme, it was 230 feet long and 52 wide, and displaced 5,000 tons. Its 1,100-horsepower engine enabled it to do fourteen knots, driven by single-bladed propellers 16 feet in diameter. It also carried 30,660 square feet of sail.

It was at about the same time that the English began to build the *Great Eastern*, which was launched in 1859. This "liner" was made of iron; it was 692 feet long and 83 feet wide, displaced 32,000 tons and could carry 10,000 passengers; it was propelled, paradoxically enough, by two wheels 59 feet in diameter and one enormous screw propeller (5,000 horsepower).

Jules Verne, the creator of the fictional *Nautilus*, whose name was to become attached to the history of the conquest of the poles, was one of her first passengers. The *Great Eastern* distinguished herself particularly through her part in laying the first transatlantic cable.

The year 1870 was notable too for the voyages of the German Karl Koldewey on board the *Germania*, during which he reached 77° N. to the east of Greenland; of the Swedish Baron Nordenskjöld who made his way 32 miles into the inland ice of Greenland;[1] and of Elling Carlsen, a Norwegian, who discovered Barents's winter quarters.

On November 8, the American Charles Hall died after drinking his morning coffee and was buried in Greenland at 81° 45′ N. on a peninsula bearing the name of his ship, the *Polaris*, running off a land bearing his own name, Hall Land. The contribution of Hall (a former blacksmith turned newspaperman) to polar technique lies in the construction of the *Polaris*, an enormous ship of 800 tons, specially fitted out for the Arctic winter.

After Hall's death, the whaler Buddington who had taken his place, became so troubled by the ice battering against the ship that he ordered all provisions to be thrown pell-mell overboard onto the ice pack. This same gesture was often to be repeated by the later polar aviators, whose faltering flying machines were to prove too heavy.

It was in this same period (1872-74) that the Austro-Hungarians, in the persons of Julius von Payer and Karl Weyprecht, discovered the Franz Josef Land peninsula. Their ship, the 220-ton *Tegethoff*, had both sail and steam, and carried only twenty-three men and eight dogs, and three years' provisions. When they were forced to abandon their own ship, they were picked up by Captain Voronin of the Russian ship *Nicholas*.

In 1872, Baron Nordenskjöld, who was to become famous for his discovery of the Northeast Passage, wintered with forty reindeer at Spitsbergen, with the aim of reaching the Pole in the spring. Through the carelessness of their Lapp guardians, the reindeer escaped, and the planned expedition thus became impossible; Nordenskjöld did not admit defeat however; he began preparations to set out again.

---

[1] His Eskimo guides refused to go any farther.

But it is unarguable that, along with Nordenskjöld, these years were dominated by the personality of the Englishman George Nares, who, like most British polar explorers from Frobisher to Fuchs, earned a knighthood by his exploits.

He began by heading the famous round-the-world cruise of the *Challenger* between 1872 and 1875. This was a purely scientific cruise, aimed at making an inventory of all living undersea species and formulating general oceanographic laws. The *Challenger* was a steam-driven corvette of 2,306 tons. Its auxiliary engine produced 1,234 horsepower. As the ship was equipped with the most modern scientific instruments, steam was also used to work the windlass, thus sparing the men work.

In February 1874, the *Challenger* crossed the Antarctic Circle at 78° 22′ E. The voyage's achievements could hardly have been more satisfactory; from the fifty volumes published on Nares's return, it was for the first time possible to deduce that Antarctica was indeed a continent.

On his return, Captain Nares shifted his attention from one pole to the other and, in the *Challenger*, set sail for the north. It was not entirely unknown to him, even then. As second-in-command on the *Resolute* (under Kelett in 1852) he had learned his first lessons from the master, McClintock, now knighted and an admiral, who was superintendent of Plymouth dockyard, where the expedition was organized in 1875. His two ships, the *Alert* (a 751-ton sloop with seventeen guns, 157 feet by 33, commanded by Albert Markham) and the *Discovery* (a remarkable 668-ton sealer, 164 feet by 30, commanded by Stephenson; this second ship was bought on the advice of Sir Clements Markham, who was to exert a great influence on British exploration), sailed from Portsmouth on May 29, 1875.

At Proven (in Greenland), Nares took aboard fifty-five dogs, all of whom died during the course of the winter, or else ran away, victims of *piblokto*, a peculiar sort of madness suffered by dogs in those regions. The expedition's sledges were specially designed by McClintock; each had its own flag and, at Sir Clements Markham's suggestion, its own heraldic device: the cross of St. George at the hoist, with a swallow-tailed fly bearing the colors and crest of the sledge commander. (Captain Scott was to adopt this system later.) The Geographical Society presented Nares with a volume containing papers on Arctic geography and ethnology, while the Royal Society prepared a digest on various branches of science connected with the regions to be visited.

The daily rations were: 16 ounces of pemmican; 14 ounces of biscuits; 4 ounces of bacon; 2 ounces of potatoes; ½ gill of rum; 1 ounce of chocolate; 2 ounces of sugar; ½ ounce of tea; ⅛ ounce of salt; 1/20 ounce of pepper; ¼ ounce of onion-and-curry powder. Nevertheless, the crew suffered badly from scurvy. In 1917—forty-two years later—Rasmussen was to discover, to the north of the Humboldt Glacier in Greenland, six crates, each containing "four tins of preserves and nine pounds of Australian mutton, as fresh and as good as if they had been left there the day before."

Nansen sums up the importance of this voyage thus:[2]

> In later times, the point from which the Pole has been most frequently assailed is Smith Sound, probably because American explorers had somewhat too hastily asserted that they had there descried the open Polar Sea, extending indefinitely towards the north. Every expedition was stopped, however, by immense masses of ice which came drifting southwards and piled themselves up against the coast. The most important expedition by this route was the English one conducted by Nares in 1875-76, the equipment of which involved a vast expenditure. Markham, the next in command to Nares, reached the highest latitude till then attained, 83° 20′, but at the cost of enormous exertion and loss; and Nares was of opinion that the impossibility of reaching the Pole by this route was fully demonstrated for all future ages.

Markham reached this latitude on May 11, 1876, with sixteen men hauling their own sledges over the chaotic ice pack. "Sail-driven sledges are convenient," Markham noted good-humoredly in his journal, "when one is travelling on flat, soft snow, but we have rarely had the advantage of such snows. . . ."

On the scientific side, Nares believed that he had found in the Arctic Ocean traces of the old paleocrystic ice, thickened over the course of centuries into floebergs scores of feet high which had stopped Parry and McClure at the coast of Banks Island, and con-

---

[2] Fridtjof Nansen, *Farthest North.*

cluded from this phenomenon that the Arctic Ocean was a single unit; this opinion was confirmed by his study of the tides.

And just as George Nares was returning with his ample scientific findings, notably the certainty that Greenland was an island, another stubborn man was setting out to sea. This was Baron Nordenskjöld, who was to discover the Northeast Passage.

Not at all disheartened by his successive fruitless voyages to the north, the baron obtained the assistance of a patron, Oscar Dickson, and left Tromsö in June 1875 on board a small sailing ship, the *Proven;* he reached the mouth of the Yenisei. In August 1876, he did the same route over again, in order to prove that the way he had opened answered to the requirements of regular shipping traffic.

Finally taken seriously by the Swedish government, Nordenskjöld was able to fit out the *Vega,* a sail-and-steam ship of 300 tons, 150 feet long by 29 feet wide, with a screw propeller and a 60-horsepower steam engine. The staff included two engineers and three Norwegian sealers. The ship carried 300 tons of coal and provisions for two years. It was to be accompanied by three cargo ships which were to transport Siberian wheat back to Sweden.

As the *Vega* became icebound on September 27, 1878, at 67° 07′ N. by 173° 31′ E., the expedition was forced to winter in temperatures of 58 degrees below zero. The scientists took advantage of this time to build a snow observatory, while the crew made contact with the native Chukchi. Worthwhile exchanges (Swedish bread for hides, whale or seal blubber and tools) were made, and a serious study of the way of life of the tribe was carried out.

The expedition's most eminent visitor was a native *starosta,* or headman, a pagan despite the Christian name given him by the Russians, Vasili Menka. He came to the ship in a sledge respectfully drawn by his men and was "dressed in a beautiful white reindeer-skin tunic, under which a flannel shirt was visible." He was a small man with a dark complexion and an emaciated face. The moment he arrived he displayed a certificate in Russian giving official acknowledgment of his position in his tribe, as well as his receipts for his taxes, which were paid in the form of hides; he made several signs of the cross before the few religious images in the expedition's back room, but soon ceased this sham when he realized that his hosts, who were Evangelists, were not joining in; he lavished his majestical joviality on everyone, gave and received presents, danced to the music of the barrel organ and then took his leave.

On July 18, 1879, the *Vega,* in its turn, took leave of the Chukchi, for the ice had begun to break and open a passage. Finally, on the twentieth, at 11 A.M., Nordenskjöld fired off a five-gun salute to the eastern cape of Bering Strait and arrived on September 2 at Yokohama without any incident in the meantime; the Northeast Passage had been forced.

It was to take two generations for this passage to become a reality. The Northern Sea Route has been in operation since 1932; it was the icebreaker *Sibiriakov* which opened it and the cargo ship *Chelyuskin* which, in the following year, first traveled through it without having to make winter camp. In 1937, the commercial traffic had reached 350,000 tons of merchandise; as navigation was restricted to a few summer months, the ports were equipped with powerful machines that enabled them to load and unload in the minimum time.

Today, the passage is a private affair; the U.S.S.R. is the only nation to use it commercially and, more important, militarily; the time has long since passed when the ports of Murmansk and Archangel received American war material (5,000 tanks, 7,500 airplanes, 4,000 vehicles, 1,500 radar sets, 250,000 tons of plastics, et cetera, between 1941 and 1944). But it was Adolf Erik, Baron Nordenskjöld, a Swede, who opened the way to the Russians' immense activities in these regions.

Nordenskjöld's nautical exploit had revealed only one detail in the over-all superstructure of the Arctic Ocean: the summer gap between the ice pack and the north Asian coast. The first real knowledge ever acquired of this immense region of more than 4,000,000 square miles—the world's true Mediterranean—was the result of a hazardous enterprise which ended in catastrophe: that of the *Jeannette* (in 1879-81).

Basically, it was the public's infatuation with polar exploration which was the pretext, since it was James Gordon Bennett, the proprietor of the New York *Herald,* who financed the voyage. Bennett bought the *Pandora* from Sir Allen Young; it was one of the Admiralty's old, but very fast, gunships (a three-masted bark

THE CONQUEST

EMIL SCHULTHESS, BLACK STAR

The brilliant landscape of the Antarctic.

The *Fram*, icebound, January 1895.

BLACK STAR

Man in the Antarctic. This photograph was taken by Emil Schulthess during the International Geophysical Year, and shows an American geologist returning from the ascent of Mount Glossopteris. But it also represents the eternal struggle of man against the barriers of cold and ice.

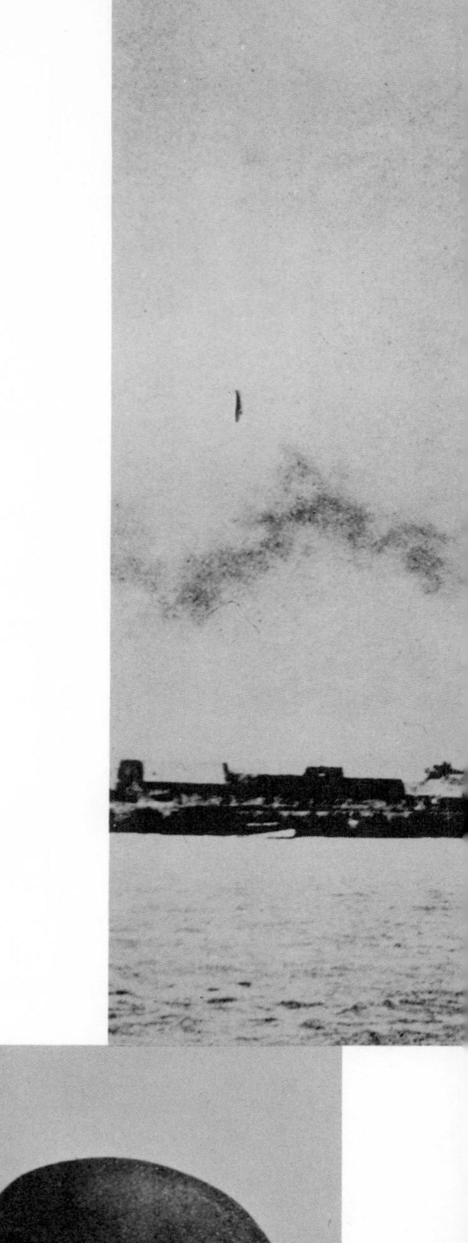

SWEDISH GEOGRAPHICAL SOCIETY

Charcot's *Pourquoi-Pas?* leaving St. Malo in July 1908.

(LEFT) Andrée's balloon; taken immediately after landing on the ice floe, July 14, 1897.

SCOTT POLAR RESEARCH INSTITUTE, CAMBRIDGE, ENGLAND

Dr. Edward Wilson's sketch—"Three men in a tent"—showing Robert Scott and his companions working in their tent by the light of a lantern.

(LEFT) April 1909. Peary and his companions stand at the North Pole.

AMERICAN GEOGRAPHICAL SOCIET

General Nobile, seen in the porthole of the dirigible *Italia.*

(LEFT) "The three polar stars": Amundsen, Shackleton and Peary.

FOK
JOSEPHINE FORD
BYRD ARCTIC EXPEDITION
FOKKE
BA

(LEFT) The *Italia* mooring at Spitsbergen.

(BELOW LEFT) The first airplane to fly over the North Pole.

(BELOW) George Wilkins' submarine, the *Nautilus*, in which he attempted to cross the Pole by cruising under the polar icecap.

INTERNATIONAL NEWS PHOTOS, INC.

(RIGHT) A view of the North Pole taken through the periscope of the U.S.S. *Seadragon*, showing the submarine's crew walking on the ice.

The U.S.S. *Skate*, a nuclear submarine, surfaces at the North Pole.

U.S. INFORMATION AGENCY

U.S. INFORMATION AGENCY

JACQUES MASSON, EXPÉDITIONS POLAIRES FRANÇAISES

(LEFT) A helicopter in the Arctic. Here, a French machine is picking up supplies.

A French camp in the Arctic during a blizzard.

J. J. LANGUEPIN, EXPÉDITIONS POLAIRES FRANÇAISES

EMIL SCHULTHESS, BLACK STAR

A party of three Snocats pulling sledges, during the I. G. Y.

with an auxiliary engine). He took away her old name and gave her that of *Jeannette*.

Sir Clements Markham points out that the custom of changing the names of Arctic ships generally brought bad luck; the names of all the ships but one in the Franklin search were changed, and the only ship that was not lost was the *Fox*, whose name had not been changed.

Command of the *Jeannette* was given to United States Navy Lieutenant De Long, assisted by Lieutenants Chipp and Danenhower (whose son Sloan was to be a member of Sir Hubert Wilkins's staff on board the first polar submarine).

The expedition, which consisted of thirty-two men and forty dogs, learned during a stop at Serdze Kamen that Nordenskjöld had wintered, then set out again for the east. Having lost his headline in the *Herald*, De Long made a senseless decision, and one which gives a fair idea of the degree of ignorance prevailing at the time; he resolved to go to the North Pole aboard ship. From this point forward, the *Jeannette*—which was not equipped for the battering of the ice floes—was doomed to annihilation.

After discovering two new islands (Jeannette Island and Henriette Island), De Long was forced to stand by, powerless, on June 13, 1881, at 77° 71′ N. by 155° 48′ E., while his ship was crushed to pieces. "It looked like a staved-in barrel," Danenhower noted. Then there began, on the northward-drifting ice pack, an exhausting, spiraling retreat to the south. At 77° 42′ N. De Long concealed the results of his observations from his crew. On July 10, at 76° 38′ N., he touched land at Bennett Island.

As the sea was freer now, he was able to launch three longboats that the men had been hauling with them. In the final result, thirteen men returned out of the thirty-two who had started out. In October, Gordon Bennett got his headline; it was not at all what he had wanted, since the New York *Herald* had to run: "Polar Catastrophe: The De Long Expedition Crushed by the Ice."

Polar catastrophes went on one after another, brought fatter and fatter headlines in the papers and went on confirming the poles' murderous reputation. In 1884, the news of Greely's tragic failure broke.

The Austrian Karl Weyprecht had been the first to suggest the idea of scientific co-operation of all nations in polar exploration. The International Polar Conference in Hamburg in 1879, presided over by Dr. Georg von Neumayer and including representatives of eleven nations, decided on the First International Polar Year for 1882-83.

France was not absent from the project; her Cape Horn station, directed by Captain Martial and Lieutenant Courcelle-Seneuil from September 6, 1882, to September 3, 1883, made excellent observations and drew further distinction from the publication of these observations, "unequaled," as Greely[3] himself pointed out, in their "typographic beauty by any other of the International Polar publications."

The other nations were spread out over forty-nine scientific stations (mainly magnetic and meteorological). The United States was assigned, among others, the regions accessible via Smith Sound, as a result of the work of Kane, Hayes and Hall. But the United States was not yet in the Byrd era; financial support was parsimonious and Lieutenant Adolph Washington Greely of the United States Army had at his disposal only a single, quite modest ship. Moreover, through a special—incomprehensible and inadmissible—order of the Congress, the members of the expedition had the right to resign and to go on strike. The full crew numbered four officers and nineteen men from the Army, and it included one photographer and two Eskimos.

Greely installed himself at Fort Conger on Hall Basin in August 1881, sending sorties into Greenland, Grant Land and Grinnell Land. One of these sorties, which was led by Lieutenant James Booth Lockwood and included David Legge Brainard and the Eskimo Christiansen, with one dog sled and twenty-five days' provisions, enabled the United States to win the record for latitude up to that time: 83° 24′ N., at Lockwood Island north of Greenland.

As the ship that had brought him did not come back to pick him up, Greely attempted to return south with the aid of his steam-driven launch and his two barks. After a terrible journey, the men reached Cape Sabine, where they built a stone cabin. With hope running out and with scarcely fifty days' provisions, they waited. Scurvy broke out. One man was shot for having stolen another's food. One by one, the others died in an infernal atmosphere of hatred and cannibalism.

---

[3] A. W. Greely, *Handbook of Arctic Discoveries.*

When the sailors of the sealing ship *Thetis* discovered the six survivors, on June 22, 1884, a horrible spectacle was offered to their eyes:

> The tent had fallen down. None of those underneath could move. One of the rescuers then took his knife, made a rip in the cloth and looked inside; a man with his jaw hanging free and glassy eyes seemed dead. Ellison, who was nothing more than a human wreck, without hands or feet, had a spoon attached to the stump of his right arm. Greely was on his hands and knees, with long hair in pigtails; he resembled a skeleton, and all his joints were bulbous and swollen. He could not stand up. The three others were scarcely any better off. All the food that remained in the tent was two repulsive-looking cans of jelly, which had been obtained by boiling strips cut from their sealskin clothing.[4]

It was possible to save Greely, and he lived to become a general.

Coming after the Franklin disaster and that of the *Jeannette*, this catastrophe shrouded polar expeditions in a sinister veil, which Nansen's and Peary's exploits barely managed to dissolve. For this end of the nineteenth century was marked by the appearance of exceptional men, who were to seize on all available knowledge and on every possible technical means with which to launch the final offensive against the poles.

It was the inland ice of Greenland that was to serve as their proving ground. It was a tempting spot; no one could say what the immense (850,000 square miles) interior of Greenland was like, though its contours were practically all known. It had long been thought that the heart of this vast island (of which 700,000 square miles are covered by ice) was free and even inhabited; it was in part to verify this that old Baron Nordenskjöld, who was still in the midst of the fray, took up his old project for crossing the island ice in 1882. He scaled the glacial icecap in Disko Bay and sent his Lapps eastward, but had finally to give up, leaving the glory of being the first man to cross Greenland to one of the giants of polar exploration: Fridtjof Nansen.

---

[4] Dr. R. Wheeler, *The Polar Hunters*.

16

THE "FRAM"

IN 1905 SWEDEN had an army of 70,000 men; Norway one of 3,500—but she also had Nansen. Thanks to him, Norway was to seize her independence, breaking the iron grip that had held his country under the Swedish crown for ninety years.

If a miracle was required anywhere in the world, all that was necessary was for Nansen to put in an appearance. When the League of Nations put him in charge of the repatriation of prisoners after the 1914-18 war, Nansen ran up against the Soviet Foreign Minister Chicherin, who refused to receive him. This was a mistake. It was Nansen who collected and repatriated 430,000 prisoners at a cost of $8.60 a head, when the experts had predicted a cost of $200. To help with the reclassification of the million and a half White Russians wandering over the face of Europe, Nansen created a passport which still bears his name and which, accepted as official by fifty-two nations, enabled these unfortunate people to find asylum.

It was Nansen, again, who was in charge of the victims of the Greco-Turkish War; he proposed an exchange of populations; a half million Turks returned to Turkey, while a million Greeks returned to Greece.

During the Russian famine of 1922, Nansen once again made his voice heard, and his efforts resulted in the feeding of a million people. When he received the Nobel Peace Prize in 1922 every country in the world rejoiced, and no one was surprised to hear that he had donated the money that came with the prize to charitable works and to the Greek refugees. And then when, on a spring afternoon in 1930, he died in his armchair, sitting in the garden of his small house in the Oslo suburbs, the whole world wept.

But this apostle of peace and liberty, this tireless benefactor, this subtle negotiator, was also—and above all—one of the greatest Arctic explorers of all time. He was like a character out of the Scandinavian sagas; gigantic, with blue eyes and blond hair, he was—as McClintock said—a "true Viking." Bold, durable, obstinate and "always ready," Fridtjof Nansen resembled a force of nature; he achieved the highest rank among the conquerors of the Pole by dint of exceptional intelligence and intuition.

From a very early age, he shunned the city, where "personality is softened," and sought escape in the solitary open spaces. Born on September 6, 1861, and trained for a career in natural science, Nansen was barely twenty-one when he embarked as a zoological observer on the whaling ship *Viking*, plying between Spitsbergen and Greenland. The spectacle that met his eyes was so like a fairy tale that he decided to devote himself to "the great adventure of the ice, deep and pure as infinity." The magic of the north had had its effect.

A reading of the accounts of Nordenskjöld's voyages convinced him all the more; he decided that he would succeed where others had failed, by crossing Greenland. And, as if to make his idea seem the madder, he announced in 1888 that he was going to do it on skis.

His plan, however, seemed simple, and it was not lacking in logic;

setting out from the inhuman east coast of Greenland, which was ravaged by immense concentrations of floating ice, he would head across the icy desert toward the more hospitable west coast, where the climatic conditions were easier and where the landscape was dotted with Danish trading posts and Eskimo villages.

Baron Nordenskjöld, charmed by the brilliant young Nansen's fiery personality, supported his request for backing. The failure of an American beginner named Peary (the future conqueror of the North Pole), who in 1886 was halted in his attempt to make the same crossing, was not designed to encourage potential patrons. Nansen, who claimed that "things that might seem impossible can be done when you have to do them," ended, nevertheless, by obtaining the means necessary for him to undertake his journey.

His preparations for this adventure were a model of their kind. Nansen gave proof here of his intelligence and of his practical sense. The characteristics of the equipment he took with him can be summed up in a very few words: lightness, simplicity, efficacy. The very nature of his trip, since it would require him to travel over every form of ice, required lightness, and Nansen was led to design a new type of sledge which was to remain down to our day and with practically no modifications the model for the expedition sledge.

The Nansen sledge (he built five of them) weighed about 31 pounds and measured 10 feet long and 20 inches wide. It was made of ash; its upper part was light and delicate. The ⅓-inch-wide, slightly convex runners had narrow blades made of German silver (an alloy of zinc, nickel and copper). The sledge was raised at both ends.

The tent designed by Nansen was made of five pieces of weatherproof cloth stretched on bamboo poles. The reindeer-skin sleeping bags included a hood which could be turned down over the sleeper's head. All the clothing was wool.

Particular attention was paid to the choice of footgear; as the expedition was to use skis, this would be the basis of its success. Woolen socks covered the skin directly, then came thick goatskin slippers, over which were worn Lapp *finnesko*, all fur on the outside and lined with dried grass, as was the Lapp custom. Heavy woolen gloves and caps with flaps completed the equipment.

Finally, there were the famous skis. Used by the Scandinavians for centuries, and popularly called "Norwegian skates," the skis were long narrow strips of wood, from 7½ to 10 feet long and 3½ inches wide. Never yet had an expedition used this means of transportation; only the Canadian snowshoes (like Franklin's) were in use, and then mainly on fresh snow. Nansen, who had used skis since his childhood, was a virtuoso on them, as were the three Norwegians and the two Lapps who accompanied him.

The scientific equipment included a pocket sextant, an artificial horizon using mercury, an azimuth compass, four chronometers, a theodolite with its base, thermometers and barometers.

Four sledges carried loads of 220 pounds each; the fifth carried double that figure. The food to be taken had been planned so as to be as light as possible—dried fruit, dried meats, various powders (cocoa, biscuits, soup, lard and tea)—thereby freeing the party from having to carry the usual heavy sealed tins.

Last of all, the equipment included an innovation: the famous "Nansen Cooker," invented by the explorer himself, which was to be of such great value to so many of his followers.

> The cooking apparatus [Nansen wrote] had the advantage of utilizing to the utmost the fuel consumed. With it we were able to cook food and simultaneously to melt an abundance of drinking water, so that both in the morning and in the evening we were able to drink as much as we wished, and even a surplus remained. The apparatus consisted of two boilers and a vessel for melting snow or ice in, and was constructed in the following manner:
>
> Inside a ring-shaped vessel was placed the boiler, while underneath this again was the lamp. The entire combustion output was thus forced to mount into the space between the boiler and the ring-shaped vessel. Over this was a tight-fitting lid with a hole in the middle, through which the hot air was obliged to pass before it could penetrate farther and reach the bottom of a flat snow-melter, which was placed above it. Then, after having delivered some part of its heat, the air was forced down again on the outside of the ring-shaped vessel by the help of a mantle or cap which surrounded the whole. Here it parted with its last remaining warmth to the outer side of the ring-vessel, and finally escaped, almost entirely cooled, from the lower edge of the mantle.[1]

[1] Fridtjof Nansen, *Farthest North*.

Nansen took neither tobacco nor alcohol; he thought them harmful.

His companions, five picked skiers, were: Otto Sverdrup, Dietrichson and Kristiansen (all Norwegians) and the Lapps Balto and Ravna.

A sealing ship, the *Jason,* agreed to transport the expedition to the dangerous east coast of Greenland, not far from Angmagssalik, where, on July 17, 1888, it set out in two small boats, twelve miles from land. Twelve days were required to cover the distance; the men had to fight their way through the waves and moving ice, with a drift that took them south to 60° 14′ N. Then for two weeks they worked their way back over the more than three hundred miles that separated them from their planned point of departure, the Sermilik Fjord.

On August 10, 1888, they camped at Umivik, and by August 22, the six men with their 1,300-pound load had scaled a rocky wall more than three thousand feet high; the crossing could now begin, over rough, uneven, hardened snow, whipped by violent winds. On September 14, the expedition, which was now heading toward Godthaab, reached an altitude of 8,900 feet in 40-below-zero cold.

"Me old Lapp and me silly old fool," remarked the veteran Ravna, "me don't think we never get to coast."

"That's quite true, Ravna, you are a silly old fool," Nansen replied.

Their advance became more and more painful; tying the sledges together, and using a tarpaulin for a sail, they were able to make better time with a following wind. "Our ship," Nansen reported, "flew over the waves and drifts of snow with a speed that almost took one's breath away. Our ship rushed on faster and faster, the snow flew round us and behind us in a cloud which gradually hid the others from view."

The moon rose. "It was a curious sight for me to see the two vessels come rushing along behind me, with their square Viking-like sails showing dark against the white snowfield and the big round disc of the moon. . . ."

They made out a peak in the distance and headed for it; they entered a valley on foot, where they were surprised to find a stream. A swarm of black flies swooped down on them.

The descent was as difficult as could be imagined; on September

23, they reached the rocky coast and lit a great grass fire on the banks of the Ameralik Fjord. Then, with ski poles, fragments of the sledges and bunches of dwarf willow, they built a canoe frame, and covered it with a waterproof tent. With this improvised *umiak* and using their skis for paddles, they reached Godthaab on October 3, 1888; the ship that was to pick them up had already left; they were forced to winter there. Nansen took advantage of this time to study the Eskimos' ancestral techniques, from which he picked up many bits of information that were most useful to him later on.

When he returned to Norway, Nansen published his scientific observations; the structure of the Greenland plateau was described, and certain aspects of its meteorology proved to be of the greatest interest and importance (among other things, Nansen found that the hygrometric condition obtaining in these regions approached saturation).

At the age of twenty-eight, Nansen was the first man ever to have crossed Greenland, and he became the idol of youth everywhere; in the crowd that thronged the Norwegian capital for Nansen's triumphant welcome home was a high-school boy of seventeen, whose name was Roald Amundsen and who was destined to achieve a glory equal to Nansen's own.

The conqueror of the inland ice took up his old post at the University of Oslo; but already a new project was germinating in his mind. Even now, the boldness and subtlety of this plan seem overwhelming. Before Nansen, everyone had imagined that the Arctic Sea was covered with ice; the explorers had sailed their ships up to the ice barrier and then tried to reach the Pole on foot. Moreover, it was felt that a ship that became icebound at a very high latitude was sure to be irretrievably lost.

But, surrounded by the fairy-tale immensity of the Greenland glacier, Nansen was thinking ceaselessly of an article by Professor Henrik Mohn in the Norwegian paper *Morgen Bladet*. Mohn told how the Eskimos had discovered debris from a shipwreck at the southwest tip of Greenland in 1884; this debris was authenticated by a cap and a jacket bearing the personal markings of two explorers, Noros and Ninderman.

Noros and Ninderman were two sailors from the *Jeannette*, De Long's ship which sank off New Siberia in 1881; thus, the wreckage had taken three years to drift southward, around Greenland,

and then drift north again; such was Nansen's conviction, for he also knew that Koldewey had found Siberian larchwood among the driftwood washed up on the east coast of Greenland. Finally, Nansen himself had found diatoma (brown microscopic algae) identical to those fished up by the *Vega* (then commanded by Nordenskjöld) in the Chukchi Sea.

A great idea was born. In 1891, Nansen presented his project to the Royal Geographical Society of Christiania (now Oslo):

> If a floe could drift right across the unknown region, that drift might be enlisted in the service of exploration. . . . This piece of wood was carried from the west coast of Alaska over to Greenland by a current, the whole course of which may be assumed to flow very near the North Pole, or at some place between it and Franz Josef Land. . . . From the Atlantic to the south of Spitsbergen and Franz Josef Land, a belt of low atmospheric pressure (minimum belt) extends into the Siberian Arctic Sea. In accordance with well-known [meteorological] laws, the wind must have a preponderating direction from east to west on the north side of the minimum belt, and will consequently produce a westerly current passing across the Pole toward the Greenland Sea. . . .
>
> The ship will simply be hoisted up [by the ice] and will ride safely and firmly. . . . To reach the exact mathematical point that forms the northern extremity of the earth's axis is intrinsically of small moment. Our object is to investigate the great unknown regions that surround the Pole.

This project, as Greely emphasized, "ignored the accepted canons of ice navigation." The general, who was decidedly hostile to the plan, added that he considered such a voyage suicide. England spoke unanimously (except for the magnificent McClintock) and openly of his folly. Along with Nares, Sir Joseph Hooker expressed the wish that Nansen "dispose of his admirable courage, skill, and resources in the prosecution of some less perilous attempt to solve the mystery of the Arctic Area."

Norway, fortunately, followed Nansen's advice; the government and the parliament enthusiastically granted him 280,000 kroner; a further 164,000 kroner was contributed by the King of Norway and Nansen's generous countrymen. Thus, he was able to devote himself to preparations for his voyage, and, above all, to the choice of his ship.

Since he needed an exceptionally sturdy ship, capable of withstanding the onslaughts of the ice, Nansen decided to build one himself according to his own specifications. The Norwegian engineer Colin Archer drew up the plans, following Nansen's directions; the first ship designed and built specially for the ice was about to be born. On October 26, 1892, Mrs. Eva Nansen broke a champagne bottle over the bow, crying: "I name thee *Fram!*"

Fram means "Forward!" in Norwegian. This word depicts Nansen quite fully. In 1926, in a lecture given before a group of Scottish students, Nansen confessed: "Let me tell you one secret of such so-called successes as there have been in my life. It was to burn my boats and demolish my bridges behind me. Then there is no choice for you but *forward.*"

In the original plan, the *Fram* was to be as small as possible and was to displace only 170 tons. (She turned out larger than planned: with 402 tons' gross and 307 tons' net capacity.)[2] She also had to

[2] Details of the *Fram*'s construction were:

Length of keel	102	feet
Length at waterline	113	feet
Length on deck	128	feet
Greatest width	36	feet
Depth	17	feet
Draft with light load	12½	feet
Displacement with light load	530	tons
Draft with heavy load	15	feet
Displacement with heavy load	800	tons

Both the bow and stern were reinforced with special care; the stem was made of three strong oaken beams with a combined thickness of four feet, while the stern was armor-plated and so built that the rudder and propeller could be retracted in a matter of minutes, by means of a capstan. The rudder was placed very low, so that a floe running against the ship could not reach it, because of the stern part.

The oak that was used had been kept dry for thirty years. The total thickness of the ship's sides was from 24 to 28 inches. The upper deck, at the stern, was higher than the main deck, because of the space taken by the engine. The keel consisted of two heavy blocks of American elm fourteen inches thick, though only three inches were allowed to extend below the frame. The rigging was simple, light (to give the least possible hold to the wind, when the engine was in operation) and strong; the *Fram* was rigged like a three-masted fore-and-aft schooner, with 6,000 square feet of sail. The

be short; a long hull is an inconvenience in the ice. Her sides were to be smooth to allow the ice to slip off, and, as her load would be a large one, it was clear that the *Fram* should be very wide. Her width was, in fact, almost equal to one third of her length; and with her rounded lines and smooth surfaces, she looked like a nutshell. As Nansen put it, she could "slip like an eel from among the ice blocks when they begin to press too hard around her." Nansen realized that the *Fram* was "not precisely elegant," but she was the ideal ship for the Norwegian's undertaking.

During the construction period, he busied himself with preparations for the voyage. "If the voyage itself took three years," he pointed out, "the preparations took no less time, while the scheme was conceived thrice three years earlier." Every element in the provisions underwent chemical analysis and was packed with minute care; the biscuits, for example, were kept in zinc boxes; rations were planned to last five years.

There was a large amount of scientific equipment, and it was all "good" and "complete." It included: thermometers, barometers, psychrometers,[3] anemometers, a large quantity of self-registering instruments, one large and two small theodolites, several sextants, four ship's and several pocket chronometers, and instruments to measure the magnetic declination, inclination and intensity.

The *Fram*'s crew consisted of thirteen men. "After the success of our expedition," Nansen notes, "the ancient and puerile superstition attached to this number no longer has any justification."

---

engine was of the "triple expansion" type; in case of a breakdown, each cylinder could be isolated from the others. It had 220 H.P. and could drive the boat at six to seven knots. (The two spare propellers and the spare rudder, never had to be used.)

The hold was divided into three watertight compartments, in case a leak developed. The living area was in the stern, under the poop deck; four one-bunk and two four-bunk cabins were grouped around the salon, thus protecting the central room from the cold. The ceiling, walls and floor were treated with a layer of insulation and waterproofing. The ship's sides were fitted with a protective layer about fifteen inches thick, consisting of air, felt, deal paneling, reindeer hair and linoleum. The *Fram* was lighted by electricity (from a dynamo attached either to the ship's engine or to a windmill). There were two large and four small ship's boats. (The steam-launch, "run on an oil-burner," was never anything but a source of bother.)

[3] From the Greek ψυχρὸς, cold, humidity; and μέτρον, measure. (An instrument for measuring the relative humidity of the atmosphere.)

Otto Neumann Sverdrup, the first officer, was thirty-eight years old and had been Nansen's companion in Greenland. The crew consisted of picked men; in order to participate in the voyage, Lieutenant Hjalmar Johansen had even signed on as a stoker. The expedition included a doctor, an electrician, a watchmaker, and a harpooner.

On June 24, 1893, the *Fram* sailed off toward the "threshold of the kingdom of cold."

At Khabarova, a small Samoyed village, Nansen took aboard thirty-four Ostyak dogs in perfect condition, which had been bought by Baron Eduard von Toll, the famous Russian explorer of northern Siberia. Von Toll had, moreover, assembled a second crew, which was now waiting for the *Fram* at the mouth of the Olenek. His friendliness went to the point of setting up depots of provisions in the New Siberian Islands for the Nansen expedition in case they should suffer any unexpected accident.

The stop at Khabarova lasted several days, the time required to clean the boiler; then, as he saw no sign of the coal tender that he had expected, Nansen decided to weigh anchor on August 4. After the "terrible" Kara Sea and Chelyuskin Strait (on September 10), the *Fram* ran into the ice barrier at 77° 44′ N. on September 20. Nansen moored his ship to a great ice block, and, during the period when he was waiting to be taken by the ice, ordered a ship-wide bug hunt: steam-hosing of mattresses, sterilization of clothing, et cetera.

On September 24, the *Fram* was icebound. The temperature was 8½ degrees above zero. The drift could begin. The rudder was removed, and the ship prepared her winter quarters. The engine was taken apart and stored, then the windmill (off which the dynamo worked) was set up; the mill had to be watched continually in order to keep it facing in the right direction.

Scientific work began, and it went on night and day; meteorological observations, in particular, were made every four hours, sometimes every two. Bearings were taken every second day. Once a month, each man was weighed by the doctors, and a count was made of his red corpuscles. Temperature, salinity and other characteristics of the sea were taken and studied by Nansen himself; he was also in charge of observations on the aurora borealis. Soundings and dredgings were made all along the course of the drift.

The menus were varied: hard bread, cheese, corned beef, corned mutton, ham, tongue, bacon, cod roe, anchovies, oatmeal biscuits, potatoes, green vegetables, macaroni, orange marmalade or jelly, tea, coffee, or chocolate. The dogs' rations consisted of half a dried codfish per dog, and biscuits. Pipes, cigars and cigarettes were prohibited except in the galley.

Leisure activity consisted of reading, playing cards, playing the organ or the accordion (the most popular tune was "*Oh, Susanna!*"). In the evenings, Nansen went for walks on the ice pack. "Nothing more wonderfully beautiful can exist than the Arctic night," he notes in his journal. "To what end all this beauty, with not a creature to rejoice in it? Now I begin to divine it. *This* is the coming earth—here are beauty and death. . . ."

An October sounding gave a depth of 800 fathoms (4,800 feet). "This rather disposes," Nansen notes again, "of the story of a shallow polar basin and of the extreme coldness of the water of the Arctic Ocean."

The drift was still very slight; then it became negative. Nansen did not despair. Moreover, on November 7, after an 83-mile southward drift, the *Fram* began to turn back toward the north. She was under pressure from the ice from October 9 onward, but the boat behaved exactly as Nansen had planned; she slid on her hull, and, despite the most furious assaults of the ice, she never went under:

"It begins with a gentle cracking and moan along the side of the ship, which gradually sounds louder in every key. Now, it is a high, plaintive tone, now it is a grumble, now it is a snarl and the ship gives a start up. The noise steadily grows till it is like all the pipes of an organ; the ship trembles and shakes, rises by fits and starts or is sometimes gently lifted. Outside, the ice is ground against our ship's sides, the piles of broken-up floe are forced under her heavy, invulnerable hull. . . . One feels oneself to be in the presence of Titanic forces. . . . All round you there is thundering and roaring, as of some enormous waterfall, with explosions like cannon salvos. . . . Still nearer it comes. . . . But now the disturbance begins to calm. . . ."

Then everything grew calm, and the crew could fish again with the Murray net, a silk net for dredging at various depths; it was used to gather ostracodes, copepods, amphipods and other crustaceans.

The crew killed bears; time passed. Nansen relaxed by playing the organ or going for walks, thinking often of his little daughter, who was only a year old. Under the keel, the *Fram* had ice from 10 to 23 feet thick; the temperature fell to 32.3 degrees below zero. On December 10, the doctor founded a newspaper, the *Fram Sjaa* ("Fram Lookout").

Christmas was coming; not a flake of snow had fallen. On December 21, a sounding of 1,150 fathoms was made; the line did not touch bottom. Morale was excellent. "The Arctic night," Nansen wrote, "has had no aging, no weakening influence of any kind on me; I seem, on the contrary, to grow younger. . . ." On January 3 the thermometer stood at 40 degrees below. The battering of the ice continued, but it did not discommode the *Fram*, which continued her zigzagging drift. With the temperature at 57.3 degrees below zero, Nansen made several excursions by dog sledge. His method of harnessing was simple, if not particularly efficient; a rope or a bit of sailcloth was passed around the dog's belly and tied to the collar by another rope. The traces were attached under the belly and passed under the legs. Nansen noted that four dogs could pull two men.

He found the drift "terribly slow"; he calculated that, at their present speed, the journey would take eight years, and he began to suffer from the enforced inactivity: "No struggle; no possibility of struggle!"

On April 6, an eclipse of the sun took place and enabled him to test the performance of his chronometers. On July 11, Nansen, who thought he had run out of his supply of cigars, discovered to his joy a forgotten reserve of Londons. The summer passed in scientific observations, including even the discovery of certain bacteria by microscope; the lengthened sounding-line gave the sea depth as 2,132 fathoms.

But Nansen, exasperated by the slowness of the drift, was secretly planning a northward march; he overhauled his equipment and, foreseeing a catastrophe during his absence, had six kayaks built; each weighed 67 pounds, measured 10 feet by 31½ inches, was 16 inches deep and could carry two men.

On August 21, 1894, at 81° 04′ 02″ N., Nansen nevertheless thought that the *Fram* would be home "in two years"; this prediction was carried out, moreover, nearly to the day. On October 4, there remained on board one hundred tons of coal and lamp oil enough for ten years. The second winter began, the sun disappeared on October 17, with the party at 81° 47′ N. On the twenty-first, they reached 82° and celebrated the achievement in weather of 33 degrees below zero.

On November 16, Nansen revealed to Sverdrup—who approved of it—his plan for proceeding toward the Pole on foot. Nansen chose for his traveling companion a remarkable skier, Lieutenant Johansen, and announced his departure to the crew on November 20. He had two lighter kayaks built with sleds of the same length (12 feet); he then proceeded to test his equipment; the famous Nansen cooker furnished about 3 quarts of boiling water and 5¼ quarts of cold water in an hour and a half, the cold water being melted down from 31-degrees-below-zero ice; the oil consumed was not more than 3½ ounces.

By December 12, the *Fram* had got 82° 30′ N., a latitude never before reached by any ship; the Pole was now only 520 miles away —"the distance from Paris to Marseilles," Nansen observed. To celebrate Christmas, Nansen invented a drink with a blackberry-juice base, which he named "83° north latitude champagne," and for New Year's, the crew was allowed a bottle of *akvavit*.

On January 5, 1895, a terrifying alert was called; the ice was threatening the ship on all sides, and the scientific equipment just barely escaped being lost and the dogs narrowly missed being drowned. "I heard a thundering and crashing outside in the ice, as if doomsday had come . . ." It was, fortunately, no more than an alert, and Nansen took advantage of it to "photograph the *Fram* by moonlight, in the afternoon. . . ."

On March 14, Nansen and Johansen left the ship (at 84° N.), to the cheers of the rest of the crew. They carried very carefully selected equipment with them: two kayaks, three sledges and twenty-seven dogs. One of the sledges was fitted with a device that registered the distance traveled—the wheel of an old anemometer attached to the side of the last sledge. The camping equipment included a sleeping bag with a double reindeer-skin covering, and a silk tent weighing just over two pounds, as well as a Nansen cooker. Their guns were double-barreled rifle-shotguns, one barrel rifled for large game, the other smooth-bore. They carried 180 cartridges and 150 shotgun shells. A small theodolite, a pocket sextant, a spirit level, aneroid barometers, three quicksilver sling psychrometers, two minimum spirit thermometers and a camera made up the scientific equipment.

The provisions consisted principally of dried and powdered fish and meat, biscuits, and 86 pounds of butter. For clothing, each man took two woolen shirts, a camel's-hair coat and a thick jersey, two pairs of woolen underdrawers, knickers, loose gaiters, and a great oilskin for protection against the powdery snow. Lapp moccasins and felt hats completed their equipment, which weighed 1,460 pounds in all.

"If we wish to turn back," Nansen noted, "we have absolutely nothing to return to, not even a bare coast." It was indeed a risky business; on their return, it would be impossible to find the drifting *Fram* again, and they would be forced to make their way to Spitsbergen or to Franz Josef Land on their own. Before Nansen set out, Captain Sverdrup took him aside and asked whether he were thinking of going to the South Pole when he got home, and if so, whether he would wait for Sverdrup to join him.

Nansen and his companion advanced slowly over the tortuous ice, at temperatures between 43 and 47 degrees below zero. They lost their mileage recorder along the way and spent much of their time lugging their heavy sledges over the hummock ice. It was a terrible, exhausting march, in clothing so stiffened by the cold that it cut deep gashes in their flesh.

Nansen's equipment had not been perfectly designed and caused him terrible disappointments; the two men were at the mercy of the slightest hitch, any one of which might precipitate a catastrophe. "It is astonishing that we have not got farther," Nansen noted on April 3. "Beginning to doubt the advisability of continuing north much longer . . . over such ice as this and with these dogs. If only we had more of them. . . ."

On April 8, in temperature of 36 below zero, Nansen hoisted the Norwegian flag at 86° 13′ 06″ N. by 95° E., the most northerly point yet reached by man, less than 250 miles from the Pole.

The retreat toward Franz Josef Land began. On the twelfth, Nansen forgot to wind the watches; longitude could no longer be determined except approximately. On April 20, in the midst of ice, they discovered the trunk of a Siberian larch tree, standing on the ice pack; they inscribed: "F.N.—H.J.—85° 30′."

On May 2, the dogs' provisions ran out; they would have to be done away with one by one. The incoherent drift of the pack and the thaw that was just beginning transformed their march into a nightmare, and it was clear that provisions were running short. On

May 26, Nansen's favorite dog, Kvik, had to be killed, to feed his eight remaining companions.

The month of June was terrible; the two men did not gain a single degree in their southwestward march. On June 21, in the depths of despair, they managed to kill a seal, which saved their lives.

On July 10, three bears appeared, as if by a miracle, and on the twenty-fourth, they sighted land. It was to take them twenty days to reach it. They presumed it to be one of the northeastern islands of Franz Josef Land.

On August 6, they had to do away with their last two dogs, Caiaphas and Suggen. The faithfulness and the courage of these two animals earned them the honor of being shot; the others, in order to conserve precious ammunition, had had their throats cut.

At the end of August, they set up a winter camp, not knowing that, only 94 miles away from them, the Jackson-Harmsworth expedition (which, it should be noted, was the first ever to use ponies) had built a comfortable base. They improvised a stone cabin, where they lived till May 19, 1896, killing and eating bears. Their bear-grease lamp covered them with soot and grease, but their condition remained satisfactory.

On June 17, they reached Cape Flora, barely escaping the attack of a school of walruses by driving their gutted kayaks onto the ice. Toward noon, Nansen left Johansen in the galley and climbed up on a hummock. He thought he heard the baying of dogs in the distance. In the afternoon, he found footprints in the snow, and then, with his heart beating wildly, he met a man:

"I raised my hat; we extended a hand with a hearty 'How do you do?'

" 'I'm immensely glad to see you.'

" 'Thank you. I also.'

" 'Have you a ship here?'

" 'No, my ship is not here.'

" 'How many are there of you?'

" 'I have one companion at the ice edge.'

"As we talked, we had begun to go in toward land. Suddenly he stopped, looked me full in the face and said quickly, 'Aren't you Nansen?'

" 'Yes, I am.'

" 'By Jove, I am glad to see you!'

"And he seized my hand and shook it again."

The two rescued men were washed, clothed and given every comfort, but no one knew anything about the *Fram.* On July 26, the *Windward* arrived with fresh provisions for Jackson and departed again with the two men aboard; on August 13, they landed at Vardö. It was Captain Brown, of the *Windward,* who informed Nansen of the discovery of the X ray by Roentgen, the defeat of the Chinese at the hands of the Japanese, and finally, the Swede Andrée's plan to reach the Pole by balloon; Andrée was even then waiting for a favorable wind to enable him to depart.

Nansen and Johansen rushed to the Vardö telegraph office and sent off more than two thousand words. The town, which had already learned of Nansen's return, was decked out in all its splendor.

On August 21, the *Windward* dropped anchor at Hammerfest, where Nansen met Sir George Baden-Powell and where Mrs. Nansen came to meet him. But there was no news yet from the *Fram.*

On the morning of August 26, on board the Baden-Powell yacht, Nansen received a telegram:

> Fridtjof Nansen,
> The *Fram* arrived in good condition. All well on board. Shall start at once for Tromsö. Welcome home.
>
> OTTO SVERDRUP

Nansen had predicted that the *Fram* would be home by the autumn of 1896; he had not been wrong. The *Fram*'s drift had been accomplished without serious incident. In October 1895, she reached 85° 57′ N. On August 13, after thirty-eight days of "Herculean effort," she was pried loose and began to make her way south toward Vardö. On the way, at Dane Island, she met the Andrée expedition, which had not been able to depart that year.

On August 27, Nansen rejoined his ship, amid cheers and embraces. On September 9, Norway gave them a triumphal welcome at Oslo. "Still," Nansen wrote, "we have done nothing but our duty. . . ." But a duty which was recognized throughout the world as "the greatest human exploit of the nineteenth century." The exploit was also scientific; Nansen had proved the accuracy of his theory of transpolar currents, and he had revealed the nature of the Arctic basin, thanks to his continuous and thorough observations.

This was Nansen's last expedition; he was to devote the rest of his life to the easing of human misery. But he never gave up entirely the idea of setting out again, and he thought seriously about the possibility of using a submarine to circumvent the polar icecap, as Wilkins was to attempt to do in 1931.

In 1930, the year of his death, he was planning to fly over the Pole aboard the *Graf Zeppelin.* He never stopped thinking of leading an expedition to the South Pole, down to the day when his young compatriot and admirer, Roald Amundsen, came to him in 1917 to ask that he lend him the *Fram.*

"But," as Nansen says in his journal (these were his last written words), "what would life be worth without its dreams?"

17

THE FIRST ICEBREAKER

WE MAY SAY that with Nansen the nineteenth century came to a beautiful close. His name, certainly, eclipses all others. But for anyone who is interested in the technological progress that led to the conquest of the poles, it is impossible not to take into account a series of innovations which were to crown the last years of the century.

It was in 1899 that the first tests on the icebreaker *Yermak* took place off Spitsbergen. The Russian Admiral Stepan Makarov reached 81° 28′ N. by 20° E. thanks to this revolutionary vessel, which was to become indispensable for convoys in the Far North.

Contrary to popular belief, the icebreaker does not ram the ice;

it shoves its bow onto it, and the ice is broken by the bow's descending weight. Later, tanks were added at the bow and along the sides of the ship, into which water could be drawn and from which it could then be ejected. The *Yermak* did not have such tanks, but the principle had been found all the same. The construction, which had been carried out under Makarov's supervision in 1890, was so sturdy that the ship remained in service till 1957 and, moreover, set a record for Arctic navigation (by a ship that was not icebound) in 1938, reaching 83° 06′ N.

It was in the south, on the other hand, that two of the most important events of the end of the century took place; two expeditions in a row were the first to winter on the Antarctic continent—one at the edge, the other in the interior. Since Ross, Wilkes and Dumont d'Urville, exploration had practically come to a halt in the south; in 1901, Scott was to bring the region back into the limelight. He was, however, preceded by the whalers Larsen, Evensen, Svend Foyn and Kristensen, and especially by the two expeditions which first wintered there.

The earlier of these was organized by the Belgian Adrien de Gerlache, whose *Belgica,* a three-master equipped as a scientific laboratory, sailed from Antwerp in 1897. His preponderantly Norwegian crew included, as first mate, Roald Amundsen, who was to become the conqueror of the South Pole fourteen years later. As for the ship's physician, Dr. Frederick Cook, he was, twelve years later, to set off one of the greatest controversies in polar history, by claiming that he, rather than Peary, deserved the glory for having conquered the North Pole.

After having passed through the strait that now bears his name, Gerlache, who like so many others before him was also seeking the South Magnetic Pole, became icebound at 70° 20′ S. by 85° W.; when the ice pack opened up following a storm, Gerlache hurled himself into it, against the advice of his staff.

His drift, which lasted from March 1898 to March 1899, bears a special importance in light of the fact that the *Belgica* was the first scientific ship ever to visit the Antarctic and that she was able to carry out continuous observations. For the first time, the terrible southern winter was forced to give up its secrets. Gerlache brought home a large amount of information of various kinds, and also proved that it was possible to winter in the south.

The second expedition proved, for its part, that it was equally possible to winter on the continent itself. Its chief, the Norwegian Carsten Borchgrevink, decided to set up camp on Cape Adare; the sealing ship *Southern Cross* deposited him there on February 17, 1899, with his scientific instruments and his crew of Laplanders, whose job it was to take care of the dogs. The *Southern Cross* picked up the winter party again on February 2, 1900; they had made numerous observations and had shown that it was possible to live through the terrible Antarctic winter without ill effects.

On the return journey, the ship explored the edges of the Ross Barrier, which the steamship was able to come much closer to than the *Erebus* and the *Terror* had done. It was noted that, since 1845, the contours of the barrier had receded, as much as twenty-six miles in some places. It was further noted that, at about 164° W., the height of the barrier dropped to sea level.

But it is to the north that we must now turn our attention once again, despite the interest offered by these two winterings, to consider two remarkable events: the first flight over the polar ice pack—with unfortunate results, as it turned out—and the first appearance on the northern ice of the future conqueror of the Pole, Lieutenant Robert E. Peary of the United States Navy.

"Even if explorers," Nansen had written in his account of the *Fram*'s odyssey, "have to live in Eskimo fashion and content themselves with the barest necessaries, they may, provided they are suitably equipped, make good headway and cover considerable distances in regions which have hitherto been regarded as almost inaccessible." This was Peary's program.

Peary did not have a scientific mind; he was first of all an engineer, a technician, a soldier. For him, the Pole was, more than anything else, a target, an objective to be reached. For many, many years, he prepared himself, with astounding intelligence and obstinacy. All his Arctic adventures before the great final one, were, in fact, rehearsals, or training sessions, during which Peary never ceased to work at perfecting his techniques and equipment for the final assault.

He discovered his vocation one day when he was reading a description of the inland ice by Nordenskjöld in a popular magazine. Being the young man he was, his imagination took fire, and from that day on, he never stopped affirming that the Pole was his "principal aim."

He asked for leave from the Navy[1] and, at the beginning of 1886, arrived in Disko Bay, in the west of Greenland. With a friend, the Danish Lieutenant Maigaard, he attacked the inland ice, carrying thirty days' provisions on two sledges (9 feet long and 13 inches wide, weighing 29 pounds). From June 8 to July 2, they struggled against the violent winds, but in the end they were forced to give up. Their return was made easier by the following wind, which they harnessed by attaching a sail to the sledge. They returned to the coast on July 24.

But Peary, undaunted, decided to carry his project through to the end. Nansen's success in crossing Greenland in 1888 reinforced his determination, and, in 1891, having found the necessary funds, he was able to set out once again for the north.

A steamship dropped him off north of Baffin Bay; he was accompanied by his wife, by Dr. Frederick Cook (then twenty-six years old) and by Matthew Henson, his Negro manservant from Virginia. He set up the portable house he had brought with him, in order to winter on the spot and to be able to undertake the crossing of Greenland along a more northerly line than the one Nansen had taken, thus beating him on his own home grounds.

His great talent lay in understanding the advantages of the Eskimo technique. His first act was to invite an Eskimo family to come and live with him, and to make him a full set of fur clothing. A deep friendship grew up between Peary and the Eskimos, and it lasted through the American's long Arctic visits. He spent two winters with them, and from them he learned how to dress for the Arctic as well as how to travel with dogs. This was not, as we shall see, quite all there was to the total adoption of Eskimo technique in the manner of Stefansson and Rasmussen, but Peary was to draw from certain of the Eskimo methods sufficient technical knowledge to go down in history as the conqueror of the North Pole.

In April 1892, Peary set out with two men; on June 27, he reached Independence Fjord on the northeast coast, and on August 5, he got back to his base after an absence of seventy-six days.

He returned the following year with thirteen men and his wife,[2]

---

[1] He was, in fact, a civil engineer employed by the United States Navy, with the equivalent title of lieutenant.

[2] He had married Josephine Diebitsch in 1888; she was to give him exemplary aid and support all through her life.

who gave birth to a little girl, Mary Anighito,[3] in Greenland at 77° 40′ N. His second long-distance run took place in April 1894; accompanied by Lee and Henson, he returned after twenty-five days with a single dog, without provisions, and having advanced only 125 miles in the direction of the northeast coast of Greenland, which, we may note, he was to reach the following year.

Calmly but obstinately, Peary continued his polar apprenticeship, as no one had ever done before; when he set off at the age of fifty-two, in 1909, he would be the master of his techniques, with an elaborate plan, the stages of which, as we shall see, were to be linked with an absolute logic.

As for the attempt made by the Swede Andrée to reach the North Pole in a balloon, it comes more under the heading of foolhardiness than of exploration. The bizarre appearance of this round monster over the ice nevertheless forms a part of the great polar story, which has included so much greatness, so much misery—and also so much folly.

It was Baron Nordenskjöld who had, indirectly, led Peary to his vocation. It was he too who infected Andrée with the Arctic virus. Following a meeting of the Swedish Geographical Society on March 16, 1894, the baron fell into conversation with Andrée, who was already known for his talent as an airman, and asked him whether he believed it would be possible to use the balloon on polar expeditions. This question, which must have seemed commonplace enough to an experienced researcher like Nordenskjöld, immediately set Andrée's imagination on fire.

Salomon August Andrée, head of the technical section of the Patent Office, was forty years old and full of blind self-confidence. He also had absolute faith in technology. He was convinced that he had succeeded in eliminating the major difficulty in the lighter-than-air craft of the period, that of their being almost impossible to steer; and he was indeed the inventor of a process which enabled a balloon to follow a course which veered as much as 30 degrees from the direction of the wind. To do this, he had used sails and "guide ropes," or heavy cords hanging from the nacelle; when the balloon became wet and heavy and began to sink,

[3] Anighito means "snow girl." The Pearys also had a son later on.

the guide ropes trailed along the ground and relieved her of their weight. The balloon thus maintained a regular altitude.

Andrée decided then to set off from the most northerly point to which his equipment could be transported, that is, Spitsbergen. He hoped that, with a south wind, he could travel the 690 miles that separated him from the Pole at an average speed of about 15 miles per hour. But two major gaps made this plan a pipe dream: first, no one knew anything about the wind pattern over the Arctic Ocean; and second, no one, not even the specialist Andrée himself, could say how the balloon would behave in such a climate, although he denied that icing presented any danger.

But with this imprecise, not to say totally obscure, plan, he was able to work absolute marvels of ingeniousness. He began by convincing the Swedish Geographical Society, with Nordenskjöld's support, of his chances for success. He encountered greater skepticism at the Royal Geographical Society in London from Sir Albert Markham and A. W. Greely, but this did not stop him. He went on stubbornly seeking the 130,000 Swedish kronor that he needed; it was Alfred Nobel,[4] the inventor of dynamite, who gave him one half the sum, the other half being raised by King Oscar and other patrons such as Baron Dickson.

Andrée then threw himself into the construction of the world's largest balloon; the contract was given to the French builder Henri Lachambre, who promised delivery by Christmas, 1895. The balloon, which was finished a few days ahead of time, was put on display on the Champs de Mars in Paris, where the French president, Félix Faure, came to see her.

She was a gigantic monster, 98 feet high, whose double Chinese-silk envelope contained 190,000 cubic feet of gas. The wicker and bamboo car consisted of three sections: the roof supporting the mast and sails (990 square feet), the galley (placed 32 feet lower to avoid fires) and the hold. The guide ropes were planned to maintain an altitude of about 820 feet.

Andrée first christened his balloon the *North Pole*, then the *Örnen* ("Eagle"). He took her to Spitsbergen in June 1896, on board the steamer *Virgo*. Andrée had the *Örnen* inflated; accompanied by Strindberg (the playwright's nephew) and Dr. Erkholm, he was preparing to set out, when the *Fram* arrived at the

---

[4] See Robert de La Croix, *Les Disparus du Pôle*.

Isle of Danes on August 14. From Sverdrup, he learned that there was no permanent wind from the south in the Arctic in the summertime. Discouraged, Andrée gave up and returned to Sweden.

One year later, however, on July 11, 1897 at 1:50 P.M., the *Örnen* took off. On board were Andrée, Strindberg and one other crewman, the engineer K. Fraekel, with hunting gear, portable sledges and thirty-two homing pigeons, with which to inform the world of their progress. But, as she went up, the balloon broke her guide rope.

On July 16, a whaling captain, Hansen, shot a strange bird that had come to rest on the mast at 2 A.M.; the bird fell into the water, and Hansen resisted the impulse to fish it out. During the day, he described the incident to another whaling captain, who immediately thought of Andrée's homing pigeons. Hansen retraced his course and was lucky enough to recover the dead bird. Under its wing was attached the following message:

> *July 13*
>
> 12.30 midday, Lat. 82° 2′, Long. 15° 5′ E., good speed to E. 10° S. All well on board. This is the third pigeon-post.
>
> ANDRÉE

Then silence fell. Uneasiness increased, and, as in the case of Franklin, the search for Andrée began. It was not till two years later, on May 14, 1899, that two fishermen found a buoy released at 82° N. by 25° E. washed up on a sandbank north of Iceland. On August 27, 1900, a second buoy was found north of Norway, and this was to be the last trace of the Andrée expedition.

The world would have to wait till August 6, 1930, thirty years later, to learn the three men's fate; that day, the Norwegian ship *Bratvaag*, transporting a scientific expedition led by Gunnar Horn, landed at White Island, on the way to Franz Josef Land. Searching for a spring, two sailors came upon an unexpected pot lid, then, a little farther on, a black mass—a boat. Eliassen, the commander of the *Bratvaag*, searched the boat; the first thing he found was a sack labeled: "Andrée Polar Expedition, 1896." Gunnar Horn, the head of the expedition, rushed to the spot and gathered a large number of miscellaneous objects from the boat: navigational instruments, kitchen utensils, rifles, sewing kit, et cetera, all caked together by water, ice, snow and time. In the bottom of the boat, Horn discovered Andrée's corpse. Several yards away was Strindberg's grave.

The discovery had an overwhelming effect on the people of Sweden, to whom the news was brought by another ship, the *Terningen*, which had crossed the *Bratvaag's* path. Journalists hastened to White Island; one of them found Fraekel's remains, Andrée's and Strindberg's journals, the *Örnen*'s logbook, and Strindberg's camera; the rolls of film, which were developed by Swedish specialists, turned out to be exceptional documents.

It is known that the *Örnen* was abandoned on July 16, five hundred miles from the Pole, and that the three men arrived at White Island after an exhausting journey, on September 18. A winter camp was prepared. Then suddenly, on October 17, the notes stop, with the mystery only half explained. The exact cause of the three men's death is not known; there were still provisions and oil remaining.

The lack of experience, of equipment or of warm clothing: none of these hypotheses satisfies the experts. As two of the bodies were found next to one another close to a cooker in good condition, it has been suggested that their death was caused by carbon monoxide.[5] This is obviously nothing more than a supposition.

And so is the notion that the three flying explorers died of trichinosis.[6] According to Andrée's journal, the three men ate thirteen polar bears in the course of their journey. Moreover, the Danish physician Ernst Tryde has found traces of *Trichinella spiralis* in the remains of a bear found at the White Island camp. Although it is easier to imagine that Andrée and his companions died of exhaustion, discouragement and cold, we shall probably never know the exact cause of their death.

This mad escapade, this illogical sacrifice was to have at least one merit: it announced the coming of the great era of airborne exploration of the twentieth century. The nineteenth century had contributed in large measure to the conquest of the ice. The two passages, the northeast and the northwest, had been forced, but

---

[5] Kaare Rodahl, *North*.

[6] Trichinosis is a parasitic disease produced by the trichina (*Trichinella spiralis*), a tiny nematoid worm from 1/25th to 1/8th inch long. It attacks men as well as animals. In the polar regions, sled-dogs as well as bears may be struck by it, sometimes mortally. Man is usually infected by eating badly cooked pork, containing tumorous trichinae.

man had not yet succeeded in conquering the poles. They had not been able to get closer than 250 miles.

Louis of Savoy, Duke of the Abruzzi, wintering on his ship in Teplitz Bay to the north of Franz Josef Land, ordered a splendid fireworks display to be set off on December 31, 1899, in the midst of the polar night; the century thus closed with a gesture of man's defiance of the Pole.

18

SCOTT AND CHARCOT

WE COULD CHOOSE no more magical name than that of Captain Scott to symbolize the opening of our century. Amundsen, Peary, even Nansen, and a few others will always be remembered in polar history, but their names will doubtless never enjoy the popular adulation of Scott's. Scott is synonymous with adventure, intrepidity, risk. He is rather like the hero of the kind of novel that children and dreamers love. Had he lived under the Vikings, the sagas would have made his story into a legend. In fact, of course, it has neither more nor less merit than the story of Shackleton or Amundsen. It is Scott's tragic end that has so greatly enhanced his popular reputation.

Robert Falcon Scott,[1] a thirty-year-old lieutenant on board a torpedo vessel, was walking in the streets of London one afternoon in 1899, when he met Sir Clements Markham, the president of the Royal Geographical Society and a great promoter of expeditions.

Sir Clements Markham had noticed young Scott in 1887, when he was the guest of his cousin Sir Albert Markham in the Antilles; Midshipman Scott had won the regatta and had dined at the table of honor. Sir Clements had been struck by "his intelligence, information and the charm of his manner."

When England was committed to sending a great expedition to the south, on the occasion of the "Antarctic Year" of 1901-03, which was brought into being by the Geographical Congress of Berlin in 1900, Markham had no hesitations; he appointed Scott to command it. He did more than this, he secured the appointments of two young officers in the merchant marine, one of them an expert on the ice, the other on sailing: Albert B. Armitage and Ernest Henry Shackleton, whose name was to become famous in the Antarctic. On June 9, the ship's articles were signed, and on the thirtieth, Scott was promoted to commander and transferred to the *Discovery*.

The choice of ship was the source of great discussion. The committee (which included McClintock, John Murray, Nares and Albert Markham) decided that it should be made of wood, and that its lines should roughly resemble those of Nares's old *Discovery* of 1876; but it would not have the configuration of Nansen's *Fram*, for, as Markham points out in a curious note,[2] "there is not the same likelihood of severe nips in the south."

For 34,050 pounds sterling, the shipyards of Dundee built an oak three-master with an elm keel. Her length was 177 feet, her beam 33 feet and her capacity 483 tons. The 400 horsepower engines were to cost 10,322 pounds. A system for retracting the rudder was built in. The forty-three-man crew was trained for both sail and steam navigation. Rather extreme measures were taken during the building period to ensure accurate compensation of the compasses; everything conceivable was done to avoid the possibility that mag-

---

[1] He was born near Devonport on June 6, 1868, and became a Naval Cadet in 1881.

[2] Sir Clements Markham, *The Lands of Silence*.

netic observations might be thrown off by the proximity of iron particles, and so all iron was excluded from within a radius of thirty feet around the compasses. The lighting was electric, the electricity being produced either by a dynamo or by storage batteries.

On March 21, 1901, Lady Markham christened the *Discovery*, the sixth ship of that name (Hudson, Baffin, Cook, Vancouver and Nares had each commanded a *Discovery*).

The *Discovery* carried 335 tons of coal and provisions for two years. Captain Scott expended a considerable amount of attention on matters of practical organization. He would leave to no one else, for example, the task of choosing provisions; it was he himself who visited the canneries of Beauvais and Copenhagen. Dr. Collin Grigg examined the food containers one by one and rejected 265 pounds out of 11,300. To combat any danger that might arise from preserved food, Scott took aboard fresh meat in the form of forty-five live sheep.

As England had lost the habit of equipping polar expeditions, Scott was forced to go to Norway to buy fur clothing, reindeer-skin sleeping bags, four bales of Lapland grass and seventy pairs of skis (7 feet long, 11 inches wide), as well as nine Nansen sledges, 9 feet long with all their accessories.

The scientific equipment was, of course, the best available at the time and included, among other things, alcohol thermometers that would go as low as −90° Fahrenheit, a Dines pressure gauge, pendulums and seismographs, as well as a photographic spectrometer for the observation of the aurora borealis. A highly perfected sounding device and dredging nets were provided. From the scientific point of view, the *Discovery* had at her disposal equipment unique in the period.

But the most original instrument Scott carried in his hold was a captive balloon[8] which he intended to use for aerial observations in the manner of the Frenchman Gaimard on Spitsbergen in 1838-40. Several models of the Army's captive balloons were taken along; six enormous gas tanks from which to fill them were stored on deck. One officer and two men took a special course, before departure, to familiarize themselves with balloon technique.

The Geographical Club gave the officers a farewell dinner; the

---

[8] See R. F. Scott, *The Voyage of the* Discovery.

Bishop of London blessed the *Discovery;* the King and Queen visited her. Then, on August 5, 1901, Scott weighed anchor.

On January 9,1902, the *Discovery* called at Cape Adare in the Antarctic, in the Ross Sea. On the twenty-first, at an altitude of 1,300 feet, at the peak of Cape Crozier on Ross Island, Scott was able to admire, for the first time, the upper surface of the immense Ross Ice Shelf. Observations were begun, photographs were taken, and on February 4 Scott had the honor of being the first man ever to contemplate the Antarctic from a balloon, at an altitude of 790 feet. Shackleton made the next flight, to take photographs.

The *Discovery* then established winter quarters in McMurdo Sound, where the Americans were to build their great supporting base for their 1956 expeditions. To relax from the work of observation, the men held skiing races and played rugby; they edited a newspaper, the *South Polar Times,* under Shackleton's direction, and put on theatrical productions.

Numerous exploring parties were undertaken by Scott and his collaborators; it was at this time that the captain was making a serious study of the problem of sledge travel in the Antarctic. He concluded that traveling conditions in the south were significantly different from those in the Arctic (which, we ought to point out, he knew of only at second hand).

In his study of traveling techniques, Scott made the greatest mistake of his life; he became convinced that it was preferable to use men, rather than dogs, to haul the sledges. This error, which was tragic in its consequences, demonstrates the degree to which a lack of experience can be dangerous for a polar explorer, even one of Scott's stature.

It is true that before his departure Scott had conferred at length with Nansen, who had offered his advice on the matter. But, just at this moment, Sverdrup and Peary were learning from the Eskimos how to use dogs in the Arctic, and they were unable to give Scott the benefit of their experience. When they were at last able to, they encountered Scott's stubborn refusal to accept the idea; dogs ought to be treated "humanely," he claimed.

"There were two ways of treating them," Sir Clements Markham[4] wrote in defense of Scott, "there was the idea of bringing

[4] *Op. cit.*

them all back safe and well, which was McClintock's way and there was the way of getting the greatest amount of work possible out of them, regardless of everything else, and using them as food, which was Nansen's and Peary's. If dogs are treated with humanity, they are, in the writer's opinion, not so good as men in a long journey;[5] and Scott had an unconquerable aversion to the employment of them in the second way. The dogs, twenty in number, were obtained from Siberia, but five were lost in various ways. . . ."

We can hardly account for this aversion in terms of the British temperament, since Shackleton was to say, "fourteen dogs did as well as or even better than eighteen men," while Sir Douglas Mawson, an Australian, was to write, "There can be no question as to the value of dogs as a means of traction."

There was something at once poignant, great, and childish, in Scott's feeling about dogs. At the moment when his competitor Amundsen was preparing to drive toward the Pole with his pack of fifty-two animals, he wrote in his journal, "If he gets to the pole, it must be before we do, as he is bound to travel fast with dogs."

This sentimental and slightly dated stubbornness, this total refusal to use the one technical means that was generally regarded as effective at the time, in order to "make the conquest more nobly and splendidly won" doubtless goes far toward illuminating Captain Scott's exceptional character.

Thus, the commander of the *Discovery* decided that he would use human traction. Each sledge was designed for a crew of three; it carried their tent and their full equipment. The heavy cloth tents were supported by five bamboo poles seven feet long meeting at the top. With its ground cloth, the weight of a tent was thirty-three pounds.

The daily ration per man was approximately the following: 12.7 ounces of biscuits; 1.6 ounces of oatmeal; 8.8 ounces of pemmican; 2.7 ounces of bacon and pea flour; 2 ounces of plasmon; 2.1 ounces of cheese; 1 ounce of chocolate; 0.7 ounce cocoa; 3.5 ounces of sugar. Each three-man crew received a further weekly allowance of 12.3 ounces of tea; 8.8 ounces of onion powder; 4.4 ounces of

[5] This opinion has been proved false many times over. The efficiency of humanely treated dogs is higher than that of ill-treated dogs and much greater than that of men. The question may be put, moreover, in the following way: Is it preferable to treat dogs like human beings, or men as if they were beasts of burden?

pepper and 7 ounces of salt—a total of just over 34 ounces per man per day.

Each sledge's equipment included an aluminum model of the famous Nansen cooker. A Primus stove, a mechanism first used by the same Nansen, was also provided; the fuel used was petroleum gas, a gallon can of which had to last each crew ten days. The total load of each sledge was more than 660 pounds, or 220 pounds per man.

For the harness, Scott had developed an original system. The weight, instead of being concentrated on the shoulders, was spread over the upper part of the body by a broad band which was held in place with braces. A rope was attached to two iron rings at the ends of the band. The haulers wore Lapp *finnesko* on their feet.

Scott and his man made a good number of runs in this way. During one of them, he and Shackleton reached 82° 17′ S. along the coast, and he noted that the mountain range bordering on Victoria Land seemed to continue on toward the South Pole, from which he was then only 460 miles away.

In the meantime, in London Sir Clements Markham was trying to gather funds with which to send the supply boat that had been promised to Scott. He opened a great campaign. But gifts came in only at a very slow rate, in spite of the reminder of Franklin's expedition, which had been lost through the lack of a rescue ship. Money came from the farthest corners of the empire; schoolchildren took up collections; one little boy even deprived himself of the five shillings he had put aside to buy a bicycle. The Prince of Wales gave 50 pounds, and The King 100.

In Norway, Markham was able to acquire the *Morgen*, which then became the *Morning*. She was 140 feet long and displaced 452 tons. Her engines were old but sturdy and had proved themselves in the whaling trade. Her builder was none other than the famous Svend Foyn, the inventor of the harpoon gun.

The *Morning*, under the command of Captain William Colbeck, managed to reach the *Discovery* in January, 1903, after having discovered two islands which were christened the Scott Islands. The new supplies were painfully transported over the ice (14 tons over a distance of six miles), and the *Morning* returned home, taking with her the sick and wounded men from the Scott expedition, including Shackleton, who had fallen victim to an odd sort of exhaustion.

Stocked with fresh provisions and cheered by news of their families, Scott's men were now prepared to undertake their second winter, without apprehension. In November 1903, Scott scaled the Ferrar Glacier, which ran up from the camp toward the east, and reached a point 146° 30′ E. on the Antarctic plateau. In the course of another sortie, he reached a point 79° 30′ S. In January 1904, the *Morning* returned accompanied by the *Terra Nova;* toward the middle of February, the ice freed the *Discovery*, which was able to set sail and return to London with her two companion ships.

The Scott expedition was a remarkable success; its achievements have been summed up by J. Gordon Hayes in the following table, giving the mileage of its geographical discoveries:

West Coast Barrier	350 miles
Glaciers	200 miles
Continental ice	200 miles
King Edward VII Land	150 miles
Land discovered	900 miles
Barrier	150 miles
Land and shelf ice discovered	1050 miles
Lands explored	200 miles
Total	1250 miles[6]

The mass of observations, geographical, meteorological, biological, oceanographic, et cetera, led Sir Clements Markham, Scott's mentor, to remark, "Never has any other polar expedition returned with so great a harvest of results."

The results of the other expeditions of the Antarctic Year were more modest, but they were nevertheless of some importance.

The Germans had sent the *Gauss*, an improved model of the *Fram*, with Erich von Drygalski, the head of the previous expedition to Greenland from 1891 to 1893. The *Gauss*, which had been specially built for this expedition under the sponsorship of Dr. Neumayer, measured 164 feet and had a capacity of 650 tons. She remained icebound from February 1902 till February 1903. The expedition sent out a number of sledging sorties along Wil-

[6] J. Gordon Hayes, *Antarctica.*

helm II Coast, as well as a captive balloon, which made observations similar to Scott's. After this expedition, the Germans abandoned polar research and sold the *Gauss* to the Canadians.

Sweden sent Baron Nordenskjöld's nephew Otto, an eminent geologist, to study the east coast of Graham Land. His ship was called the *Antarctic*. One of the scientists on this expedition, Dr. Anderson, even discovered an abundant fossil heap, thereby proving that, in the Jurassic period, the region had been covered with lush forests and that Graham Land had once been attached to Tasmania.

At the end of 1902, the *Antarctic* was unable to reach Nordenskjöld's winter quarters (Snow Hill) and was crushed by the ice pack in February 1903 (at 63° 50′ S. by 57° W.). The crew took refuge on Paulet Island and was rescued a year later by the Argentine gunboat *Uruguay* under Captain Irizar. This rescue made a great impression in Argentina, which immediately became interested in exploring to the south. Dr. William S. Bruce, the head of the Scottish expedition, ceded the Laurie Island weather base to Argentina, and she has never failed to send an annual expedition there since that time.

As for France, it was to Dr. Jean Baptiste Charcot that she owed her presence among the expeditions organized for the Antarctic Year. Dr. Charcot was the son of a famous neurologist at the Salpêtrière Hospital in Paris. A doctor of medicine himself, Charcot was astonished by the fact that France should not be represented among the other nations in the van of human progress in the polar regions.

He succeeded in collecting 450,000 gold francs and had Gauthier Senior, of St. Malo, build him a 250-ton polar ship, the *Français*, which was 105 feet long, with a beam of 25 feet; he followed the advice given him on shipbuilding by the Belgian Adrien de Gerlache. The bow was reinforced; the keel was curved sharply toward the bow; the engine was bought secondhand.

Charcot's staff included a naval ensign, Rey; Pléneau, a photographer; Turquet, a naturalist; Gourdon, a geologist; Matha, a hydrographer; and Dayné, an Alpine guide. Charcot deplored the French custom of drinking half a pint of wine with every meal, and he also felt that wine barrels would be a useless encumbrance in the hold. Being the good classicist that he was, and to make up for his decision on wine, he stocked the ship's library with Virgil,

Dante, Cervantes, Swift, Saint-Simon, Hugo and Michelet. He had the happy experience of watching his men grow interested in the works of these authors as the voyage progressed.

Charcot was, moreover, an extremely sensitive man; he was moved to tears by the death of his dog Sogen and of his pig Toby; and one day on the ice pack he took a new-born Weddell seal in his arms like a little child. Charcot was also an explorer who believed in technology; his equipment was modern in the extreme, and on board his later ship, the *Pourquoi-Pas?*, built in 1907, there were a searchlight, a motor launch, telephones, and cables with which to light stations set up on land by electricity.

On board the *Français*, Charcot explored the west coast of the Antarctic peninsula,[7] completed Gerlache's series of readings, corrected those of the whaler Dallmann, explored the Biscoe Archipelago and wintered before Wandel Island. In 1904-05, he explored Alexander I Island and Loubet Coast, named for the President of the Republic. It was during this cruise that the *Français* ran against a rock. The watertight partitions had to be knocked down to allow the water to siphon off to the stern where the pumps were (the pumps were hand-operated). On March 5, 1905, the *Français* called at Patagonia with seventy-five cases of collected materials and scientific notes. The Argentine government bought the *Français*, but did not get to use her for long, for she was lost on the Rio de la Plata in 1907.

Having returned to France, Charcot had a new ship built, again at St. Malo, at a cost of 780,000 gold francs. She was to become famous throughout the world and to bear the French colors proudly: the *Pourquoi-Pas?* She had a capacity of 800 tons, was 131 feet long and 30 feet wide, and her engine developed 550 horsepower.

The moment he was in possession of his new vessel, Charcot set sail for the south. At Wiencke Island (64° 45′ S. by 63° 30′ W.), the *Pourquoi-Pas?* ran onto a rock, which did serious damage to the keel. This injury, over which the deep-sea divers were later to shake their heads, did not prevent Charcot from carrying out his program.

In 1908-09, he discovered that Loubet Coast was identical with

---

[7] Graham Land on English maps; Palmer Peninsula on American; Terra San Martin on Argentine; Terra O'Higgins on Chilean.

Biscoe's Adelaide Island, but that it stretched seventy miles farther on. He also discovered Fallières Coast, so named in honor of the new President of the Republic. Charcot's work in this region was considerable, and the maps of it which he drew up were practically the only ones in use in 1935, some twenty-five years later, when the English began the scientific exploration of Graham Land.

Nor must we forget that, if France has taken the interest in Adélie Coast that we know she has, she owes this also to Charcot, who, in 1925-26, persuaded the government to promulgate the decrees affirming France's rights in this Antarctic sector.

"Dr. Charcot," affirms Sir Clements Markham, "has won the admiration of all who know him, and all true Britons feel a regard for the gallant Frenchman when they remember his consideration and affection for Captain Scott." In the conquest of the poles, Charcot represents the qualities of calm, lucidity and balance, the very same qualities which were to make Peary the conqueror of the north.

It was, paradoxically enough, the contrary qualities which characterized the struggle for the conquest of the South Pole; while in the north the duel between man and the environment was only a question of time and technique, in the south the struggle took on a dramatic new light, in which the Pole was no longer anything but the stakes in a gigantic free-for-all between men who would sacrifice their safety for success.

19

THE FIRST MAN AT THE NORTH POLE

Had it not been for Roald Amundsen, the century would have gotten off to a bad start in the Arctic. One after the other, Otto Sverdrup (on board the famous *Fram*), Peary (icebound on April 20, 1902, at 84° 17′ N.) and Baldwin (who with his 420 Siberian dogs and 15 ponies never got past Franz Josef Land), failed in their efforts to approach the Pole. Even Edvard von Toll, who distinguished himself most notably by aiding Nansen during his voyage on the *Fram* and who discovered real fossile treasures, met his death in 1902 on Bennett Island.

It was only shortly afterward, on the night of June 16, 1903, that Roald Amundsen sailed from Christiania on board the *Gjöa*, with the intention of forcing the Northwest Passage at one go. McClure had achieved this exploit before him, but had had to abandon his ship, the *Investigator;* it was on foot that he had completed the journey.

Amundsen was only thirty-one, but he possessed, in addition to a highly tempered character, one considerable advantage: steam. The *Gjöa* was not, certainly, one of those great three-masters with a slender smokestack sticking out of them, whose classic silhouettes immediately call to mind Scott or Charcot. She was minuscule; her capacity was 47 tons and her engine only 14 horsepower; it was, however, this little 72-foot sealing cutter which first forced the passage from one end to the other and was the first ship with an auxiliary engine to navigate in Arctic waters.

Roald Amundsen was born at Borge, in 1872. After learning his first lessons in the hard school of the sealing trade, he participated in Adrien de Gerlache's Belgian expedition in the Antarctic. He earned the reputation of having an authoritarian and difficult character, but a lucid and enterprising intelligence.

Having gathered the necessary funds by borrowing, even from his own brothers, Amundsen bought the *Gjöa* at Tromsö and took aboard provisions for five years, ten tons of fuel, a quarter ton of pyroxylin (or guncotton), six Eskimo dogs (a gift from Otto Sverdrup) and six crewmen. It is said that the *Gjöa* then slipped out of port in the middle of the night, to avoid being seized by a creditor.

By sail ("and out-and-out luck") he reached Beechey Island; he then set his engine going in order to force a passage through Peel Sound. On September 9, he dropped anchor off the south coast of King William Island, where he was forced to remain for two years. It was during these two winters that Amundsen familiarized himself with the Eskimos' techniques and that he learned how to become a great dog sled driver. On the scientific side, he succeeded in reaching the Magnetic Pole and in calculating its elliptical course.

On August 12, 1905, he set out once again toward the west; and, having wintered for the third time, and then lost the *Gjöa*'s propeller, Amundsen arrived on August 30, 1906, at Nome; luck and boldness had paid off and the Northwest Passage had been vanquished for good. This feat of prowess was never to be repeated till September 1954, the date on which the two American icebreakers, the *Burton Island* and the *Northwind,* having set out from the Baffin Sea, were to succeed in entering the mouth of McClure Strait.

When the world learned of Amundsen's exploit, Peary had been carrying on his Arctic training and his attempts to reach the Pole for twenty years. He had unambiguously defined his objective, which was, purely and simply, to plant the Star-Spangled Banner on the roof of the world. Nansen and Amundsen, Papanin and Byrd—and, in general, all the great polar explorers—always began by setting themselves more modest objectives.

But Peary had no complexes whatever. The conquest of the North Pole was the aim of his life, and he was to devote all his energies, all his intelligence and all his courage to this exploit, which comes more under the heading of sport than of science. It was to become a veritable obsession with him, and one from which he would be freed only on April 6, 1909, when he was to become the winner of the "last great geographical trophy," as he called it in his own words, which took no notice at all of the South Pole.

The chronology of his voyages and the progress of his results bear witness to his tenacity.

In 1886 Peary tried, without success, to cross Greenland from west to east, starting from Disko Bay.

In 1891-92 he stayed for thirteen months among the Eskimos at the entry to Smith Sound. In the spring, he succeeded in crossing the north of Greenland.

In 1893-95 he barely escaped death after reaching Independence Fjord on April 1, 1894, and returned to his base with a single dog.

In 1896-97, he brought back to the United States meteorites found at Cape York, and submitted his final plan for the conquest of the Pole to the National Geographic Society.

From 1897 to 1899: In London, he took possession of the *Windward* (which Nansen had returned to England in 1896), equipped with a tiny engine, on which she could do three and a half knots. The *Windward* carried Peary back to the north, via New York. With his Eskimos from Cape York, Peary traveled the length of the Ellesmere Island coast, leaving depots of meat and equipment all the way, in view of future expeditions. On January 6, 1899, he called at Fort Conger, Greely's former base, in 58-below-zero cold; on his return to the *Windward,* his frostbitten big toes had to be amputated. At the end of March, he set out once again with a column of three detachments in the direction of Fort Conger. Then he pushed eastward to Cape Morris Jessup (83° 39′ N.), so named for the president of the Peary Arctic Club, which was founded in 1898. Peary went as far as 83° 50′ N. On his way back he picked up from a cairn the document that Lockwood had deposited there seventeen years earlier. He returned to Fort Conger on June 10.

In 1900, he tried in vain to push farther north.

In 1902, he led a new offensive in the direction of the Pole. On March 3, six sledges under the command of his Negro butler Henson left Etah; then, on March 6, a second convoy of fourteen sledges took off at 9:00 A.M. Peary himself brought up the rear at noon. Fort Conger was the planned rallying point. Peary set off again on March 24 with nine sledges and followed the coast as far as Cape Hecla. On April 20, at 84° 17′ 21″ N., he was halted by the chaotic pack ice.

In 1905, Peary analyzed his failure at length. Since he had made six degrees by starting at 78° N., all he would need to do would be to apply the "Peary system" and start at 84° N.

To do this, he needed a larger, sturdier and faster ship than the ailing *Windward*. Launched on March 20, 1905, this ideal ship—150 feet long, 33 feet wide, with 1,500 tons' capacity and an engine developing 1,000 horsepower—was "built of American timber in an American shipyard, engineered by an American firm with American metal, and constructed on American designs. Even the most trivial items of supply were of American manufacture." This was a national enterprise, and no one was surprised to learn that the ship had been given the name of the President of the United States, *Theodore Roosevelt*. The hull was made of wood, the sides were two feet thick and reinforced with steel. The bowsprit was narrow, the stern was rounded, and the rudder was retractible.

During the course of the summer, Peary rejoined his Eskimos in Inglefield Bay and took aboard several families (forty individuals in all) and more than two hundred dogs. Time after time, the ship was icebound, then got free, only to become icebound again; but the *Roosevelt*—whose captain, Bob Bartlett, encouraged her from his perch in the crow's-nest with cries of "Rip 'em, Teddy! Bite 'em in two! Go it"—succeeded in forcing the Robeson Channel and rounding Cape Union at the farther end, then dropped anchor off Cape Sheridan. She was moored to an ice ledge, which had been carved into an inclined plane to facilitate the raising of the hull in case of an increase in pressure.

On September 16, 1905, the long-awaited offensive came; an ice floe driven by the north wind began to constrict the ship in her ice dock. This was a dramatic moment; the deck swelled, rivets gave way here and there, while the joints shook with cracks that sounded like pistol shots. But the hull held, and the ship rose out of danger.

On February 19, 1906, four groups including six whites, twenty-one Eskimos and 120 dogs set out in the direction of Cape Hecla. Peary, who was then fifty years old, had decided to beat Cagni's record (86° 34′), to set up a base at this latitude and then to head for the Pole on an ultrarapid run.

The first part of the journey went off extremely well. Then the cold became more intense and the conditions terrible; Peary, seeing the morale of his Eskimos falling, his dogs becoming skeletal, his own tracks disappearing in the snow, gave the order to fall back at 87° 06′ N. The return journey was difficult; it was all the more rigorous, as the crew was ravaged with ophthalmia and the ice pack had drifted eastward. He decided to head for the north of Greenland. With only two dogs and accompanied by Clarke and three Eskimos, Peary touched land at Cape Neumayer, where their lives were saved by a small herd of musk oxen (two males, three females, and three calves).

Peary was able to get back to the *Roosevelt* in May 1908. Once again, he analyzed his failure. His journey had not been entirely useless, since, besides achieving a new record latitude, he had brought back a description of the north coast of Ellesmere Island, where he had observed vast ice floes, 200 feet thick, breaking off from the coastline; the phenomenon of "the Great Land ice slab, or glacial fringe," was to be of considerable interest to the Americans in 1952, when they used one of these floating islands as the site of their first permanent drifting station.

Having observed the drift, Peary decided to compensate for it by choosing a route slightly tilted to the west. It was 1908. When Peary, at age fifty-two, set off on his last polar journey, he was the master of his techniques and had worked out a minutely elaborate plan, each of the parts of which followed from one another with the logical rigorousness of a game of chess. He applied the "Peary system," which he had worked out from his twenty-seven years of Arctic apprenticeship, down to the minutest details. This system consisted in making maximum use of Eskimo techniques, while still "thinking European."

In the lead, small groups were to be dispatched, whose mission it was to clear a path, with ice axes if necessary, to build igloos and to leave caches of provisions. In this way, the men and dogs participating in the final assault would gain time and would avoid difficulty. Behind them, there would also be intermediary crews in charge of remaking the path of the trail that had been demolished by drift.

Peary assigned this crucial scouting work to his fifty Eskimos. As far as he was concerned, the highest praise he could bestow on them was the fact that he was using their own techniques of travel and of survival.

For the journey, Peary had at his disposal 250 dogs, from which he formed nineteen teams of seven dogs each. The sledges were adaptations rather than faithful copies of Eskimo prototypes; some were 10 feet long, and some—the "Peary model"—were 13 feet long. It would be inaccurate, however, to make comparative reference to a "standard Eskimo model," since there were several different types of Eskimo sledge.

In the east of Greenland, the Angmagssalik sledge never exceeded 5½ feet in length or 14 to 18 inches in width and was made of driftwood floated from Siberia by the polar drift. Its upper part was composed of juxtaposed planks, with the front one slightly raised, thus forming a toboggan in case of deep snow; the runners would then dig all the way into the snow. The undersides of these runners were covered with bear bones (long bones were used). They were not parallel, the distance between them being between 2 and 3 inches greater at the rear; they operated rather like a snow plow. The sledge was held together with sealskin straps. The bone plates were nailed under the runners with bone nails. (In our day, bone has been replaced by iron, and the runners are usually parallel.)

On the west coast of Greenland, the types of sledge varied from district to district and sometimes from family to family. They were never longer than 5½ feet either, but they were wider (27½ to 29½ inches).

Peary's Eskimos used sledges about ten feet long, held together with leather thongs. Peary's personal sledges were 13 feet long and

2 feet wide. They were built of oak and bound with strips of seal- or walrus-skin, and their runners were equipped with steel blades 1 ½ inches wide.

The load, which was to last fifty days, was standardized. It included (from the bottom of the sledge to the top): the dogs' pemmican in red tins; the men's pemmican in blue tins; tins of condensed milk and tea; cans of fuel, a musk-ox skin and a sealskin for bedding; snowshoes; an ice axe and a snow knife; Eskimo sealskin *kamiks* for a change of footwear. Scientific instruments were regarded as extras.

The daily ration for each man consisted of: one pound of pemmican, one pound ship's biscuit, four ounces condensed milk, half an ounce of tea, six ounces of liquid fuel. For each dog it was one pound of pemmican.

It is clear enough that Peary used his dogs to the maximum; though at the same time, no one could think of speaking of "inhumanity" toward them, as Scott did. Scott was, moreover, to pay with his life for his stubbornness in disregarding one of the basic theorems of the Far North: A sled dog pulls approximately his own weight; and each time a sledge is lightened by 77 pounds, one dog becomes superfluous.

The efficiency of dog-sled transportation is so great that even in our own day, when the technical means of surface travel have reached something like a state of perfection, this age-old means of transportation remains the ideal under certain conditions, in the south as well as in the north. Of course, on hard, flat, uniform surfaces, there is no question of the superiority of motorized vehicles. But on a route running over floating ice or mountainous surfaces interrupted by crevasses, sled dogs alone can be used both successfully and safely, although their speed and the burdens they can transport are limited.

In our own day, Eskimos, trappers, traders, policemen, and Arctic missionaries still use the dog sled. The air forces of the United States and Canada have used them successfully for salvaging airplanes and on rescue missions. Ground troops use them for transporting supplies, or as ambulances, on terrain where it is impossible to operate with motorized vehicles or helicopters. The Eskimo continues to hunt seal and walrus in the wintertime by sledge. In summer, the dogs are used as pack animals to transport light loads. These loads (of up to 35 pounds) are carried in a sack with two pockets which is thrown over the dog's back and strapped under his belly.

In order to understand Peary's performance in attacking the Pole with dogs, it may be useful to say a word or two about these admirable creatures. We must first make clear that these dogs are descended from wolves only insofar as crossbreeding has taken place between individual sledging bitches and wolves. Their reputation for savagery is ill-founded. Treated with understanding and benevolence, they are as good friends to man as the German shepherd. It is true, on the other hand, that they do display a strong tendency to fight among themselves. On a journey as perilous as Peary's, where every drop of energy was precious, the loss of a dog in a brawl would have been a very serious thing.

The American Kennel Club recognizes four distinct breeds: the Alaskan *Malemute* (heavy and powerful, with an excellent reputation); the Eskimo (most of Peary's dogs were of this type, as well as Amundsen's and Byrd's); the Siberian husky (the fastest of all); and the Samoyed (which has a good character, though it has proved to be better as a guardian for reindeer than as a sledge hauler). Their colors vary from white to black, with all shades of gray; their weights run from 45 to 110 pounds; their maximum age is nine years. The record for speed and endurance in sled dogs was established on the famous serum run from Nenana to Nome, in Alaska, during the winter of 1925. By relays, nearly 700 miles were covered in five and a half days at an average speed of 125 miles per day, under extremely harsh weather conditions.

The harness is a very important part of the sledge's equipment, for there is a danger that it will injure the dog and reduce his efficiency. A good harness centers the pull in the dog's shoulders and breast. In the high-traction harness (used by most Eskimos and by all the French and English expeditions), the traces are fastened over the back next to the hindquarters in order to avoid sending the dog sprawling and fatiguing him, at least on this count. The harness may be made of leather, of cloth or of lampwick. Cloth is harder for the dog to chew through; it is also cheaper and does not need to be oiled and looked after. The Siwash harness, made of low-traction cloth, has been much used by the Russian and American expeditions.

Whether the dogs appear to be friendly or not, they ought always to be tied up. To fail to do this is to run the risk of losing an animal in a fight, at the very moment when he is most indispensable. On the trail, the dogs ought to be chained at night; each dog is chained to a common rope fixed to a steel or wooden stake which has been driven into the ice.

The traces are very often eaten through by certain dogs; this habit is remedied by plunging them in a solution of tar or creosote, or else by using a thin chain.

As snow and ice may become lodged between the toes of the dog's paws and cause serious cuts, protective boots are often used; they may be open or closed, duck cloth or gray sealskin, depending on the preference of the driver. These boots have to be taken off at night.

While driving, the Eskimos generally use a whip with a short, sturdy handle and a thin sealskin lash 20 to 30 feet long. A good driver knows how to handle this whip with great accuracy, but makes use of it only in extreme cases. A slender and supple leather whip, about 6½ feet long, is generally preferred for ordinary use, and particularly in the case of a free-for-all between dogs. A whip has to be greased and taken care of, if it is to keep its suppleness.

For the sled dog's food, meat and fish are recommended: walrus, seal, cachalot, whale, narwhal, bear, reindeer, caribou, salmon, et cetera. Shark meat is thought to be harmful, if it is not boiled for several hours or aged for several days. One to two pounds of dried fish or two to three pounds of fresh meat per meal will keep a dog in excellent working condition. Cod-liver oil is added to his diet twice a week. Some dogs stubbornly refuse to try a new kind of meat; in this case, the best solution is to allow the meat to rot slightly, after which it will be accepted by the dog as excellent nourishment. Peary had planned on one pound of pemmican per dog per day; thus, it is only the more astonishing to note the fantastic run his animals made to the Pole—which, by the way, they were the first to tread on, since they came in the lead.

Peary's team was composed of Professor Ross Marvin (his scientific assistant, who was drowned on the return journey); Dr. J. W. Goodsell (a physician specializing in diseases of the lung); MacMillan (a former football player); Robert Bartlett (a Newfoundlander and captain of the *Roosevelt*); and George Borup (the only one of them on his first polar expedition). There was also Matthew Henson, Peary's Negro manservant, utterly devoted and incredibly competent at all polar techniques.

On March 1, 1909, the sledges set out one by one for the north, from Cape Columbia, with Bartlett in the lead, parading before the Commander for one final inspection. On the second day, Markham's record was beaten, but a "river" which opened up in the ice cut off part of the column. The advance began again on the eleventh. On the twelfth, a temperature of 49 below zero was recorded, and on the thirteenth, 67 below. "The brandy was solid, the petroleum was white and viscid." The system of relays and caches began to go into effect. The men were well protected from the cold by their Eskimo clothing, made of seal- and walrus-skin and sewn by the native women.

On March 19, Borup beat his retreat as planned, at 85° 20′ N., and the lead was taken by Bartlett and Henson. Peary followed, a day's march behind, with Marvin, and so took advantage of the work done on the trail by the forward echelon, sleeping, for instance, in igloos which had already been built. On the twenty-sixth, Marvin set out for home in his turn with two Eskimos and one 17-dog sledge. Each time the superfluous sledges were left on the spot for the return journey.

On the twenty-seventh, the 87th parallel was crossed, and Peary beat his own record (of 87° 06′). On the thirtieth, in 22-below-zero cold and at 87° 46′ N. Bartlett came to a halt and turned back to the south; all that remained were Peary's and Henson's detachments, with four sledges and forty dogs, the best of the 140 that had left the *Roosevelt*. The four remaining Eskimos were Ootah, age thirty-four; Egingwah, twenty-six; Seegloo, twenty; and Ookeah, sixteen; the last of the four had set out for the Pole in order to win the hand of a young Whale Sound beauty. The provisions were ample for forty days and could be stretched to sixty, as the dogs were butchered when they became useless.

On April 2, Peary set out in the lead, leaving the others to load their sledge; the final sprint had begun. Sleeping time was reduced to the minimum and the dogs were spurred to a trot, sometimes even a gallop; the first day's march trimmed 23 miles off the 155 left to go.

On April 5, at 89° 25′, the camp was awakened a little before midnight (since the 87th parallel, it had been day around the clock). After making thirty-five miles in twelve hours broken only by a rapid meal, the march came to a halt at 10:00 A.M. Position: 89° 57′ N.

A meal; double rations for the dogs; the building of two igloos; a siesta. When Peary woke up, he seized his journal and wrote: "The Pole at last. The prize of three centuries. My dream and goal for twenty years. Mine, at last! I cannot bring myself to realize it. It seems all so simple and so commonplace."

As the overcast weather prevented him from making observations, Peary pushed on for several miles (a nautical mile equals one minute on the terrestrial arc) with two Eskimos, one sledge and all his instruments. The sky cleared. New observations gave a reading of 89° 55′. A sounding was made: 10,000 feet without touching bottom.

Peary went back a few miles by sledge; he could neither sleep nor keep still. He went on pacing over the ice field, taking more and more readings, and meditating on the strange position he was in: at the summit of the world; everything around him, in every direction, was the south. The east, the north, the west, no longer existed.

Five flags were then raised before a great hummock: a silk American flag that Peary had carried with him for fifteen years, leaving a fragment of it behind on each of his record expeditions; the flag of the United States Navy; the pennant of the Bowdoin chapter of Delta Kappa Epsilon; a Red Cross banner; the "World's Ensign of Liberty and Peace."

Thus, Peary, his four Eskimos and his Negro manservant were the first men to tread the earth of the North Pole. When the American flag was ready, Peary said, in English (he usually spoke only Eskimo): "We are going to plant the Star-Spangled Banner at the North Pole."

Then after three hearty cheers, Peary shook hands all round and gave the signal for a "lavish feast." The Eskimos did a dance on the roof of the world, exclaiming again and again, "*Ting neigh timah ketisher!*" ("We're there at last!") In a glass bottle, the commander deposited a brief account of his journey and a document affirming that he had taken possession of the area in the name of the President of the United States. He then wrote a postcard to his wife.

Everyone tried to sleep, but without success. After a short time Peary got up; "Come on, Matt," he said, "let's go home!" And the race south began on April 7, at 4 P.M. They traveled sixteen hours out of every twenty-four; as the weather remained clear and as the weight of the sledges diminished as they went along, they were able to keep up the rhythm, in spite of their fatigue. On April 23, at

6 A.M., Peary arrived at Crance City; the work of his life was done.

On April 27, the crew of the *Roosevelt* gave him a triumphal welcome. One of his first acts on returning to the civilized world was to send a telegram to his friend Beaumont in New York, announcing Marvin's death and urging him to break the news to the man's mother before the papers got hold of it.

But the papers had quite other headlines to keep them busy, for, five days before Peary's return, a "sportsman" named Harry Whitney, who had come on board the *Roosevelt* to do some winter seal-fishing, noticed three human outlines and a single dogless sledge along the coast. Whitney spoke to the only white man in the group, who said: "I am Doctor Frederick A. Cook, and I have come from the North Pole."

Thus, at the finish line, Peary was about to be robbed of the results of twenty-three years of hardships and stubborn effort. This was, obviously, to be only the opening shot in an interminable controversy, which has not yet died down, even in our own day. In a general way, however, we may say that Peary is thought to have been the only "certain" conqueror of the Pole.

The least that can be said for Cook's story is that it is obscure and seamed with inaccuracies. But Cook was far from an unknown figure in the polar regions—he had participated in an expedition led by Peary himself in 1891 and in the Gerlache expedition of 1898.

Aided by a patron, Richard R. Bradley, he had set out from New York on July 3, 1908, under the banner of the Explorers Club (a rival, more or less, of the Peary Arctic Club). On February 19, 1908, with ten Eskimos, eleven sledges and 105 dogs, Cook, who knew of Peary's failure in 1906, had set off for the north. He returned on April 18, 1909, without dogs, with one sledge in very bad condition and two Eskimos.

These facts alone are certain. For the rest of the story, we must take the word of Cook himself. Cook's notes and instruments were entrusted by him to Whitney, who was supposed to bring them back to the United States on the *Roosevelt*. Peary refused to allow this, and the notes were deposited in a cache which has never been found.

There are two arguments that merit examination: the moral argument and the geographical argument. Can we believe Cook morally? His detractors have no hesitation in recalling that he got into difficulties and was punished by the law, but all this took place long after 1908.

But the geographical argument is decisive. Cook declared that he had established the existence of Crocker Land; but Crocker Land does not exist, as MacMillan demonstrated in 1914. Cook saw, described, situated and photographed Bradley Land; but the ceaseless aerial reconnaissance which has been made since then has determined that it too does not exist. Finally, the only land discovered in the vicinity by Stefansson in 1916 is Meighen Island. As its coordinates lie between 98° and 100° W. and between 79° 40′ and 80° 15′ N., Cook would have had to see it on his left on his return journey, according to the itinerary he claimed to have followed. He could not have failed to perceive it when taking the bearings for the point 79° 32′ N. by 101° 22′ W., which he claims to have occupied.

At this point, two hypotheses present themselves: Either Cook was "a liar, a faker and a madman," as some of Peary's partisans have claimed, who made up his imaginary story out of whole cloth; or else he committed serious errors in his astronomical observations, though this would hardly jibe with the flattering opinion Peary expressed of him in 1891. On this theory, he could have confused Meighen Island with his own Bradley Land (his description of the latter fits reasonably well with the description of Meighen), and so might have reached a latitude of 85° or 86° N., which would stand as quite a remarkable exploit in itself.

The dispute immediately became an acrimonious one in America, with the flames being fanned by the two rival clubs. Peary's partisans, writing in the New York *Times*, carried on a verbal brawl with Cook's friends, whose organ was the New York *Herald*.

Peary himself never did believe in Cook's success, although he did not hesitate to say that he admired "his unruffled patience and coolness in an emergency." [1] He did, however, reproach him violently for having plagiarized his "Peary system," and for enticing away from his service Eskimos whom he had trained for years in scientific exploration. Cook, for his part, accused Peary of having misappropriated a $10,000 load of hides, and of having carried on an orgy of debauchery among the young Eskimo girls. It was, as

---

[1] Frederick J. Pohl, in his preface to Cook's *Return from the Pole.*

one of Cook's partisans, Russell W. Gibbons,[2] affirms, the "American Dreyfus case."

The great explorer Knud Rasmussen, who knew both of the rivals, the Eskimos, and the whole set of polar problems, all equally well, had no hesitations whatever; he asserted his admiration for Peary and held Cook to be nothing more than a despicable mystifier. The Royal Society of Copenhagen was called upon to pronounce judgment; again without hesitation, the society rejected the unfortunate Cook's evidence with two simple words: "Not Proved."

Cook was expelled from his own club, the Explorers. This act caused General Greely's resignation from the same club and from the Arctic Club of America in December, 1909. Cook left America in dishonor and went to Argentina, then Europe. He did not return till 1911, the year which saw Peary finally and definitely accepted as the true conqueror of the Pole.

The scandal did not prevent Cook's book from being an enormous success; *My Attainment of the Pole*, an account larded with irrelevant romanticism and self-dramatizing, sold more than 100,000 copies in three years.

Still defended, in spite of everything, by Amundsen, Otto Sverdrup, Otto Nordenskjöld, Greely and many other eminent polar figures—which only goes to prove how difficult it often is to get at the truth—Dr. Cook died on August 5, 1940, without history's ever having revised her verdict.

We ought, however, to recognize that in this controversy, two points seem unarguable, and are indeed unargued: 1) Peary certainly reached the North Pole on April 6, 1909; 2) there is no conclusive proof that Cook did *not* reach it before him.

The true measure of the controversy was given by a cartoonist of the period who showed Uncle Sam sighting the Pole through a pair of binoculars and saying: "After all, whether it's Cook or Peary, the winner is still an American."

---

[2] Russell W. Gibbons, *An Historical Evaluation of the Cook-Peary Controversy.*

20

THE FIRST MAN AT THE SOUTH POLE

THE MODERN READER who first discovers the Pole in magazine photographs must feel that it resembles the surface of the moon. "The steel monsters, the caterpillar tractors bristling with antennae, riding roughshod over the snow and ice at inhuman temperatures," all seem to him to go hand in hand with the bizarre landscape of a new age of exploration just beginning. For him, the modern explorer seems entirely dependent upon perfect equipment. The sight of a man encased in fur, hauling his own sledge through the blizzard, would hardly seem to him evidence of a serious exploration.

However, it was thus that most of the great exploits of the great polar pioneers were accomplished. Peary, Nansen, McClintock and Nordenskjöld did not have Sir Vivian Fuchs's "Snocat" tractors at their disposal, nor the Weasels of the French Polar Expeditions, nor the 30-ton mobile laboratories that the Soviets used during the International Geophysical Year.

Today the poles can be reached in comparative comfort by atomic submarine and jet aircraft; and the Emperor penguin no longer displays the least astonishment before man or his ubiquitous machines.

There was, however, a day when the first motorized vehicle rolled over the ice pack, thus signaling the beginning of the formidable mechanization to come. It was January 3, 1908, after Scott's first voyage and just as Peary was about to set off to conquer the North Pole at the head of his dogs.

In this period of violent industrial confusion, the least we can say is that the automobile too was in a state of confusion. But there have always been enterprising men who have been ready to make use, in their forward march, of all the inventions, and even the boldest among them, that the progress of technology put at their disposal. It was in just this way that the first compass, the first rudder, the first steamship, the first propeller, the first free balloon, the first automobile, the first airplane, the first submarine have made their appearance in polar territory, where man, face to face with the elements, had need of them to complete and exploit the conquest.

Sir Ernest Shackleton, Scott's former companion and now one of his rivals, was one of these men, and he had the genius to foresee the immense service that the new invention of the automobile could give in the polar battle.

We ought to point out here that, if the conquest of the North Pole was earned by the endurance and the perseverance of a man like Peary, that of the South Pole took on the aspect of a free-for-all among three great explorers, and that no device, whether revolutionary or not, could possibly have been neglected. Each of these three men, Shackleton, Amundsen and Scott, was to go so far as to risk his life, and one of them was to give it up, for the simple gesture of planting a pennant at the southernmost point of the world. Each prepared his expedition with extraordinary care and attention to detail, neglecting nothing whatsoever in his attempts to snatch the victory.

Shackleton set out first, in 1907. This Irish giant had managed to set up an expedition, despite the fact that Scott's having sent him home in 1901 for "physical collapse" had not earned him a highly favorable reputation. But Shackleton's wounded pride was a powerful motive, and all the more so as he had just undergone a new series of failures; the Navy had refused to make him an officer, and he had been beaten as a Liberal candidate in the most recent elections.

In 1906, his luck finally turned; Beardmore, the industrialist for whom he worked, agreed to finance his expedition, despite the indignant disapproval of Sir Clements Markham. Shackleton was able to organize the expedition all the more quickly, due to the fact that he did not have to report to commissions, subcommissions or any other of the various sorts of official administrative bodies; he was his only master.

He settled on his plan, which was published in the *Times* on April 12, 1907. From the base camp at Hut Point where Scott had wintered, Shackleton was to send out three teams, the first into the unknown east, the second toward the geographic Pole, the third toward the Magnetic Pole.

Scott, who was then in command of the *Albemarle* at Gibraltar, found the story in his newspaper over his morning tea. He immediately took pen in hand and wrote to his former second-in-command that he looked forward to organizing an expedition of his own in the very near future. And the odd thing was that he asked him not to use the *Discovery*'s former winter quarters. This was a severe blow to Shackleton, but, being the true gentleman that he was, he lost no time in letting Scott know that McMurdo Sound and the Bay of Whales would henceforth be considered as sacrosanct.

In the same day's mail Shackleton found an enormous list of candidates for the expedition, through which he carefully combed. For his staff he chose the physician Dr. A. F. Mackay, the scientist Raymond Priestley and the two Australians, Douglas Mawson (a professor of physics) and T. W. Edgeworth David (a professor of geology). Though he never exerted overmuch discipline, Shackleton succeeded in welding his team together and lost no time in establishing the smiling authority that earned him the name, "Boss."

The Irishman chose the ship he could afford: the *Nimrod*, a forty-year-old, 200-ton sealer, but a fine sailer and capable of making six knots with her brand-new engine.

The equipment that Shackleton took with him was for the most part identical with Scott's; the sledges equipped with petrol tanks came from the same factory in Christiania (there were ten models 12 feet long; eighteen, 11 feet long; and two, 7 feet long); all the clothing was made of wool, though a watertight gabardine had been originally planned on; the sleeping bags were fur-lined, and there were "classic" Lapp *finnesko*.

There was nothing revolutionary about the provisions either, except their packaging in small tins of light rations—ancestors of the K ration—which had been invented by Shackleton himself. He also took a collapsible house 33 feet by 19, and about 12 feet high, insulated with felt and cork; it was lighted with acetylene lamps and heated with anthracite coal.

After much hesitation, he had also taken nine Siberian dogs and fifteen Manchurian ponies; impressed by Scott's expedition, Shackleton was to make the same error as had his predecessor in neglecting the use of dogs. It is true that he intended to resolve all his transportation problems by using the automobile. It was the secret weapon with which he intended to snatch the victory over the Pole from Scott, though Amundsen was to snatch it from him in his turn. He unloaded the car on January 3, 1908, at Cape Royds on Ross Island, fifty miles from the great Ice Shelf.

It was a 12–15-horsepower New Arrol-Johnston. The four-cylinder engine had an air-cooling system; water would, of course, have frozen. A jacket had been put around the carburetor; the exhaust was thus recovered and used to reheat the engine. The ordinary car-frame was reinforced to withstand the low Antarctic temperatures. Special oil was used; but the fuel was ordinary gasoline.

Knowing the difficulty of the terrain, Shackleton designed a number of different sorts of wheels, including some wooden ones. The expedition's engine specialist, Bernard Day (who was to accompany Scott in 1910-13) presided at the unloading, which proved a delicate operation, for the ship, tiny as she was, was heavily loaded (she had to be towed to the very edge of the ice pack).

While the house (which was divided into seven cabins, each housing two men) was being set up and the equipment being brought ashore, Day got his automobile in shape and solemnly announced that the first test was about to begin. Before the eyes of the admiring expedition members, the Arrol-Johnston started up magnificently and began its first journey, the first ever to be undertaken by a motorized vehicle in the polar regions. It was not a long journey, however; after about a hundred yards, the vehicle came to a pitiful halt, its wheels sunk in the deep snow. The second attempt was no more successful. On the third, the machine went half a mile before coming to a stop; it had to be pushed before it would consent to return to the camp.

Disappointed, Shackleton now understood that it would be hard to count on the internal combustion engine to enable him to get to plant the British flag at the South Pole. He did not, however, give up the idea entirely; he claimed that, by using the appropriate wheels, he would manage to make the automobile into a useful ally on his polar runs; he even announced that, with its help, he would reach an average of 95 miles a day.

The mechanic, Bernard Day, spent long hours trying to get the engine tuned up; feeling that the machine's weight was the major obstacle, he got rid of the body and kept nothing but a seat riding on a bare chassis. Despite the intense cold, the engine behaved valiantly, and at −31° F., the special lubricant worked efficiently.

On September 19, 1908, the final trial run took place. Day and two assistants climbed into the machine and set out to establish a depot at the foot of the volcano Mount Erebus; a 750-pound load was piled onto the chassis. Despite the 22-below-zero temperature, the vehicle managed to go seven and a half miles before running into deep snow; after a certain amount of difficulty, it nevertheless succeeded in making the journey to within a few hundred yards of the Erebus lava flow. The return trip was like a Sunday outing. When it returned to the garage, the machine had covered more than thirty miles between 9:30 A.M. and 6:45 P.M., at an average of between three and fifteen miles per hour. The work it had done would have taken six men from two to three days.

Later on, depots to service the team on its way to the Magnetic Pole were established by the "tractor"; only one serious incident occurred; Dr. Mackay broke his wrist while turning the starting crank. On November 1, Shackleton, Day and James Murray made the seven and a half miles from the base to Inaccessible Island in twenty minutes—an excellent performance even for our own day.

The machine went on doing important work till December 1; on that day, after it had just transported 1,300 pounds of provisions over a distance of 12½ miles in the direction of Ferrar Glacier, it fell into a crevasse. It took two hours to work it free. The odyssey of the first Antarctic automobile closed on a prosaic note—in a report written for Shackleton, who was at that time off on his run to the South Pole, "This was the last journey of the car in the Antarctic, for it was laid up when it got back to the hut."

Shackleton had sent off his expeditions without counting on the machine. On April 5, 1908, David and Lieutenant J. B. Adams scaled the 13,350 feet of Mt. Erebus in 22-below-zero temperature; they estimated the depth of the crater at between 800 and 900 feet, its width at half a mile.

On September 19, 1908, the first group (David, Mawson and Mackay) set out from Cape Royds in the direction of the Magnetic Pole; taking neither dogs nor ponies, they were forced to haul their 2,200 pounds of equipment, with breast harnesses. After undergoing great hardships, the David team reached the South Magnetic Pole on January 16, 1909, and, after an exhausting journey of more than 1,200 miles on foot, returned to the *Nimrod* on February 4, bringing back a remarkable set of scientific notes on southern Victoria Land.

Shackleton had kept the task of exploring the Geographic Pole for himself. During the winter, he had calculated the distance as the crow flies from his Cape Royds base to the Pole: it was 11° 35′, or 695 nautical miles; in other words, more than 800 land miles had to be covered going and coming in ninety-one days, at an average rate of twenty miles a day. Shackleton was absent from the camp for 117 days—and failed.

He set out on October 29, 1908, accompanied by Adams, Dr. E. Marshall and Frank Wild, with four sledges pulled by four ponies (the others had died) and provisions for ninety-nine days. The horses fell into crevasses, broke legs, dropped from exhaustion; they had to be killed one after the other.

On November 26, Shackleton beat Scott's record, but soon grasped the horrible reality; to reach the Pole, he would have to get across a mountainous barrier 10,000 feet high. Before him, however, there opened up an indentation; this was Beardmore Glacier (named for his silent partner). Twenty-two days later he emerged onto the highland; the Pole was 235 miles ahead.

On January 9, the four men came to a halt; they were at 88° 23′ S., and there was now only 110 miles between them and the Pole. They could attempt to reach it, with forty days' provisions, and still get back, if everything went well on the return journey.

Shackleton hoisted the Union Jack and prudently turned back, having "done his best."

The return journey was terrible; exhausted, laid low with dysentery, held up by a blizzard, weakened by hunger, the four men arrived at Hut Point on February 28; their 99 days' rations had lasted 117 days.

When the *Nimrod* weighed anchor for the north, the expedition had discovered more than 500 miles of new mountains, explored two great glaciers, collected coal specimens and fossilized plants, discovered the South Magnetic Pole, taken the first motion pictures and introduced the first automobile in the Antarctic.

During all this time, Scott had been "waiting," not wishing to undertake anything without knowing of Shackleton's results. He was in the front row of the mob that came to welcome the expedition home at Charing Cross Station. With Shackleton out of the way, Scott was finally able to organize his own expedition. At the same time, without any publicity, with the calmness and modesty of the true scholar, Dr. Jean Baptiste Etienne Auguste Charcot on board the *Pourquoi-Pas?* was drawing up minutely accurate maps of the Antarctic which were to remain the only reliable documents of their kind down to 1935. Before setting out, Charcot had, moreover, helped Scott test a sledge equipped with a motor and caterpillar tracks in the Alps; Scott took three of these with him.

In May of 1910, Scott attended the triumphal lecture which Peary gave at the Albert Hall; then, on June 15, he left England on board the *Terra Nova,* the largest of all the Scottish whaling ships. He took 19 ponies, 34 Siberian dogs, 45 sledges and three caterpillar tractors, which naturally meant three separate teams of specialists. The Scott expedition had a marked scientific character. It included two physicists, three geologists, two biologists and a motion-picture cameraman. The program consisted of explorations in the eastern and western sections of the Ross Sea, and then the run to the Pole.

A disagreeable surprise was waiting for Scott at Melbourne when he arrived there with the *Terra Nova* on October 12; it came in the form of a telegram: BEG LEAVE TO INFORM YOU PROCEEDING ANTARCTICA. (*Signed*) ROALD AMUNDSEN.

Amundsen had long cherished the project of reaching the North Pole by drifting, as Nansen had tried to do, on board the *Fram;* with a heavy heart—for it meant giving up his own ambitions—Nansen generously agreed to entrust his glorious *Fram* to the hands of his young compatriot, who was making ready to set out when Peary's victory suddenly dazzled the world. Without saying anything to anyone, Amundsen then decided to turn southward.

On September 9, 1910, when Scott (who believed that Amundsen was on his way north) had already been gone two months, the *Fram* called at Madeira. There, the Norwegian announced to his crew that the expedition's aim was not the North Pole but the South, and he sent off a telegram to Scott in Melbourne. On January 14, 1911, he arrived in the Bay of Whales; he set out for the Pole on October 19.

Scott wintered on Ross Island, waiting for the spring before beginning his offensive; he set out on November 1, ten days after Amundsen. Throughout the whole winter, he never stopped thinking of the problem of transportation; the uncertainty of the automobile engine, the failure of Shackleton's dogs, and his own natural repugnance at the idea of using dogs, all led him to decide to make the final assault without tractors, without ponies, and without dogs.

This is exactly what Roald Amundsen had foreseen. The man who had forced the Northwest Passage had complete confidence in dogs as a means of transportation; he unloaded 118 of them onto the ice pack. Having studied the reports of the Scott and Shackleton expeditions at length, Amundsen extracted lessons from them which served him in the organization of his own attempt.

The provisions, which were carefully checked by a specialist, were packed in zinc and wood crates; to the traditional pemmican were added vegetables and oatmeal, while the dogs were given two kinds of pemmican (meat and fish) to which flour and powdered milk were added.

Amundsen erected a 25-by-11-foot house; it was 12 feet high, and the sides were coated several times over with tar. It could be anchored to the ice by rings fixed to the outer walls, a technique which was a necessity in the Antarctic storms. Fifteen tents for sixteen men each and six three-man tents (for sorties), ten sledges (thirteen-foot hickory runners covered with steel, ash frames), Primus stoves and Nansen cookers completed the equipment. As for clothing, while the English had only woolens, the Norwegians (who were expert skiers) wore fur.

For his dogs (which came from Greenland), Amundsen had adopted the harnesses and tandem teams used in Alaska; he felt that they made the pulling easier; also, the dogs would come up against a crevasse one after another rather than all at once. Amundsen further felt that by making his camp in the Bay of Whales, he would have a head start over Scott equal to the difference in their latitudes, or approximately sixty miles.

On February 9, 1911, he sent out the first team assigned to set up depots. It reached 80° S., ninety miles from the base, in four days, for an average of fifty miles per day; this is one of the best dog-sledge performances of all time. Other depots followed at 81° and 82°; the route was staked out with bamboo poles flying marking flags.

A first attempt on September 8 was cut short by the 68-below-zero cold, and Amundsen, having modified his plan, fixed on the great departure for October 19 with five men (himself, Helmer Hanssen, Oscar Wisting, Sverre Hassel and Olaf Bjaaland), fifty-two dogs and four sledges.

The distance was divided into daily 19-mile stages; on the twenty-ninth, the first depot was reached. The sledges were loaded. On November 3, the 82° depot was passed. On November 17, the group arrived, seated in their sledges, at the foot of the mountain range defending the Pole. There, after setting up the tent, the men made a few ski runs "to relax."

Then they attacked the glacier, which they named Axel Heiberg Glacier; making their way through mists and blizzards, past ice pinnacles and crevasses, they reached the 10,000-foot-high polar plateau on December 4, after passing through the far end of "Devil's Ballroom"; the latitude was 88° 09′ S.

The following day Shackleton's record was broken, and finally, on December 14, the Norwegian flag was taken out of its case at the South Pole.

"Five weatherbeaten, frostbitten fists they were that grasped the pole," Amundsen wrote, "raised the waving flag in the air and planted it as the first at the geographical South Pole. 'Thus we plant thee, beloved flag, at the South Pole, and give to the plain on which it lies the name of King Haakon VII Plateau.' "

The altitude was 10,000 feet. Amundsen decided to remain in the vicinity for three days, in order to ascertain the exact position of the Pole and to make meteorological observations. On his departure on December 17, he left behind a dark-colored silk tent, the thirteen-foot center pole of which flew the Norwegian standard, and a wooden plaque bearing the name *Fram.* Inside, Amundsen deposited a letter to the King of Norway, a sextant, a spirit level, several pieces of clothing, a plate bearing the names of the crew, and, to one side, an envelope on which he had written: "For Robert F. Scott." One month later, Scott was to read this note announcing Amundsen's victory.

Scott had left his base on the first of November, 1911. At the head of the column went the ponies, the slowest of them. Scott brought up the rear, while two dog sledges and two tractors (the third one had been lost during the unloading) went on ahead independently.

On November 4 and 5, the tractors stopped operating, their crank-shaft bearings burnt out. On December 9, at the foot of Beardmore Glacier, the last ponies were killed and eaten. It is curious to note that Scott had no repugnance to treating his ponies this way, despite his feeling about dogs.

On December 31, 1911, the men were halfway to the Pole, reduced to beasts of burden, hauling their own sledges. They did not know that at precisely the same moment, some ninety miles to the east, Amundsen and his companions were headed home, seated in their sledges, pulled at a gallop by their well-fed dogs, after having planted the Norwegian flag at the pole a fortnight earlier.

On January 4, 1912, Scott sent back his last supporting group under the command of Lieutenant E. G. R. Evans; the altitude was 10,000 feet, the latitude 87° 32′ S., the temperature 22 degrees below zero. Lieutenant Bowers of the Evans group was added to the final assault party, thus raising the number of men who were to go to the Pole to five: Scott, Dr. Edward Wilson, Lieutenant Henry Bowers, Captain Lawrence Oates and Petty Officer Edgar Evans.

This was the most serious possible sort of decision. It had catastrophic consequences. "Our organization—tents, rations, equipment—was built on a four-man basis," Lieutenant Evans wrote later. "Scott found that it took half an hour longer to cook for a fifth man. Moreover, on the way up, Bowers had left his skis behind at Three Degree Depot and until they reached that point on the return journey had to plod through the snow, while the others were running on skis. . . ."

It was this same Bowers, exhausted like the others, who was first to make out a black spot amid the white immensity on January 16, 1912; it was Amundsen's tent at the South Pole. Discouraged, the men knew that victory had been snatched from them. Writing of the return journey, Scott noted in his journal even then: "I wonder if we can do it." On January 19, they set out again in 22-below-zero cold.

On February 7, when they had reached the upper entrance to Beardmore Glacier, exhausted, half dead of starvation, they had the heroism to stop and gather 33 pounds of geological specimens, which could do nothing but add to the already excessive weight of their sledges. On the seventeenth, Petty Officer Evans fell to his knees, dazed; he died a few hours later. On March 16 or 17 ("lost track of dates," Scott wrote in his journal), in the midst of a blizzard, Oates, staggering, his feet infected with gangrene, went out of the tent saying: "I am just going outside and may be some time." He disappeared forever, having sacrificed his life in an attempt to save his three companions.

On March 21, eleven miles short of One Ton Depot, they were halted for good by the terrible blizzard; they had provisions left for two days and fuel for one meal.

Seven months later, on November 11, 1912, a party led by Dr. Edward L. Atkinson noticed a tent half-buried in the snow. ". . . Inside we found the bodies of Commander Scott, Dr. Wilson and Lieutenant Bowers." And beside them, opened, Scott's journal:

> THURSDAY, MARCH 29.—Since the 21st, we have had a continuous gale from W.S.W. and S.W. Every day we have been ready to start for our depot 11 miles away, but outside the door of the tent it remains a scene of whirling drift. I do not think we can hope for any better things now. We shall stick it out to the end, but we are growing weaker, of course, and the end cannot be far. It seems a pity but I do not think I can write more.

And below, in a scrawl, he had added: "For God's sake look after our people."

So ended Captain Scott's journal.

Near him were a dozen letters he had written before he died: to Mrs. Wilson and Mrs. Bowers, to his mother, his wife and his son, to friends, as well as a message to the English people. Atkinson erected a snow cairn and returned to the *Terra Nova*, which was now under the command of Lieutenant Evans. Before sailing back to England, Evans had a cross set up on Observation Hill overlooking Hut Point; it was inscribed with this line from Tennyson:

To strive, to seek, to find, and not to yield.

Scott's heroic death moved the whole world. There were even a certain number of ill-wishers who held Amundsen's success against him and accused him of having precipitated the English catastrophe. It was an Englishman, Andrew Croft, who later answered these charges in Scott's place: "The great explorer had been in the Antarctic before Scott . . . and, not unnaturally, he did not consider the South Pole in any sense British property." These ripples of discontent have fortunately died down in the meantime. Amundsen's own heroic death put an end to them.

Scott's disappearance closes the great period of polar romanticism. He had been dead only two years when the drone of the first airplane, Nagurski's *Farman*, terrified the polar bears of Novaya Zemlya, announcing the arrival of the mechanical age.

21

VIRTUOSOS IN THE ESKIMO TECHNIQUES

THE LAST PERIOD of polar exploration, that of the exploitation of the poles after their conquest, did not really begin till after the First World War, when the Great Powers were little by little to become conscious of the scientific, commercial and strategic importance of the Arctic and Antarctic regions.

This period has been characterized by one common denominator: the motor—the motor in every possible form, from the airplane to the caterpillar tractor, as well as the icebreaker, the submarine and the helicopter, as it was progressively perfected and more widely adapted. Expeditions have taken on a new style; they have become more massive, grouping hundreds, and sometimes thousands, of men, all of them specialists of one kind or another; they have enlisted enormous sums of capital, gone deeply into scientific research and prepared the ground for the coming exploitation of the territories they have explored.

There is no longer any place for a ship like Nansen's *Fram*, save in a museum, beside the old Viking *drakkars*, Zeno's map, Davis's quadrant, Leroy's chronometer and Scott's journal. The "good old days" of exploration have come to an end.

But the advent of this new mechanical era did not take place, happily enough, without the old methods' putting up a struggle for their honor; these methods had, paradoxically enough, reached a high point of perfection after Scott and before the airplane. This period of experts in dog-sledging and the other Eskimo techniques was particularly distinguished by the presence of two great men, the last, unquestionably, of the traditional explorers: Vilhjalmur Stefansson and Knud Rasmussen.

When, in 1914, the men of the *Mary Sachs* saw the Canadian anthropologist Stefansson arrive at Banks Island, after setting out ninety-three days earlier without adequate provisions, his survival seemed like a miracle to them. Not only was Stefansson alive, along with his two companions, Storker Storkerson and Ole Andreasen, but he had put on weight and appeared to be in flourishing good health. "So this was the end," wrote George Wilkins, the commander of the *Mary Sachs* (who was later to become famous for his submarine), "of the enterprise which for months I had heard condemned or deplored by Eskimos and whalers and the men of the Arctic experience in our expedition as 'one crazy and two deluded men going north over the sea ice to commit suicide.' "

These apprehensive souls never suspected that Stefansson was *in love with* the Arctic. Far from dreading or fearing it, Stefansson called it his "friend," discovered all sorts of hidden attractions in it, and adored it in much the same way as a suburbanite who throws all his passion into cultivating his little garden.

The crucial fact is that Stefansson *was no longer afraid;* he knew the Arctic and knew what he could make of it and what to expect from it. The monsters and the horrors had had their day and it was over. We ought to take note that this sudden consciousness of a "human" Arctic coincides for practical purposes with the conquest of the Pole. "There are two sorts of Arctic problems,"

Stefansson wrote,[1] "the imaginary problems and the real ones. Of the two, the imaginary are the more real, for man finds it easier to change the nature of things than to change his own ideas."

Throughout his life, in his writing and in person, Stefansson worked to demonstrate that the polar regions were not merely inhuman, inhospitable and hostile vastnesses. His *The Friendly Arctic* is a remarkable piece of special pleading for this cause, a sort of breviary from which so many later explorers have drawn inspiration. In it, the ancestral myths are demolished one by one. Even the cold itself no longer seems so terrifying: "If you spend an entire year at the North Pole, you will never see the temperature fall below −58°, while three American states, which are *inhabited*, have more intense cold: Wyoming, −67°; Montana, −62°; and North Dakota, −58°."

Going even beyond the accepted beliefs of the Eskimos, who imagined that life was impossible beyond the land or the coasts, Stefansson claimed that he could live anywhere at all in the north, and proved it. Setting off with two companions, six dogs and provisions for forty days, he crossed the Beaufort Sea, living "off the land" for ninety-three days, by hunting and fishing.

From 1914 to 1917, Stefansson's team, composed of both whites and Eskimos, alternated reconnaissance runs with stays in various winter camps throughout the whole of that part of the North American archipelago which touches on the Arctic Sea.

It was during his first voyage, in 1906-07, that Stefansson discovered what possibilities the "friendly" Arctic had to offer, and during his second stay, from 1908 to 1912, that he consolidated his convictions on this score. Having lived for a long time among the Eskimos, whom he studied with real passion, Stefansson was able totally to assimilate their way of life, their survival techniques, their hunting lore and their building methods. His mastery of Eskimo techniques was such that nothing stopped him from carrying out his program of studies point by point.

In 1915, he set out on McClintock's trail, unearthing a message of the latter's dating from 1853. For five months he traveled "comfortably" between Prince Patrick Island, Melville Island and Banks Island, discovering several smaller islands on his way. In 1916, he explored Meighen Island, thus rounding out the discovery of the

[1] V. Stefansson, *The Arctic in Fact and Fable.*

northernmost part of the archipelago. In 1917, Stefansson searched Cape John Russell and turned up a message from McClure dated April 21, 1851.

The total distance covered by Stefansson during his lifetime is impressive. General Greely summed it up as follows:

> From the unknown regions of Arctic land and sea, he has withdrawn areas amounting to approximately 100,000 square miles. These discoveries comprise about 65,000 square miles of Beaufort Sea to the north of the Mackenzie basin; 10,000 square miles of the Arctic Ocean west of Prince Patrick Island; 3,000 square miles along the northeast coast of Victoria Island; and over 15,000 square miles of land and sea to the northeast of Prince Patrick Island; in the last named region, three large and other small islands between 73° and 80° 02′ north.

That Stefansson was able to compile such a gigantic record was due primarily to his skill in using the Eskimo techniques, which he has analyzed at length in his writings. The one point in which his virtuosity was absolutely incomparable was the hunt. For Stefansson, there was game present even when it was invisible. "I have killed," he wrote, "thirteen bears in places where we had not seen one, and sixteen hares where we had not found a single print." Stefansson asserted that, despite everything that had been believed, the Arctic region "is lifeless except for millions of caribou and of foxes, tens of thousands of wolves and of musk oxen, thousands of polar bears, millions of birds and billions of insects."

He knew how to build igloos, make his clothing out of caribou hides, "dress" his sledge with cloth to convert it into a raft with which to get over a "lead,"[2] train and drive his dogs, look after frostbites, and prepare his food.

Stefansson declared that he was capable of surviving in any region whatever of the Far North, a claim which seemed impossible even to Amundsen, who wrote,[3] "I am ready to stake my reputation as a Polar explorer, and wager everything I own, that if Stefansson were to try it he would be dead within eight days, counting from the place of starting, only this experiment takes

---

[2] A channel in an ice field.

[3] Kaare Rodahl, *North*.

place on the Polar ice, which is constantly adrift on the open sea." Stefansson demonstrated the contrary, though he did not rob Amundsen of his reputation by so doing; it was, moreover, in the Norwegian's very own polar clothing that Stefansson made his first Arctic stay in 1906.

However this may be, Stefansson's appearance in polar history marks the advent of a realistic conception of the Far North. The old fears had disappeared, and from now on man was going to be able calmly, objectively and fearlessly to use the forces available in these regions to his own ends. Elias[4] called Stefansson "the man of the future in the north." He does indeed mark the transition from conquest to exploration. In him, the ice has found its master.

In Rasmussen, it found its philosopher. The son of a Dane and an Eskimo woman from the east of Greenland, Knud Rasmussen's first toy was a sledge, his first companion was a dog, and his mother tongue was Eskimo. His technical virtuosity, which came naturally to the children of his country, was combined with the Nordic qualities of endurance, will and ambition.

When, after Peary's victory, the Americans departed from the vicinity of Smith Sound, the Eskimos allowed themselves to be exploited by the whalers, in order to obtain arms from them. Rasmussen put an end to such practices in 1910, by founding Thule in North Star Bay and thus establishing Danish sovereignty over the region on a practical basis.

He had a deep admiration for the Eskimos, whom he regarded as a "naturally happy people"; he also was deeply familiar with their way of life. "No hunter exists up there," he wrote, "with whom I have not hunted, and there is hardly a child whose name I do not know."

Like Stefansson, Rasmussen believed that Eskimo techniques alone were capable of guaranteeing an exploration's success. His leading idea, which he put forward in his fascinating book, *Greenland by the Polar Sea*, was to undertake a vast coastal voyage on which he would classify and study all the Eskimo tribes in the world. Convinced that the traditions of the Eskimo people were being stifled little by little as the conquest of the whites advanced, by what he called their "civilization of enamel chamberpots," he

---

[4] E. L. Elias, *Les Explorations polaires*.

wanted to visit all the Eskimos between Bering Strait and Baffin Bay.

When he set out, in 1921, Rasmussen already had four important expeditions behind him. He christened his new voyage "Fifth Thule Expedition." On September 7, he left Upernavik with his assistant Peter Freuchen on board the *Sjökongen* (King of the Sea). On the twenty-third he began building his winter house on Denmark Island at the western entrance to Hudson Bay. At the end of November, he met his first nomadic Eskimos.

On January 27, 1922, in 58-below-zero weather, Rasmussen was making his way through a blizzard with extreme difficulty, when an extraordinary vehicle loomed into view: a 23-foot-long sledge drawn at full speed by fifteen magnificent dogs. There were five men on board under the command of the old Eskimo shaman Aua, who offered a seat to Rasmussen, while one of the Eskimos replaced him at the reins of his own sledge. It was then that Rasmussen learned a new technique which he was to use habitually later on; Aua's men coated their sledge runners with a paste made from frozen mud, which they then smoothed off with a knife, and over which they laid a thin coating, by spraying water from their mouths.

In April, May and June, Rasmussen discovered and studied the Caribou Eskimos, who followed the migrations of the reindeer herds and had never seen the sea. They also had no knowledge of the seal-oil lamp, which was a classic fixture throughout the rest of the Eskimo domains.

After wintering again on Denmark Island, Rasmussen decided to make his great departure in the direction of the Bering Sea, 1,800 miles away as the crow flies. He was accompanied by a half-breed from Thule, Qavugarssuaq, nicknamed the Eider, and by his wife, the smiling, twenty-eight-year-old Amarulunguaq.

On Boothia Peninsula, he came across the warlike Seal Eskimos, whose patriarch, Nakasuk, detained him for some time. Then, after having taken aboard a new supply of weapons delivered by the *El Sueno*, one of the ships of the Hudson's Bay Company, Rasmussen discovered bone fragments belonging to some of Franklin's men. He covered them over with a cairn, over which he raised the Union Jack in their honor along with the Danish colors.

In the spring of 1924, Rasmussen arrived at Point Barrow in a boat hauled by his last four dogs; and then, on August 31, he reached Jack London's beloved Alaska, with her prospectors, her missionaries and barroom brawls. After touching at Nome, he passed through Bering Strait to visit the Eskimos of the eastern cape—the final stop on his voyage among "the most northerly abodes of men."

Two months later, the three travelers were in New York, in the penthouse of a skyscraper dreaming of their dog sledges. His life's work was completed, and at the close, Rasmussen observed, "Nature is great; but man is greater still."

Earlier, he had written, "And from my heart I bless the fate that allowed me to be born at a time when Arctic exploration by dog sledge was not yet a thing of the past."

When Rasmussen reached the snows of Alaska, at the reins of his sledge, it was already fifteen years since the ice pack had seen its first radio set, its first Zeppelin and its first airplane.

22

THE FIRST AIRPLANE

At the very moment when Nansen, in August 1896, was returning triumphantly to Norway after his odyssey aboard the *Fram*, an important event occurred which went entirely unnoticed: Otto Lilienthal killed himself in an attempt to make a gliding flight in a strange new machine. Aviation had been born.

The following year, the French engineer Clément Ader succeeded in making the first flight aboard a machine equipped with a steam engine. In 1900 the Wright brothers adapted the internal combustion engine to a glider; the path ahead was laid out. Then came Santos-Dumont, Farman, then Blériot, who crossed the English Channel at the same time that Peary was preparing to launch his final attack on the North Pole. It is, of course, true that the great impetus to the development of aviation came only thanks to the First World War, and that Lindbergh did not cross the Atlantic until 1927. But the polar explorers, on the lookout as usual for any new technique that might help them to quench their thirst for discovery, study and knowledge, were not likely to wait until this revolutionary new means of transportation and communication had reached a perfect state of development. It was in 1912 that the airplane was to make its first official appearance on the polar ice. This was a worse fiasco than that of the first automobile.

Douglas Mawson, Shackleton's former companion and a member of the party that discovered the South Magnetic Pole with David, was then in command of his first Australian expedition to the Antarctic. On board his ship, the 600-ton Newfoundland sealer *Aurora,* which was equipped with a 98-horsepower auxiliary engine and was commanded by John King Davis, two important innovations were to be found: a wireless transmitter-receiver set and an airplane.

This collapsible Vickers monoplane had not in fact been originally intended for use on the exploration proper. Mawson's idea had been to use it to make barnstorming demonstrations in Adelaide in order to gather funds to finance his expedition. An accident occurred during the test flights and the airplane became unusable. Mawson decided to use the damaged plane as a propeller-driven sledge.

He removed the wings and replaced the lower part of the fuselage with long runners equipped with brakes; he counted on gaining extra speed and, thanks to the length of the runners, avoiding crevasses, for which he had developed a healthy mistrust while testing Shackleton's first automobile. But the Adélie Coast is, in Mawson's own words, "the home of the blizzard" and this was to prove a major drawback for a propeller-driven engine.

The trial run took place on December 2, 1912. The machine began to haul four heavy sledges when the engine failed. After numerous tries, it had to be admitted that the difficulty derived from cylinders and pistons which had been broken during the dismantling of the plane. The short life of the first propeller-driven sledge came to an end and the four sledges were hauled by the men from then on.

Although the 88-foot-high antennas were blown over several times by storms, Mawson had more luck with his radio. It served him particularly well on February 8, 1913, when, exhausted and half-frozen, he managed to return to his base, where six volunteers were waiting to tell him that the ship had already left. The *Aurora* was called back by radio, but, because of the storm, was unable to come and collect the seven men, who were not to be picked up till 1914, after spending a terrible Antarctic winter.

Mawson's 1911-14 expedition was a very fruitful one. Having got beyond the stage of romanticism, he had defined his task as the exploration of the continent. The expedition fully succeeded in exploring 20 degrees of the coastline (from 132° to 152° E.). In particular, Mawson demonstrated that the South Magnetic Pole is not a fixed point but shifts over a vast area.

The first airplane to fly over the ice pack, in 1914, was piloted by a Russian. At the very moment when Amundsen was delivering a lecture in Oslo in which he declared that the future of Arctic exploration lay inevitably with the airplane, a young Russian lieutenant named I. Nagurski was making five consecutive flights over the ice of the Barents Sea in an attempt to find Broussilov, Roussanov and Sedov, who were lost in the vicinity.

He was flying a 70 horsepower Farman equipped with pontoons and based on Novaya Zemlya; here was the real beginning of polar aviation, a prelude to the gigantic exploitation of the polar airspace.

The Russians, encouraged by Nagurski's success, were to go on steadily working in the background. Under the impetus provided by the Arctic Institute of the U.S.S.R., which Lenin had founded in 1920, they systematically explored the Arctic's aerial possibilities. Nor were the Western powers far behind. It might be said this whole period of aviation's first faltering steps was dominated by the figure of one exceptional man: Roald Amundsen.

After conquering the South Pole, Amundsen decided to add the North Pole to his laurels by succeeding where Nansen had failed with the *Fram* and where Shackleton had also failed in the south: in crossing the polar continent from one end to the other. Shackleton had in fact set out for the Antarctic with a handsome three-master, the *Endurance*. He wanted to reach the Ross Sea from the Weddell Sea where the *Endurance* was to leave him. This was the extraordinary epic of the *Endurance*.

Shackleton did not, however, succeed in making his crossing, this glory being reserved for Fuchs (and Hillary) in 1957-58. But his journey on board a small open whaling vessel from Elephant Island to South Georgia was to remain one of the greatest moments in polar history.

Amundsen learned of Shackleton's glorious failure, and his desire to carry off a new drift, in the manner of the *Fram* though farther to the north, was now all the greater. He had an enlarged replica of the *Fram*—which was old and tired by then—built, and he christened her the *Maud* in honor of his queen. The *Maud* had a 240-horsepower engine.

Amundsen then conceived the notion of using an airplane to assist the *Maud*. He chose a Junkers monoplane which had established the then-standing endurance record of 27 hours of continuous flight, and which was made of Duralumin. He tried to take the plane from New York to Seattle in May 1922, but it crashed over Marion, Pennsylvania. A new Junkers was ordered and delivered to the *Maud* by rail; at the same time, Curtiss Aircraft decided to make Amundsen a gift of a small reconnaissance plane.

On May 12, Amundsen and his pilot, Odd Omdal, made their first test flights with the new plane in Alaska. They were as catastrophic as the earlier set, and the Junkers had to be abandoned after one of its skis was severed. Amundsen was no luckier with the little reconnaissance plane, a Curtiss Oriole, which crashed on the ice pack, after it had succeeded in completing two flights. The *Maud*'s drift was no more successful, and Amundsen, by now a ruined man, gave it up in 1924.

But he did not give up hope of taking revenge on the elements. Encouraged by the success of the Swiss pilots Mittelholzer and Neumann, who had managed to take an admirable set of aerial photographs of Spitsbergen, Amundsen took off for the Pole once again on May 21, 1925.

He had obtained the funds in a miraculous way. While he was making a lecture tour in the United States in order to gather the necessary money, the telephone rang in his hotel room.

"Mr. Amundsen?"

"Yes, Amundsen speaking."

"Lincoln Ellsworth here."

Young Ellsworth was an accomplished sportsman who dreamed

of setting out on new exploits. His father was a millionaire; he financed Amundsen's expedition with $85,000.

Lieutenant Hjalmar Riiser-Larsen was in charge of fitting out the two hydroplanes; these were Dornier-Wals[1] with tandem Rolls Royce engines of 360 horsepower each. Riiser-Larsen opted for seaplanes of the hulled, rather than the pontooned, type, in order to avoid their capsizing. The hulls were made of Duralumin, a metal which is easy to work with a hammer and which withstands shocks without breaking. The planes were equipped with sponsons, or "fins," at the wing tips, in place of pontoons.

The two engines were placed in tandem, one acting as a tractor, the other as a pusher. At the outset, each plane weighed 14,000 pounds. Pure glycerine was added to the water in the radiator in the proportion of 40 to 100; it would freeze only at 0° F. During each stop on the ice pack, the radiator was carefully drained. The engines were heated with "Therm X's," six to each engine group. The Therm X is a catalytic heater which was invented by Louis Lumière and which is still used in our own day.

After piling 6,800 pounds of equipment and provisions into each plane and checking their three watches against the Eiffel Tower time-signal on the radio, Amundsen and his men took off from Spitsbergen on May 21, 1925, at 5:10 P.M. On board N24 and N25 were to be found for the first time solar compasses, invented by Amundsen and built by the firm of Goerz Optische Werke.

> The sun's image is reflected through a periscope onto a plate placed in front of the pilot. A clockwork connected to the periscope by a cogwheel is set in such a way as to make it turn 360° during the average time between two consecutive passages of the sun through the meridian. With the aid of a gauge included in the instrument, the periscope may be set in a given direction with relation to the plane's axis. If departure is to take place at noon, it is pointed exactly to the rear and at noon (local time), the clock movement is set going. When the plane is heading due north, a small reflected image of the sun appears at the center of the plate which is marked by a cross. The periscope will thenceforth follow the apparent movement of the sun, and its image will remain visible so long as the plane stays on the same course. . . .

---

1 *Wal,* in German, means whale.

The N24 and N25 also carried instruments with which to register the drift, and all their compasses worked with pure alcohol, as did their levels. All the movable parts of the instruments which were exposed to the cold were coated with a special oil that froze only at —40° F.

At 1:15 A.M., after eight hours in the air, half the fuel was consumed. Amundsen then decided to alight on the surface of the sea. This decision was all the more urgent as the rear engine on his N25 was beginning to cough. The two planes managed to come down on a free stretch of water at 87° 44′ N. by 10° 30′ W. But the N24 was separated from the N25; they had had to come down on different leads out of sight of one another. Amundsen and his crew settled in for the night in the hydroplane which they transformed into a dormitory and heated with their Therm X's.

Amundsen grasped the seriousness of the situation. He decided to build a 500-yard runway; this was the only way it would be possible for him to take off again. All the tools he had on board were three *tolleknives* (a Norwegian knife carried in a sheath attached to the belt), an ice anchor that could be used as a pick, and one large and one small wooden shovel. Amundsen had a sledge rigged, foreseeing the possibility that his plane might be crushed by the ice.

The provisions, which had been prepared originally on the basis of two pounds per man per day, to last for a month, were reduced to twelve ounces. The original daily ration was the following:

Pemmican	14 ounces
Two chocolate bars	9 ounces
Twelve biscuits	4½ ounces
Powdered milk	3½ ounces
Malted milk	3½ ounces
	34½ ounces

On the twenty-third, a full day after the planes had come down, Amundsen finally made out a tent and a flag in the distance; the crew of the N24, under Ellsworth's command, was safe. By Morse code, Amundsen learned that their hydroplane was no longer usable. Thus, he would have to take six men, rather than three, on board the N25. On their way to join their leader, two of the three men from the N24 (Dietrichson and Omdal) fell into the water at a temperature of 14° F. Amundsen gave them a drink of 194-proof pharmaceutical alcohol.

On May 25, the sounding read 12,300 feet. On the thirtieth, an attempt was made to take off from the 500-yard runway the men had smoothed off by hand, with their knives. The hydroplane, which now weighed four and a half tons, was hoisted up to the entry to the runway, but went through the thin ice. Several similar failures did nothing to diminish the courage of these men—the first ever to be shipwrecked in an airplane. They struggled unceasingly against the ice to make their new runway. They managed to haul their aircraft over 300 yards of piled-up drift ice to a point where it was facing a long stretch of uniform ice. To facilitate the take-off they attached skis to the underside of the plane, which had to be lifted by five of them; this was a labor of giants. On June 10, the daily ration was reduced to nine ounces.

On the eleventh, Omdal had the inspiration of a genius: "See," he cried. "This is what we can do instead of shoveling." He had noted that, by trampling the snow, it was possible to obtain the solid surface that they had been trying to get in depth. Everyone buckled down to the task, clearing away 500 tons of snow and ice. On June 14, the hydroplane was "prepared"; all superfluous equipment was got rid of and all that was kept was fuel for eight hours in the air, a collapsible boat, two hunting rifles with 200 cartridges, a tent, the heating units, and provisions for a few weeks: 660 pounds of baggage in all.

On June 15, at 9:30 A.M., the engines were started up. The runway was still in deplorable condition (two crevasses and a 10-foot canal intersected it), but, as Amundsen pointed out, "there was no better one in the region." At 10:30, the aircraft took off at 2,000 r.p.m. "And now," Amundsen wrote, "started the flight which will take its place amongst the most supreme in flying's history. An 1850-kilometer flight with death as the nearest neighbor. One must remember that we had thrown practically everything away from us. Even though we had managed by a miracle to get away with our lives, after a forced landing, still our days would be numbered."

Within sight of Spitsbergen the aileron warping controls stuck and it became necessary to make an immediate landing. Riiser-Larsen managed it perfectly on a patch of water at the edge of the ice pack; the aircraft was then attacked by enormous waves, but succeeded in making its way into a calmer gulf. There remained only 24 gallons of fuel in the tanks.

It was at this moment that a sailing ship, a sealer, appeared on the horizon, in the best tradition of the shipwreck novel; but she did not notice them. The whole crew jumped into the plane and set out over the water in pursuit of the boat, which they finally caught up with. The *Sjöliv* hitched a tow rope to the hydroplane, and on June 17, 1923, nearly a month after their departure, the Amundsen team arrived back in King's Bay (west of Spitsbergen), where they found their boat, the *Hobby*, waiting for them, as well as two Hansa-Brandenburg hydroplanes, standing ready to take to the air in search of them. They received a triumphant welcome. "That was the signal," Amundsen wrote, "for great excitement."

Here was doubtless the reason why this intrepid man set out for the pole on May 11, 1926, less than a year after the N25 adventure, on board a dirigible.

"As the expense of using airships was prohibitive," Amundsen's second-in-command Riiser-Larsen had written, "we could only consider the employment of flying-machines." On his return from the voyage of the N25, Ellsworth, who was by now absolutely bitten with the polar bug, put an end to this objection by advancing Amundsen the funds with which to buy a semirigid dirigible of Italian make. It was christened the *Norge* ("Norway").

Amundsen and Ellsworth were waiting in King's Bay for the arrival of the *Norge*, which was to have been delivered by Colonel Nobile of the Italian Military Aeronautic Corps, when they saw a small American cargo ship, the *Chantier*, enter the harbor. A man came ashore from her and introduced himself: "Commander Richard E. Byrd of the United States Navy."

Byrd had decided that he should succeed where the great Amundsen had failed: in flying over the Pole. He had chosen a Fokker monoplane with three 200-horsepower engines and a maximum speed of less than 125 miles per hour. Aided by his warrant officer Floyd Bennett, he began immediately unloading his aircraft, which had been dismantled and stored in the *Chantier*'s hold.

While Byrd began his test flights, Amundsen was going ahead with his own preparations. By October of 1925, the *Sörland* had delivered the 2,000 tons of building materials that would be needed for the construction of a vast hangar 328 feet long, 112 wide, and 98 high, and for the pouring of 6800 cubic feet of concrete casing. On May 7, 1926, eight days after Byrd, the Italian staff led by Umberto Nobile, the best dirigible pilot of the period, arrived in King's Bay after a 4750-mile voyage via Vadsö, where they had had special mooring masts built.

After many false starts and disappointments on both sides, Byrd was the first to be ready to take off; he headed for the Pole on May 9, 1926, at 1:55 A.M., accompanied by Floyd Bennett. He also had a solar compass on board, the magnetic compass being practically useless in those regions. The flight went off perfectly regularly despite an oil leak in the right-engine tank. They made three turns over the Pole, and Byrd threw the medal that Peary had been wearing in 1909 onto the ice pack; in seven hours, he had made the distance it had taken Peary fifty heroic days to cover.

At 5:15 P.M., they landed on the King's Bay field, where Amundsen and Ellsworth gave them a warm welcome.

"And now," said the Norwegian, "what are your plans?"

"The South Pole."

"You're right. The airplane alone can triumph in the Antarctic."

These words from the great Amundsen were prophetic, and it was Byrd who was to prove the fact.

For its part, the *Norge* went up on May 11, the day after Byrd's exploit, at 8:55 A.M., and set its course for the North Pole, the aerial victory over which had just been snatched from Amundsen by a young American aviator. On land, Byrd watched the giant, which the Eskimos were to take for a flying whale, as it disappeared into the distance.

At a temperature of 49 degrees below zero, with almost no wind, the *Norge* was cruising at 50 m.p.h., with its two 250-horsepower engines turning over regularly at 1,200 r.p.m. It was carrying seven tons of fuel and sixteen passengers, including Amundsen, Ellsworth and Nobile as well as Riiser-Larsen and Mr. Frederik Ramm —the first "polar journalist."

At 1:15 A.M., the *Norge* arrived at the pole. American, Norwegian and Italian flags were thrown overboard. Then they set off again, only to find themselves, some seconds later, at 2 P.M. on the preceding day, because of the shift in time zones. After various incidents (storm, fog, frosting, radio breakdown), the dirigible arrived at Teller, Alaska, a village some sixty miles from Nome, where it sank into the sea at the close of its 3,250-mile journey.

This successful, though laborious and almost fatal, exploit convinced Amundsen that the ideal machine for exploration would be the four-engined airplane, which was both "safer and faster than the dirigible." This was not Colonel Nobile's feeling, and the two men had already had serious differences of opinion on various points.

Irritated by the chorus of praise which seemed to be directed exclusively at the Norwegian, Nobile had sharply reminded everyone that after all it was he, Nobile, who had piloted the ship and who had overseen its construction. The Italian press followed his lead. Amundsen—who did not have a particularly pleasant personality to begin with—resented this campaign. He even revealed the fact that Nobile had committed three navigational errors which could have been fatal, and that he did not know how to manage himself on skis, and then described him as a "boasting dreamer" and an "epauletted Italian."

Wounded by this attack, Nobile decided to take his revenge by carrying out a great exploit with an entirely different Italian crew. His rather shopworn idea was to go to the Pole with a new dirigible, which he named the *Italia* and with which he wanted to demonstrate that this type of aircraft could fly with perfect safety and regularity.

A public subscription was opened in Milan and triumphantly filled, while Mussolini gave Nobile a tender-escort, the *Città di Milano*. His crew was composed of picked Alpinists, all of whom were expert skiers, and included three famous scientists: the physicist Aldo Pontremolli, the Czech radium specialist Franz Behounek, and Finn Malmgren, a Swede who had already taken part in the *Norge* expedition. As we can see, the crew was not totally Italian, but Nobile was sole master of his own craft.

Pius XI blessed ship and crew and handed General Nobile (he had just been promoted) a cross. "You will place it at the summit of the world," said the Holy Father. "It is a bit large, and like all crosses, it will be heavy to carry!"

On May 23, 1928, the *Italia* set out from King's Bay in Spitsbergen, at 4:00 A.M., in the direction of the Pole. Nobile had decided against taking the dogs that Nansen had advised him to arrange for. "Put them to sleep with a narcotic," the old master had said, "so they won't be afraid of the engine noise."

The dirigible's radio functioned normally; every receiver in the world was tuned to its wave length. At midnight, triumphant telegrams were dispatched to the Duce, the Pope and the king; the Pole was reached. "The standard of Fascist Italy," went the message to the Duce, "is floating in the breeze over the ice of the Pole." Nobile ordered that the *Italia* make a turn around the Pole, and during this circling maneuver, he served eggnog, while the phonograph played the Italian national anthem. Having thrown the cross and the flag overboard, Nobile gave the order to return at 2:20 A.M.

It was then that fog rose. The following morning, May 25, at 10:30, the airship's radio went dead; the world realized that the *Italia* was lost.

Two days later, in Oslo, Norway gave a great banquet for two aviators, Wilkins and Eielson, who had scored a remarkable success in making the Alaska-Spitsbergen run a month earlier. Their machine was a Stinson biplane, with its carburetor heated by the exhaust. All its mechanical parts which were exposed to the cold were protected with asbestos. The forward skis were made of steel, while the plane's tail rested on a wooden ski. The rest of the aeronautical equipment consisted of a compass, thermometers, an oil gauge, a speedometer, a horizon indicator, a drift indicator, a bubble octant, a pocket sextant, an aperiodic compass, an echo sounder and a chronometer accurate to 1/100th of a second. They took 264 gallons of fuel and 8 gallons of oil.

For their provisions, Wilkins and Eielson took only 11 pounds of biscuits, 22 pounds of chocolate, 5 pounds of army rations, 3 pounds of pemmican and an enormous thermos of black coffee . . . not to mention a supply of chewing gum, to cut thirst and to give the illusion of satisfying hunger. Wilkins, a former collaborator of Stefansson's, knew that his hunting lore would enable him to survive in case the airplane had to be abandoned. To this end, he brought along two rifles and 400 rounds of ammunition, a pair of field glasses, a fishing net, fishhooks and various accessories including the inevitable Primus stove as well as three forks, three knives and three plates. The radio, finally, worked on a hand-operated generator.

After a first fruitless attempt in 1927, Wilkins and Eielson succeeded in flying from Point Barrow to Spitsbergen in 1928. Wilkins was an Australian and Eielson a Norwegian. To do them special honor the veteran Amundsen (he was 56) presided over the triumphal banquet. At dessert, he was handed a telegram. "I'm ready to go right away," he whispered after he had read it.

The Norwegian government was giving him the official announcement of the disappearance of Nobile and his seventeen men and asking him to take charge of the search for them. Despite his personal feelings, Amundsen once again set out on a journey to the ice pack.

He immediately cabled his friend Ellsworth. But as he received no reply, he began to seek about on his own for "a large hydroplane or an icebreaker." As far as the icebreaker was concerned, the Russians had decided to send one directly: the *Krassin*, the largest and most powerful in the world. It was the French government which furnished the aircraft. At 11:00 P.M. on June 16, a French Navy Latham seaplane set down in Bergen Fjord to collect Amundsen and take him on to Tromsö.

Several radio messages from Nobile had finally been picked up, thus putting an end to the suspense. When the disabled *Italia* had fallen on the ice pack, the gondola in which Nobile and nine of his men were riding had broken. Freed of a heavy part of its load, the *Italia* had righted itself and taken off again, carrying with it the other men, who were still standing at their various posts.

On the ice, the nine men organized with great difficulty; one of them, Vincenzo Pomelia, had a fractured skull. Malmgren and Nobile both had broken arms. Malmgren took charge of the group, since Nobile was suffering seriously from shock. A red tent was set up. Searching through the debris of the gondola, the men found clothing, flares and, most important of all, an emergency radio set with its batteries intact.

Biaggi, the wireless operator, set to work. He succeeded in picking up messages from the *Città di Milano*, but his own transmissions remained inaudible. Ceaselessly, for eleven days, he dispatched messages to the outside world, which could not hear them. On June 6, Biaggi started with astonishment; an Italian short-wave news broadcast announced that his appeal had been picked up by a Russian amateur operator. On June 8, the *Città di Milano* announced to the shipwrecked men that the rescue operation was about to begin. But in the meantime, weary of waiting, the Italian officers Zappi and Mariano, and the Swede Malmgren had set out on foot.

While sixteen ships (including Charcot's *Pourquoi-Pas?*), twenty-one airplanes and 1,500 men were taking part in the search, Amundsen left Tromsö on June 18 at 4:00 P.M. At 5:00, his Latham OZ flew past the Ekinghen lighthouse, with which it kept in radio contact until 6:45. When the Lighthouse tried to re-establish contact at 8:00, the Latham did not reply. Amundsen was never to be heard from again. One of the greatest polar explorers of all time had earned the glorious death he so hoped for.

It has been argued that the choice of Amundsen's aircraft must have played an important part in this disaster. France had only two modern seaplanes at this time, but she had had no hesitation in making a choice between them. These two planes were a Cams 55 with two 420-horsepower, air-cooled Jupiter engines and a Latham OZ with two 450-horsepower, water-cooled Hispano Suiza engines.

The Cams, which was piloted by Lieutenant Commander Paris, set out for Africa in an attempt to establish a new series of records and was disabled by a mechanical failure in the Azores; air-cooling was not the best system for a tropical climate. The Latham, under the command of Lieutenant Commander Guilbaud, assisted by Lieutenant Commander Cuverville, Chief Engineer Brazy and Radio Operator Valette, set out for the Arctic with Amundsen, never to return; here again, water-cooling, in 40-below-zero temperature, does not seem to have been the ideal system.

In all events, it is unlikely that the mystery of their disappearance will ever be entirely cleared up.

On June 24, a small plane piloted by the Swede Einar Lundborg finally sighted Nobile's red tent and managed to land on the ice pack. "I am to take the general first," the pilot announced. Nobile was transported to King's Bay, where he received a very cool reception from the assembled journalists, while Lundborg's Fokker set off again to continue the rescue operation. He capsized on his second attempt to land, and the group of shipwrecked men now numbered one more.

Meanwhile, a Fokker reconnaissance plane from the icebreaker *Krassin* sighted three black spots on the pack ice. Full-speed ahead, the powerful ship drove toward them, but she was able to find only Zappi and Mariano, who had set off with Malmgren forty-three days earlier. Zappi was wearing three sets of clothing and seemed to be in good health. Mariano had only one layer of clothing and was totally exhausted. According to Zappi, Malmgren had died a month before. This surprised Captain Chukhnovsky, the pilot of the Fokker, who claimed to have seen three men on the ice; his crewmen confirmed his testimony.

When the *Krassin* arrived in King's Bay after picking up the last of the shipwrecked men, her commander Samoylovich asked that an inquest be opened on the circumstances surrounding the Swede's death. The Duce, for his part, had ordered that Nobile, who, contrary to naval tradition, had been the first to be saved, be put under arrest on the *Città di Milano*.

The Nobile affair caused a sensation throughout the world. Lundborg was criticized for having saved Nobile first. The latter carried a very heavy life-insurance policy, and it was said that Lloyd's had promised a ten-million-franc reward to anyone who brought him back alive. Zappi was accused of nothing more nor less than cannibalism.

An Italian court declared Nobile responsible for the disaster, took away his rank and his professorship at the Aeronautical Institute. He went into exile in Russia, where he became an instructor in aeronautics. He returned to Italy after the fall of Mussolini and stood as a candidate for the Italian parliament. He was defeated. He now lives in Rome, ruminating over the past among his trophies and his memories. His rank and his honors have been restored to him, and he won his lawsuit against the *Italia*'s builder, Hugo Eckener.

In spite of Behounek's book, *The Truth about the Red Tent,* it is likely that Nobile, who is now seventy-four, will carry the truth with him to the grave. But one day history will revise its estimate of this man, whose most serious error, after all is said and done, was to allow himself to be evacuated first.

23

THE FIRST SUBMARINE

THE SEVENTEEN VICTIMS in the Nobile disaster—eight in the *Italia*, six in the Latham, and three on Penzo's return flight—were by no means the only ones in the early days of polar aviation. In the year 1929, when 3,000 reindeer were convoyed from Alaska to Canada, and when the Russians installed a radio station on Franz Josef Land, the most remarkable of the American Arctic pilots, Carl Ben Eielson, was killed.[1]

It was Stefansson who introduced Eielson to Wilkins. From that day till his death, Eielson had more than 500 hours of flying time

---

[1] Jean Potter, *Alaska Under Arms*.

with the future pioneer of the first *Nautilus*, a feat unique in that period. In 1927, on their first long flight together, Eielson landed, after a mechanical failure, in 22-below-zero cold, on the moving ice of the Arctic sea more than 600 miles north of Alaska. All the technicians had said the thing could not be done. Their second flight, in 1928, was an astonishing performance; they had to change course more than fifty times in order to cross all the meridians from Point Barrow to Spitsbergen. Wilkins and Eielson had brought a small radio set with them to Point Barrow; they left the receiver apparatus with the local schoolmaster and took along the hand-operated transmitter. Thus Point Barrow had news of them all through the course of their long flight, though, as the town was isolated for months on end by the ice, the outside world received no word.

Scarcely was their triumphal reception in New York over when the two men turned to the south, over which they hoped to be the first to fly.

George Hubert Wilkins, who was born in Australia in 1888, had just been knighted when he set out on the whaling factory ship *Hectoria* with Hearst, Eielson, three crewmen and two Lockheed Vega monoplanes, which were designed so that they could be mounted on skis, wheels or pontoons. On November 16, 1928, he took off with Eielson from Deception Island, thus making the first Antarctic flight, though an extremely short one.

Wilkins had planned to fly across the Antarctic continent. But atmospheric conditions forced him to give up his project; the summer snow made it impossible to use anything but pontoons. As he was unable to take off except from the water, he could not carry a sufficient quantity of fuel, because of the weight. He did, however, succeed in flying over Graham Land and sighting six previously unknown islands. He was thus the first man to discover a new territory from an airplane.

Wilkins then went back north with other plans, and Eielson returned to Alaska, where he intended to work in commercial aviation. The renown he had earned so far brought him a large number of offers to fly chartered planes; the most noteworthy of these was a request to go to the aid of an American merchant vessel, the *Nanook*, which was icebound in Siberian waters with fifteen passengers and a million dollars worth of furs aboard. The Swenson Fur Company of Seattle offered Eielson $50,000 to fly back the cargo and passengers. The proposition was extremely dangerous, but tempting. With a young mechanic, Earl Borland, Eielson succeeded in making a first trip; then, on November 9, 1929, he disappeared forever. The Arctic had lost a great pilot.

But at about the same time, the Antarctic had found one: Richard E. Byrd. With Lincoln Ellsworth, Byrd was the man who assumed the major responsibility for America's efforts in the Antarctic throughout this period.

The massive winter camp, the first step toward a future polar colonization, was Byrd's specialty; in him, we no longer have simply man attacking the Pole, but the whole of modern technology, with an abundance of means that must have made old Nansen, then seventy-seven, shake his head in wonder. In his expedition of 1928-29, Byrd made skillful use of both old and new methods, taking ninety-five sledge dogs, several powerful radio transmitters, a tractor and three airplanes.

His two ships were the *City of New York*, a 512-ton Norwegian ex-whaler, which he bought on Amundsen's advice, and the steamship *Chelsea*, which Byrd rechristened the *Eleanor Bolling* in honor of his mother. The two ships sent regular dispatches to America, giving news of the expedition. On Christmas Day, 1928, Byrd set up camp in the Bay of Whales, a few miles from an inlet which he named Ver-sur-Mer, in memory of the French village where he landed after his transatlantic flight in 1927.

Amundsen's old winter quarters were, theoretically, only three miles from Little America, but seventeen years of constant drift had wiped them out. The unloading of Byrd's 650 tons of equipment was rapidly carried out and Little America I was set up. It consisted of individual rooms for the men, a mess hall, a gymnasium, a blacksmith's forge, an administrative room, a garage for the tractor and hangars for the planes, as well as 60-foot-high antennas. Smaller radio transmitters were provided for isolated runs in order to ensure their safety. The radio installation at Little America I was so powerful that on January 12, 1930, the Russian technician Ernest Krenkel succeeded in establishing direct contact with it from his own set on the Franz Josef archipelago. The two poles were now joined by radio.

The three planes were: a 425-horsepower Fokker monoplane, a Fairchild with collapsible wings, and a three-engine, 975-horsepower Ford, which could carry a six-ton load at 125 m.p.h.

The tractor was a great improvement over the first machine of its kind used by Shackleton. It was a very powerful Ford "snowmobile," with skis in front and caterpillar tracks in the rear. It had an average speed of 25 m.p.h. over the ice, and did the work of five or six dog teams.

A real competition grew up between the tractor's supporters and the dogs'. The two mechanics, Feury and Black, even went so far as to claim that they were capable of driving their machine straight to the Pole—if the road weren't cluttered up by slow-moving dog teams. They attempted a long run on October 25, the purpose of which was to tow three sledges loaded with provisions to their various depots. But, halted by a crevasse at 81° S., the snowmobile had to be turned round and was stopped for good, seventy miles from its base; it had to be abandoned. Byrd learned his lesson from this incident, and realized that, to triumph over a combination of thick snow and ice, he needed a heavier, more powerful machine.

Byrd went exploring by air several times. On January 27, 1929, with his pilot Bernt Balchen, who has since become one of the foremost specialists in polar flying, he crossed the Ross Ice Shelf for the first time. On March 7, he directed the first airborne expedition into the Antarctic continent: Balchen, June and Gould, who had touched down in a basin in the Rockefeller Mountain Range saw their Fokker literally swept up and smashed to bits before their eyes. Byrd and Smith set out in search of them and brought them back three days later, thus carrying out the first polar airlift.

On November 28, Byrd and Balchen (the latter at the controls) took off in the Ford with June and McKinley at 3:29 A.M. At 1:15 P.M., they reached the South Pole. By 8:30 P.M. they were back at Little America I, having done in 15 hours and 51 minutes the terrifying journey that took Amundsen 90 days. The airplane had been named for Floyd Bennett, Byrd's companion on his flight to the North Pole, who had died in 1927. For many years, Byrd was to remain the only man to have flown over both poles.

Meanwhile, in the north, the competition went on.

The most original expedition of this period was that of the German party led by Dr. Alfred Wegener in Greenland in 1930, using both dog sledges and propeller-driven sledges. It was the first to attempt to measure the thickness of the ice by seismic sounding.

As for the propeller-driven sledges, they proved somewhat less valuable than Wegener had hoped. They had been built by a factory in Helsinki, Finland. They were of ultralightweight construction; they had hickory skis, Siemens SH 12-112 PS airplane engines, 44-gallon fuel tanks and air-cooling systems. The principal difficulty was that they were very hard to start in below-zero weather. They sometimes had to be unloaded in order to scrape free the skis which had got stuck to the ice. They often required long and complicated handling; to unload, turn the sledges 180 degrees round, reload and start the engines by running down a slope often took a whole day. Moreover, because of the altitude, the engine's power, which was 112 horsepower at sea level, would fall to 85 horsepower at 10,000 feet. Wegener's two sledges nevertheless covered 2,100 miles. Their maximum speed was 44 m.p.h., and they consumed 17 gallons of pure airplane fuel per 100 miles. They could efficiently carry a load of between 1,100 and 1,300 pounds.

The most remarkable expedition of the period was nevertheless the British one of 1930 under Gino Watkins, who, with a perfectly lucid comprehension of the problems of the future, proposed to chart the polar air routes. Watkins was an enterprising young man (he was twenty-three) and a convinced partisan of the pure Eskimo technique. After his expedition to Greenland, he intended to cross the Atlantic, but he was never able to carry out his second project, for he drowned while seal-hunting in Greenland in 1931. Thanks to their dog sledges, kayaks, two motor launches and two Havilland planes, Watkins's team succeeded in making an excellent survey of the east coast of Greenland and gathered the first clear idea of the meteorology of the inland ice.

But it is incredible to think that the most astonishing event of the year 1930-31 was the appearance of the first submarine under the ice pack. The idea, which originated in Jules Verne's inventive mind in 1869, had been in the air for a long time.

An Australian explorer, Auschutz-Kampfe, had worked out a plan for getting to the Pole by submarine and had published it in the French magazine *L'Illustration*[2] in 1901. And in 1922, the great Stefansson, who, in his own words,[3] found himself "broke in Washington," wrote a long article in the *National Geographic* for

---

[2] *L'Illustration*, October 19, 1901.

[3] In his preface to George Hubert Wilkins, *Under the Pole*.

$1,000; in it, he outlined his plan for future trans-Arctic commerce, consisting of both aerial and submarine traffic.

Sir Hubert Wilkins, who had once been Stefansson's aide, made up his mind to attempt the adventure, which, from a scientific point of view, looked extremely promising. Fascinated by this new idea, Wilkins set to work in October 1930, after having read Jules Verne's *Twenty Thousand Leagues under the Sea,* while his two specialists, Simon Lake and Commander Danenhower, set about refitting and readapting an old submarine, the *0-12,* that Wilkins had bought from Navy surplus after it had already seen thirteen years' service. By transforming the *0-12* into the *Nautilus,* Lake made the dream of his life come true. He had written an article in the New York *Journal* thirty-three years earlier, on February 6, 1893, which began: "To the North Pole in a submarine boat with dynamite to blow holes in the ice . . ."

In the winter of 1904, Lake had tried out the submarine *Protector,* which he had personally designed and built; he had succeeded in making her travel under an eight-inch-thick floe in Narragansett Bay, which she broke through as she returned to the surface. Some years earlier, in 1898, the first great voyage ever made in a submarine had been carried out by Lake on board his *Argonaut;* this feat had earned him an enthusiastic telegram from Jules Verne. Lake, the son of the unlucky captain of the *Jeannette,* was the man Wilkins needed; he was made the commander of the *Nautilus.*

The former *0-12* had been built in 1918 and had cost a million dollars. The firm of Lake and Danenhower, Inc., rented her for five years at a dollar a year, on the condition that she be used only for scientific research. She had a submerged displacement of 550 tons and a maximum speed of fourteen knots. Her twin screws were powered by two 500-horsepower engines; air intake was controlled by two 200-horsepower engines. She had a 500-ampere battery which weighed 60 tons. The *Nautilus* was fitted with a hydraulic cushion forward, to counteract shocks, a retractable periscope, a hinged arm with which to "follow" the ice, in much the way a trackless trolley follows its wire, and, finally, three vertical drills with which to pierce holes in the ice. She had an underwater cruising range of 125 miles at a speed of about three knots. After traveling this distance, she had to surface and recharge batteries for eight hours.

Danenhower had calculated that it would take forty-two days to cover the 2,300 miles from Spitsbergen to Alaska, by way of the pole. The *Nautilus* could dive 200 feet without danger. The problem of "holes" in the ice pack came up as it was to come up again for the American atomic submarine *Skate* at the moment when she surfaced at the Pole. Like Captain Nemo's *Nautilus,* Wilkins's sub was equipped with an observation chamber in the conning tower, which would enable the captain to make an astonishing series of motion pictures during his trial runs under the ice pack.

She was also equipped with a special sounding winch for collecting plankton at very great depths, a "photographic balloon" inflated with helium, cameras, a gyroscopic compass (with synchronous-transmission of reading to repeaters in various parts of the boat), various sorts of explosives (for clearing ice), tents, sledges, various accessories required for survival in the Arctic and an outboard-motor boat. This delightful toy cost a small fortune ($250,000), which Sir Hubert succeeded in raising thanks to Lincoln Ellsworth, William Randolph Hearst, the Texas Oil Company, and his own writings.

Christened the *Nautilus* in a ceremony attended by Jules Verne's grandson, the submarine weighed anchor in June 1931. After being delayed by a long series of accidents, she finally reached the ice barrier in the region of Spitsbergen, where she was driven farther north by the Gulf Stream. But, as she was about to dive, the captain noticed that his submarine had been sabotaged; part of the diving mechanism had quite simply disappeared.

Wilkins went ahead, and ordered that the dive be made. The *Nautilus,* having submerged, tried several times to surface by breaking through an ice floe at 81° 59′ N. She did not succeed in piercing it. Wilkins then decided to give up and ordered the crew to return to Spitsbergen.

He had lost every penny he owned and had been able to salvage from his cruise nothing more than the joy of having sailed his ship to a higher latitude than any other vessel had ever reached on its own power. As was agreed in his contract, he had to scuttle the *Nautilus* and she was sunk in Bergen Fjord at a spot 600 feet deep; it was to the very same harbor that the American submarine *Skate* returned, twenty-seven years later, after having accomplished, point by point, the *Nautilus*'s ambitious mission: to be the first submarine to surface at the Pole.

24

PAPANIN AND BYRD

It is possible to say, as Vilhjalmur Stefansson did, that after the year 1930, the leadership in polar exploration passed out of the hands of the Western powers and into those of the Russians. The Soviet Union threw herself into the conquest of the Arctic regions with considerable technical means and a triple motive: scientific, economic and political. At the cost of a colossal technological effort, the Russians were to succeed, within twenty years, in turning their immense frozen empire into a formidable and profitable machine, both from an economic and a strategic point of view.

This success, which has been due in large measure to the action of an enormous impetus in a single direction, began with Papanin's sensational drift in 1937, a feat which was preceded by intense aerial preparation. The opportunity came with the voyage of the *Chelyuskin,* which attempted to trace a northeastern route with an eye to its future commercial development. This route had been explored from the air first by Krassinski, who flew from Bering Strait to the Liakhov Peninsula in 1929, then by the German dirigible, the *Graf Zeppelin,* which flew over Cape Chelyuskin in 1931.

Franz Josef Land was first circumnavigated by Zubov, aboard the *Knipovich,* in 1932, while in the same year the small icebreaker *Sibiryakov,* commanded by Voronin and with the scientist Otto Schmidt aboard, steamed into the "passage." She lost her propeller in the Chelyuskin Sea and drifted for thirteen days. When the spare propeller was also lost, Voronin hoisted makeshift sails, succeeded in getting his ship out of the ice, and reached the Bering Strait, where he was taken in tow by a trawler.

But Otto Schmidt would not acknowledge defeat and decided to force the Northeast Passage with the *Chelyuskin* in 1933. An intense amount of activity was going on in the Arctic at that time, it being the second International Polar Year; the idea for this project came from the great German meteorologist Dr. Johannes Georgi, who had wintered under atrocious conditions in the heart of Greenland as a member of the Wegener expedition.

The U.S.S.R. was participating in the Polar Year with fifty-two stations scattered from North Cape to Kamchatka. The series of observations which indicated a considerable increase in the warmth of the water and of the climate to the west of Taimyr led to a renewal of Soviet activity in those regions. Otto Schmidt was named director of the *Glavsevmorput* (a word composed of the first syllables of four Russian words meaning Central Administration of the Northern Sea Route), the aim of which was to pursue the methodical industrialization of the Russian Far North.

In order to study the possibilities for trans-Arctic communication, Schmidt then decided to attempt to do with the *Chelyuskin* what he had been previously unable to accomplish with the *Sibiryakov;* a decision that was all the more natural as he had in any case to relieve the winter camp on Wrangel Island and to enlarge the station there. He wanted to determine to what degree it would be possible for cargo ships to navigate in the North Siberian seas, and just how the teamwork among cargo vessels, icebreakers and aircraft ought to be organized.

The excellent icebreakers that were available to the Glavsevmorput, the *Krassin,* the *Yermak* and the *Lenin,* had not been designed for long journeys. Thus, Schmidt chose a semi-icebreaker, the *Chelyuskin,* which could, if necessary, call on the aid of a full-scale icebreaker, the *Krassin,* which was then in the vicinity of Cape Chelyuskin.

Provisions for eighteen months were loaded on the *Chelyuskin,* as well as 2,995 tons of coal, 500 tons of water, three year's food supply for the winter camp on Wrangel Island and all the necessary polar equipment. There were 112 men aboard, including 53 sailors, 28 members of the expedition, 18 men on their way to the Wrangel winter camp, 12 carpenters, and a poet! There was a most valuable machine in the hold: an amphibious aircraft. Voronin was in command of the ship. He was a veteran in polar navigation. In the summers he ran scientific cruises, while in the winters he hunted big game in the White Sea (which earned the state more than 100,000 gold rubles each season).

The *Chelyuskin* left Leningrad on July 12, 1933. She began her scientific work immediately, sowing her path with large wooden balls and bottles partly filled with gravel so as to keep them floating upright. In this position, the bottles were driven not by the winds, but by the currents, the direction of which could be determined each time a bottle was recovered. They carried a message: "This bottle has been set afloat with a view to the study of marine currents. Whoever finds it is requested to inform the Arctic Institute of the U.S.S.R. in Leningrad."

Ill-adapted as she was to the battle with the ice, the *Chelyuskin* did not reach Wrangel Island. She was icebound on November 4, 1933, in Bering Strait, whence the drift carried her toward the northwest. On November 10, the *Chelyuskin* called on the icebreaker *Litke* for aid, but, as the latter suffered an injury herself, she could be of no assistance. On the seventeenth, the *Chelyuskin* lost her N4 plane, which was wrecked on take-off by an ice block. Three months later, on February 13, 1934, in 22-below-zero weather, the ship was battered by the ice and sank in the midst of a snowstorm.

The rescue operation was immediately organized. Various sorts of planes (twin-engined Ant 4's, which could carry fifteen passengers, and N4's, which could carry eight) succeeded in evacuating the "Schmidt camp" in March. Lyapidevsky, Levanevsky,

Kamanin, Molokov and Vodopyanov, the pilots of these planes, were thus the first team ever to carry out a polar airlift of any dimension. During the two following years numerous polar flights were made, including that of Levanevsky, who went from Los Angeles to Moscow via the Arctic in thirty-seven days.

With Papanin's drift and the first great polar flights, 1937 was a memorable year.

Ivan Papanin, who was born in Sebastopol in 1895, began his career as a telecommunications specialist. He made his first Arctic voyage in 1931 aboard the *Malagin*. Papanin's idea, like Nansen's several years earlier, had a grandiose simplicity. It consisted in establishing a weather station at the Pole by airplane and in letting it drift. Stalin ordered him to begin in 1936, and Papanin went straight to work on his minute preparations.

An enormous amount of equipment and provisions was assembled, including: fuels, medical supplies, notebooks, fire-lighting devices, hides, scissors, axes, linen, furniture, razors, chess sets, books (Lenin, Stalin, Gorki, Tolstoy, Balzac, Stendhal, Dreiser, et cetera), powdered eggs, chicken rissoles, cranberry jelly, sugar, chocolate, pepper, bay leaves, coffee, vitaminized candy, tea, lemonade and concentrated milk.

By the end of the summer of 1936, Papanin announced that all was ready. He went north aboard the icebreaker *Russanov,* which also carried the expedition's equipment in her hold; he set up his base camp on Rudolph Island (the most northerly island in the world—82° N.). A vast landing field was carved out of the ice, and on March 21, 1937, the aerial squadron arrived on the island.

On May 21, two months later, the lead plane, an N170 piloted by Vodopyanov, took off in the direction of the Pole, followed by three other four-engined aircraft. At 11:00 A.M. the N170 landed (at 89° 53′ N.), followed immediately after by the others.[1] When the planes took off again, only four men stayed behind: Papanin, two scientists, Pyotr Shirshov and Eugen Fedorov, and the radio operator Ernest Krenkel, the very man who had established contact between the North and South Poles in 1930.

The fact that the whole expedition had been transported by air set a limit on the baggage weight. The pink silk tent weighed less than 15 pounds, including the beds; it was 12 feet long, 8 feet wide

---

[1] I. Papanin, *Life on an Ice Floe.*

and 6½ feet high. Double-decker cots were used. The flooring was six inches thick (it was made of a combination of eider down and tarpaulin). The clothing was made of reindeer skin, the caps of wolverine and the underwear of merino cashmere. On the ice floe, the expedition members changed their clothing every two months. Everything was planned, down to the toilet water and a supply of toothbrushes.

The total weight of the highly sophisticated scientific apparatus was a half a ton. The radio set worked by a windmill-powered motor, or else with the aid of a motor operated by hand and by foot, which was nicknamed the "soldier motor" and was built in the shape of a bicycle. On dead-calm days the men of North Pole Station I recharged the battery by pedaling.

The provisions consisted of forty-six different products shared out among seventy watertight cans containing 97 pounds each; everything was wrapped in cellophane and tinfoil. Each can contained 52 ounces of pressed caviar. Two specially designed gas heaters with a capacity of 12½ quarts were used in cooking. The nested "china" was made of aluminum, wood and bakelite. In intensely cold weather, it took three hours to do the cooking, but the "Papanites" never lacked warm, freshly prepared food throughout the whole of their 274-day drift.

Rifles, soldering irons, plywood, sheets, sledges and canoes were all provided as part of the equipment, as well as Soviet F.E.D. and German Leica and Contax cameras. "We set out for the Far North," Papanin wrote in 1940, "with the confidence that had been instilled in us by the party of Lenin and Stalin. We were confident of our strength and knew that standing behind us was the whole of our beloved Motherland, that with us was our dear Stalin, who would not forsake us in a difficult moment."

Making ceaseless scientific and weather observations, which were immediately retransmitted to the Rudolph Island station, and writing articles for the major Soviet newspapers, the four men began their drift with a dog, Happy, for company, the first polar dog that was not also a sledge dog. A first sounding gave a depth-reading of 13,800 feet, and a sampling of the sea bottom below the Pole produced a greenish-gray slime.

On June 10, 1937, a message from Moscow arrived at NP1: "Supply weather reports and radio contacts for Chkalov's flight to America over North Pole." On June 11, at midnight, the weather was so mild that the sun had heated the tent to an indoor temperature of 75° F. On the nineteenth, the roar of an airplane engine overhead indicated that Chkalov was on his way to America. Having set out at 4:00 A.M. on the seventeenth, he was to land at Portland, Oregon, after covering more than 5,600 miles on board his Ant 25. On June 20, NP1 was at 88° N.; the sounding was 14,675 feet.

On June 25, Papanin noted in his journal, after his observations for the day: "It is 28° F. out of doors, but inside the tent the temperature is between 39° and 46°. We sent a telegram to Moscow today welcoming the issuing of the Government Defense Loan. Altogether, we four subscribed 10,000 rubles." On June 27, Krenkel was still listening in to stations all over the world with his own 25-watt receiver. He managed to converse with a French operator in Reims, then with another in New York. On the twenty-eighth, Papanin received by radio the news of his nomination as a "Hero of the Soviet Union," while the other three received the Order of Lenin.

On July 4, the temperature was 33° F., the height of the Arctic summer. A new order came from Moscow to transmit weather bulletins for Gromov's flight. On July 5, the first of the Party-Komsomol group meetings of NP1 was held. The scientist Shirshov was admitted as a "sympathizer." On the twelfth, Gromov passed not far from them; he was to land at San Jacinto, California, after a formidable flight of more than 6,200 miles. But he did not catch sight of NP1, despite the fact that immense red circles had been painted around it on the snow.

On August 12, 1937 (NP1 was at 87° 20′ N.), S. A. Levanevsky set out in a four-engined N-209 with a five-man crew and flew over the Pole on the thirteenth. Shortly afterward, he reported a malfunction in one engine; then his radio went dead. The search undertaken by the icebreaker *Krassin* and by Sir Hubert Wilkins (who made ten flights of nearly 40,000 miles) was in vain.

On August 18, it rained! On September 8, a kerosene lamp was lit for the winter; the Arctic summer was over. On September 11, all the equipment was secured to sledges in anticipation of any emergency.

On October 2, the position was 85° 28′ N., and the temperature was −18° F. On October 3, the drift became more marked; its speed was 2,300 feet per hour. "Rudolph Island informs me,"

Papanin noted on October 9, "that on the basis of our observations, Soviet meterologists are reviewing the earlier theories of anticyclones in the Central Polar Basin. This is of considerable importance to the science of meteorology." On the eleventh he noted: "The Atlantic Ocean is more and more revealing its secrets. Formerly, the water temperature at 10,000 feet was one degree above freezing. It is now one and a half."

On November 5, a telegram brought them the news that the model of the NP1 tent had won first prize at the Paris International Exhibition. On December 1, the position of NP1 was 82° 46′ N., nearly 500 miles from the Pole, after six months of drifting. On December 26, it was 80° 32′ N. On January 5, NP1 crossed the 79th parallel, with a sounding of 531 feet.

Disturbed by the speed of the drift, Moscow decided to send the whaler *Murmansk*. On January 18, 1938, the temperature fell to 53 degrees below zero. On the twentieth, a storm cut Papanin off from the neighboring ice floes. The icebreakers *Taimyr* and *Yermak* were sent to sea in their turn. On February 7, the camp area was smashed up into several pieces; NP1 was now only 100 feet by 30. On the eighth, Krenkel suddenly cried out, "Land!" The high mountains of Greenland rose in the distance. On the twelfth, the *Taimyr*'s searchlights swept across the horizon, and on the sixteenth, the icebreaker's reconnaissance plane, piloted by Vlasov, sighted NP1 and landed on the ice pack.

On the 19th, Papanin, Fedorov, Krenkel and Shirshov were taken on board the *Taimyr* after 274 days of drifting. Papanin was the last to leave the ice pack, after raising the red flag and sending off a message to Stalin. "It is pleasant," Papanin wrote, "to realize that all our plans have been carried out; that we, four ordinary Soviet citizens, have justified the hopes placed in us by our Party, our people, our Government and our beloved Stalin, who reared us and on whose initiative our Motherland has acquired a new waterway linking up the east and west of the Union of Soviet Socialist Republics."

We may say that with Papanin's adventure the great period of exploration, properly so called, came to an end. The immense progress, particularly in aviation, that resulted from the Second World War enabled man to undertake the practical conquest and the exploitation of the polar regions. This is not to suggest, however, that the activity in the decade preceding the war was any the less great.

The most spectacular over-all operation was an American one, again under the leadership of Admiral Byrd.

Byrd arrived in the Antarctic in October 1933, with two ships, the *Jacob Ruppert* and the *Bear of Oakland*, which had been launched in 1874 and had brought back six of the survivors of the Greely expedition. The equipment of the expedition was considerable. Byrd had three planes: a Pilgrim, a Curtiss-Wright Condor and a Fokker, as well as a novelty: a gyroplane, the first helicopter-type aircraft ever seen on the southern continent.

Little America II was built over Little America I, some of the traces of which were still to be seen, despite the attacks of the ice. "One saw taking form in the glittering white vacuum," Byrd wrote, "one of the most remarkable cities on the face of the earth—a city which would boast, among other possessions, of electric light and power, a complete broadcasting and field-communications plant, aviation service, four modern planes and skilled personnel, various machine shops, four tractors, nearly 150 dogs, a first-class meteorological station, a scientific staff and laboratory equipped to delve into twenty-two branches of science, a dairy plant with four head of cattle, adequate medical facilities, a well-stocked galley, library, a meteor observatory, and even a motion-picture theater wired for sound."

Without any question, this expedition gave proof that motorized transport could be used in the polar regions. Its tractors covered more than 12,500 miles over snow and ice in one year. The two light tractors were built by Ford; the heavy "Cletrac" tractor, which weighed six tons and could tow a ten-ton load, was manufactured by King White's Cleveland Tractor Company. André Citroën furnished three light trucks with caterpillar tracks, which proved extremely useful for the transportation of provisions between the Bay of Whales and Little America II. In February, they were used nonstop, with the drivers taking shifts at the wheel; this wore down the engines, which had to be overhauled and reinforced. By March 1934, they had done almost 7,000 miles.

The Cletrac was too heavy to be risked on the crevasses of the Bay of Whales. It had to be used at first for shuttle service between the base and the East Barrier depot, hauling five-ton loads. By March it had covered more than 1,250 miles.

It was when an advance weather station had to be set up that the vehicles were put to their most severe test. On March 16, the latest possible date for a polar journey, the tractor squadron left Little America II. This was, for the Antarctic, the largest entirely motorized convoy to date. It was planned that each vehicle should be able to survive on its own, if it were separated from the others in a blizzard. The first day the party covered twenty-five miles.

A Citroën which had gone forward to explore the route was blocked fifteen miles ahead of the others. But without a radio, it was unable to let the others know that the terrain was dangerous. The others set out in the midst of such a violent storm that the drivers could make their way only with their heads outside the window. Numerous halts were caused by frozen carburetors and water in the fuel. One of the Citroëns had to tow the Cletrac to get it started again. The convoy finally reached the blocked vehicle, which had by now managed to get itself free, after an enormous amount of shovelwork by its two drivers. The mechanic Demas did not dare to stop the Cletrac's engine while the vehicle was at rest. It stopped of its own accord the minute the convoy started off the next day.

The three Citroëns set out alone and succeeded in reaching the spot where Admiral Byrd had decided to winter on his own, 123 miles from the base. On March 28, 1934, having left the admiral in his "snowhole," they turned back and, having recovered the Cletrac's load on their way, returned to Little America II on March 29, in 63-below-zero weather.

On August 8, the base staff, who were beginning to worry about what had become of Byrd, decided to pay him a motorized visit. A Citroën towing two sledges set out for the advance station, but after making only twenty-five miles in three days, it had to return to the base and allow a new vehicle to take its place. In intense cold and under unfavorable atmospheric conditions, in spite of the darkness, the convoy arrived at the station on August 10; they found Byrd in a condition of extreme weakness.

When the station barracks had been built (in 60-below-zero cold), several stovepipes were lost and nonairtight couplings had had to be improvised out of sheet metal taken from the oil drums. Carbon monoxide coming through these leaks were thus added to the fumes from the gas engine set up in a snow tunnel. Byrd was faced with a terrible dilemma: "To stop the burner and freeze without water or to have heat and drink while asphyxiating."

This solitary winter, which lasted four and a half months, was not the first of its kind in polar history, whatever Byrd may say in his book *Alone*. In 1931, in fact, during the Watkins expedition in Greenland, Watkins's aide Augustine Courtauld had been forced to spend more than five months alone in a tent buried under the snow on the Greenland inland ice, and this took place under infinitely more precarious conditions of comfort and security than those undergone by Byrd.

When Byrd arrived on the Ross Ice Shelf in January, 1934, he missed the American ship *Wyatt Earp* by only four days; she belonged to Lincoln Ellsworth, who was then preparing to make the first trans-Antarctic flight. After Byrd's flight over the South Pole, Ellsworth had decided to revive Wilkins's old project of crossing the continent by air. He did not manage it easily; but this son of a Chicago coal king was a real explorer; he was not afraid of the prospect of 2,200 miles over totally deserted and unexplored territory.

He chose a Northrop monoplane with a 600-horsepower Wasp engine capable of doing 5,000 miles nonstop at 230 m.p.h. It was called the *Polar Star* and was shipped aboard the 400-ton sealer *Wyatt Earp* to Little America I, where Ellsworth planned to make his first test flight; but the plane was damaged in a storm.

Ellsworth returned some months later, this time to the "other side" of Antarctica; but once again he was defeated. In November 1935, he was back again and ready to set out from Dundee Island. The *Polar Star* was hoisted onto a platform, and, after two false starts, Ellsworth, accompanied by Herbert Hollick-Kenyon, succeeded in taking flight toward the unknown at 8:00 A.M. on November 23, 1935. After fourteen hours in the air, with the bad weather closing steadily in, they decided to land at 79° 15′ S. by 102° W., and then remained pent in by a storm for several days.

On December 15, having abandoned their plane, they arrived on foot at Little America II, which was now also abandoned. They found reserve supplies of food and coal and dug in under sixteen feet of snow. On January 19, 1936, a small plane from Scott's old *Discovery II*, which had set out in search of them, parachuted them some fruit and their mail. Three days later, the *Wyatt Earp* got to them. At fifty-five, Ellsworth was at last able to enjoy a triumph of his own.

During the same period, France was quietly making a comeback in the polar world. For it was during this period that the small group from which the French Polar Expeditions were later to be born, in 1947, was beginning to work together in Greenland,[2] thanks to the efforts of Charcot, who disappeared tragically on September 16, 1936, aboard his faithful and legendary *Pourquoi-Pas?* He disappeared in the manner of a hero, and, in the history of polar exploration, he will always remain one of the purest of the legendary prewar figures.

---

[2] It consisted of Gessain, Matter, Perez and the author.

25

OPERATION HIGH JUMP

WHEN HITLER INVADED Poland, the map of the world was practically completed. Its outlines were precisely defined, the British possessions appeared in red, the French in blue, and no one could seriously expect to find adventure in purely geographical exploration any more. But while the possibilities for geographical exploration were diminished, the field for scientific research was at the same time enlarged to a fantastic degree.

The sole positive aspect of the war—that frightful affliction, that terrible tribute which we were forced to pay to our liberty—was this: It was going to make technology take a giant step forward and to give men of good will the means to complete and to secure the conquest of the poles.

Beginning in 1941, two gigantic lines of transport were established between the American arsenal and Russia. The first, an air-sea line, ran through the North Atlantic and the Barents Sea, and thousands of ships sailed over it to arrive, heavily laden, in the ports of the Murman Coast. Its nerve center lay between North Cape and Spitsbergen, where the Germans had established their own bases.

The war as it was fought in these regions seems strange and far away now. There was the raid of the battleship *Tirpitz,* which, accompanied by a fleet of destroyers, came to wipe out the Longyear installation in Spitsbergen, Longyearbyen, in 1943. There was the story of the German lieutenant named Ritter who was taken prisoner by the Danes in Greenland. He and his "guard" covered more than three hundred miles together over the ice. The journey lasted a month. The two men shared the same food, the same dangers, fatigue, storms and anguish. They became friends. They slept in the same sleeping bag to fight the cold, and they wept on parting. There was the Eskimo Rudi, nicknamed the "King of the Bear," who, when he saw a German commando disembarking from a submarine on the east coast of Greenland, escaped, half-dressed, badly shod and without a compass, heading for home like a bear, traveled nearly five hundred miles to preserve his freedom. Finally, there was the run of the German corsair, the *Pinguin,* which the Russians authorized to borrow the Northeast Passage in 1940.

Franz Josef Land received its share of Germans, who came there to set up a weather station; the fifteen men of the station's crew all contracted trichinosis and had to be evacuated in the spring of 1944.

The second great transport line, this one entirely by air, began in the very heart of the United States and ended at Moscow; it passed over the Canadian Northwest Territories, Alaska, Kamchatka and Siberia. The lend-lease bombers and fighters were put under the command of Russian crews at their point of departure; the Russians had all the aerial information necessary for the American leg of the journey at their disposal, while the Americans knew nothing whatever about what went on beyond the "line," the very line, that is, which runs down the middle of Bering Strait, between the two islets, Little Diomede and Big Diomede.

The most beneficial result of this heavy traffic was that it made the United States conscious of the importance of cold-weather techniques and of the strategic significance of the Far North. Every soldier assigned to this sector during the war carried a small work entitled the *Basic Arctic Manual,* in which he was taught how to become a perfect copy of Nansen in thirty-two lessons. Produced through the collaboration of world-renowned experts like Stefansson and Wilkins, this manual dealt with the topography of the Arctic, as well as with the best techniques for eating wild plants, hunting seal, protecting oneself from swarms of mosquitoes and driving dog sledges.

With the end of the war, an immense amount of activity in both meteorological and strategic exploration was undertaken on all sides. It has reached its logical conclusion today, with atomic submarines armed with Polaris missiles lying in ambush under the Arctic ice cap and with the explosion of 50-megaton bombs off Novaya Zemlya, eradicating all life over a vast area.

In the Antarctic, the Germans also made their presence felt. Toward the end of 1940, a German cruiser, the *Viking,* under Captain Fischer, was sent to the southern continent with orders to destroy the Allied whaling fleet and to capture the floating factories with their overflow loads of more than 50,000 tons of oil, which represented half the catch up to that time. Warned by their Secret Service, the British found themselves in an extremely difficult predicament, since they were unable to dispatch any ships from their own shores, then under the threat of German invasion. They did send an auxiliary cruiser, the *Southern Cross,* and a whaling ship fitted out with torpedo tubes to the Falkland Islands in an attempt to prevent the pirate ship from acting. The *Viking* succeeded in capturing two factory ships before she was hit by two torpedoes and sunk.

Three more German corsairs, the *Pinguin,* which had sailed through the Northeast Passage, the *Atlantis* and the *Komet,* operated in the south in 1940 and 1941. The *Komet* circumnavigated the Antarctic continent and managed to capture three Norwegian factory ships, which were taken back to Bordeaux with 22,500 tons of oil on board. The British then laid mines in the Prince Edward and Kerguelen anchorages and destroyed the Deception Island Station.

In 1939, at the moment when Europe was about to be engulfed, a monster made its appearance on the Antarctic ice; it was called the *Snow Cruiser*. It was Admiral Byrd who had brought it, on the occasion of the first United States government expedition in 1939-41, the aim of which was the systematic exploration of the as yet unclaimed Antarctic sector. Two bases were established, one at Little America III or West Base, under the command of Paul Siple, the other on Stonington Island in Marguerite Bay on the Palmer Peninsula, called East Base and commanded by Richard Black.

The *Snow Cruiser* was a ship on wheels. She was 55 feet long, 20 feet wide and 15 feet high and was a sort of "mobile base" that might very well have sprung from Jules Verne's imagination. With a total weight of 33½ tons, the *Snow Cruiser* had four individually powered wheels, each ten feet in diameter and weighing three tons apiece.

The design and construction of this monster were the work of Thomas C. Poulter, the scientific director of the Armour Research Foundation in Chicago. The *Snow Cruiser* was designed to travel over the snow in any weather and on any terrain. She carried a year's provisions and could keep four to five men self-supporting over a range of 5000 miles. Her wheels could be retracted to enable her to ski down slopes or in order to free her from a crevasse in case the snow bridges broke. An airplane was carried on her roof. She even included a dark room for developing photographs and a chart room for the navigator. She took two years to build and cost a mere $150,000. She could be turned remarkably easily in a radius of thirty feet, for her front and rear wheels could be turned in any direction at will.

On his preceding expedition Byrd had taken note of the fact that crevasses more than fourteen feet wide were visible from a rather long distance away and that only crevasses narrower than this figure remained invisible; the *Snow Cruiser*'s wheels were thus designed to cross crevasses of fourteen feet or less. Her fuel tanks held 2,500 gallons of gas and 1,000 gallons of airplane fuel. She carried a considerable amount of scientific equipment, including a seismic sounder, a gravimeter, and the full range of previously known instruments. She had two radio transmitters, one of 200 watts and one of 40 watts, as well as a 12-watt emergency transmitter.

Byrd and his collaborators put a great deal of hope into this machine. In fairness, it ought to be recorded that this marvelous object never got beyond the borders of Little America III, and that these were reached only with great difficulty; in fact, she very nearly suffered a catastrophe when she was unloaded from the *North Star*. The least hint of snow was enough to stop her dead.

Fortunately, Byrd also had Army M2A2 tanks and light tractors for each of his bases. All base work was done by teams of dogs assisted by aircraft and tractors. The tanks and tractors carried out several entirely successful missions. But the tanks had to be stripped of all their armor in order to lighten them. As for that strange monster, the *Snow Cruiser:* she was found in 1958 under sixteen feet of snow, by Captain Coykendall of Little America V. On her body, one of the former residents of Little America III had scratched an inscription with a penknife: "This is the *Snow Cruiser*. One more dream shot to hell."

When the din of battle finally subsided and man suddenly found himself faced with an incredible stock of ultra-modern technological devices, his first task was to familiarize himself with them in an entirely new way, in order to convert them to peaceful uses.

Thus it was that, in the north, the small-scale Task Force Frigid set out for Alaska to investigate modern survival techniques in the Arctic, while, in the south, the American Navy resumed its attack on the Antarctic with an immense armada and practically unlimited resources, determined to experiment with every sort of equipment in conditions of extreme cold. At the same time, France was officially making her entry on the polar scene with the creation of the French Polar Expeditions; Norway, Sweden and England were organizing a combined expedition; and Australia was preparing one too.

General Jacob L. Devers, of the U. S. Army, who was acutely aware of Napoleon's and Hitler's defeats in their operations in cold countries, decided to send a task force to Alaska to experiment on the weapons and equipment in use in 1946. The winter of 1946-47 was, by the way, propitious for these experiments, as during it the Canadian town of Snag below the Alaskan border registered the lowest temperature in its history: —83° Fahrenheit.

Between December 1, 1946, and March 15, 1947, 380 experiments were made, all of them rigorous tests of weapons, clothing, vehicles and housing. The smallest object tested was the humidity-proof match; the largest was the M26 tank, which weighed 45 tons.

The problem of starting engines in cold weather was given special attention and the best method was found to be grouping the vehicles in sets of ten or twelve and covering them with a tarpaulin. Hot air was then blown in by an air-heater. This method has the added advantage of heating the chassis. The difficulties it presents are obvious; it makes it impossible to separate the vehicles for any protracted period; it also requires a great deal of fuel. (It takes a full drumful [50 gallons] of gasoline to keep ten vehicles heated for twelve hours.)

Another method consists in diluting the motor oil with gasoline, in the ratio of five to one when the vehicles are parked at night and the temperature falls below —22° F. In the morning the mixture will remain fluid in temperatures as low as —40°. It was also discovered that pure antifreeze, which solidifies at 18 degrees below zero, will remain fluid at 67 below if mixed with water in the ratio of 60 per cent antifreeze to 40 per cent water. It was also found that diesel engines were more reliable than gasoline engines in very cold weather.

As far as accommodation was concerned, the "Wannigan," or Caravan, was discovered to be very useful. It could be used for living quarters, for latrines, first-aid stations, telephone switchboards, kitchens and dormitories. As for uniforms, Colonel Kane, the head of the task force, reported that "it is impossible to adapt Eskimo clothing for military needs, as it would be impossible to find enough reindeer and caribou skins to equip a single division."

The United States Navy's expedition of 1946, High Jump, gave an indication of America's technological power. Organized in only seven weeks, it lasted through the whole of the southern summer of 1946-47. The only preceding expedition of anything like the same scope was that of the Viking Eric the Red, who went to Greenland a thousand years earlier with twenty-four ships, fifteen hundred men, women and children, cattle and horses.

Byrd, who was in charge of High Jump, had four thousand men at his disposal, as well as a squadron of thirteen ships of various tonnages and ranging from the icebreaker to the submarine; the icebreakers were the *Northwind* and the *Burton Island;* the ships included, among others, the *Mount Olympus*, the *Yancey*, the *Merrick*, the *Pine Island*, the *Brownson*, the *Canisteo*, the *Currituck*, the *Cacapon* and the *Henderson;* and the submarine *Sennet*.

One of the men on board was Dr. Waldo Lyon, who was later to become a great specialist on atomic polar submarines. It was quickly perceived that the submarine was a useless burden to the expedition; she became icebound and was on the point of sinking even with her ballast tanks empty. The icebreaker *Northwind*, with her 6,600 tons and her 10,000 horsepower, had to return to pick her up and convoy her back to her native element, the open sea. When the submarine was once again able to travel normally, the experts discovered that the ice had staved in her pressure hull. This might logically have been accepted as a defeat, but the information that Waldo Lyon's specialists obtained from it enabled them to send a submarine under the North Pole ice pack ten years later and to make it surface through the ice.

Operation High Jump consisted of three groups. The eastern group, headed by Lieutenant Commander George J. Dufek (who was later to lead Operation Deep Freeze for the International Geophysical Year), was to work its way west to meet the western group at the entrance to the Ross Sea. The second group was headed by Lieutenant Commander Charles Bond and was to set out from 90° E. toward the Dufek group. The central group, under the direction of Admiral Richard Cruzen (the "tactical" leader of the expedition, as Byrd was its "technical" leader), went to Little America IV. Each group was organized around an aircraft carrier; the six Dakotas all had jet-assisted take-off (JATO), which they used to take off from the first Antarctic airfield, constructed near Little America IV by an advance team.

The expedition was essentially intended for aerial exploration, but the Bay of Whales base had land vehicles with which to transport equipment from the ships to the base. Captain Boyd, the head of the motorized section, had at his disposal, among other things, two 16-ton, amphibious LVT vehicles, in which men could live. Each LVT towed a sledge loaded with eight and a half tons of equipment and airplane fuel. On their various runs (some as long as 250 miles), they succeeded in getting over ten-foot crevasses.

High Jump carried out a hundred flight missions, took 40,000 aerial photographs, discovered at least 350,000 square miles of previously unknown territory, and photographed 60 per cent of the continental coast line, more than a quarter of which had never been seen before.

In February 1947, Admiral Byrd made his second flight over the Pole. His two planes, which were overloaded (with sixteen tons rather than the theoretical maximum of twelve and a half) because of the run's fuel requirements, took off from Little America IV under exceptionally favorable weather conditions on February 15 at 11:00 A.M. A breakdown in the heating system very nearly precipitated a catastrophe on Byrd's own plane, where the automatic pilot was put out of service. Everything in the cockpit was frozen. They finally arrived over the Pole, which thus received its fourth human visit since the creation of the world. Having thrown overboard a box containing all the United Nations flags, Byrd pushed on to reconnoiter in the direction of the Weddell Sea, flying over a totally unknown region. As Little America informed him by radio that the weather was growing less favorable, Byrd turned back and began his return flight. At noon he landed at his base, having flown for twelve hours at an average speed of 144 m.p.h.

Operation High Jump's results were remarkable. "Hundreds of peaks," the official report points out, were discovered, as well as twenty-six islands, and an "oasis" of temporary lakes at 104° E., the Bunger Oasis, named for the pilot who discovered the region. It was also during the course of High Jump that Dakotas took off from the aircraft-carried *Philippine Sea*, doing 30 knots into the wind outside the ice pack, and were able to land on the snow 750 miles from the ship; this was the first time that planes of this type had succeeded in landing on the Antarctic continent.

In the opinion of Admiral Lord Mountevans, who is none other than the former Lieutenant Evans of the Scott Expedition, Operation High Jump defied the Antarctic but did not conquer it. This task was to be accomplished in very large measure by the expeditions of the International Geophysical Year and by those that followed it. But High Jump was to give the American Navy the polar experience which later enabled it to carry off so successfully the complex and hazardous operations required to set up the six large American bases for the Geophysical Year. "It was, if you like," wrote Mountevans, "Dieppe but not D-Day."

High Jump was followed by another, smaller operation: Operation Windmill of 1947-48. Helicopters based on icebreakers landed at various spots on the coast in order to establish the fixed points required to prepare the maps which were being drawn up from aerial photographs taken during High Jump.

Simultaneously with High Jump, a private American expedition headed by Finn Ronne, the son of Amundsen's companion, set up its base on Stonington Island in Marguerite Bay; for the first time ever, two women wintered in the Antarctic; they were Mrs. Edith

Ronne and Mrs. Harry Darlington, the wife of Ronne's second-in-command. The expedition ran into all the difficulties ordinarily caused by the presence of women in such circumstances.

Finally, we must mention a combined Norwegian-Swedish-English expedition, under Norwegian direction, in 1950-52, as well as the establishment by Australia of Mawson Station on Mac-Robertson Coast (58° E.) in 1954. Last of all, in January 1955, the 6,000-ton American icebreaker *Atka* found the Bay of Whales base destroyed and sighted two enormous icebergs, 15 and 100 miles long, drifting in the Ross Sea with equipment left by the High Jump expedition.

As for the French, it was on January 20, 1950, 110 years after Dumont d'Urville first planted the tricolor flag on Adélie Coast, that they landed once again in Antarctica, to set up a base there and to begin a series of expeditions that were to go on one after another, year in and year out, practically without a break. An appropriation voted by the National Assembly in 1947 enabled the French Polar Expeditions to be formed within the framework of the National Center for Scientific Research. But it would not have been possible to carry out the expeditions without the co-operation and aid of private industry.

In 1947, two areas remained open to French exploration. While, in the north, the Arctic Ocean was not ideally suited for a complete program of scientific research, the interior of Greenland, on the other hand, remained practically unknown. As it was under Danish sovereignty, the country remained outside the northern no man's land where the U.S.S.R. and U.S.A. were working. In the south, the French sector of the Antarctic, Adélie Coast, was still waiting to be explored. Thus, the original feature offered by the French Polar Expeditions lay in the fact that they would work, from the beginning, at the systematic study of two separate polar zones.

The intention was to use the most recent mechanical techniques: ships, planes and caterpillar vehicles. The ship used for Adélie Coast was bought in San Francisco, transformed into a polar ship by the French Polar Expeditions, rechristened the *Commandant-Charcot*, then fitted by the French Navy and put under the direction of Commander Max Douguet, who had been second-in-command of the French Mission to Greenland during the second International Polar Year.

The first expedition took place (after an attempt in 1948-49 was halted by the ice, which was impassable that year) under the direction of André Frank Liotard in 1949-50. The cargo included a motor launch and a 165-horsepower Stinson aircraft as well as dogs, sledges and Weasel caterpillars.

The Port Martin Station contained a hut sheltering a kitchen, a washhouse, storerooms for provisions, an electric power plant fed by a diesel engine, storage batteries, and a full range of equipment with which to carry out the program of scientific research. The living conditions were rigorous, in spite of the comforts of the base. In Adélie Coast, the winds come directly from the Pole without meeting any obstacle in between, and they reach speeds of 100 m.p.h., and even 150 m.p.h. or more at certain points. There are blizzards on an average of eight days out of ten in this land near the South Pole which Mawson had christened the "home of the blizzard." Human efficiency was drastically reduced in these conditions. The efficiency of scientific equipment was also endangered; anemometers toppled over, radio antennas were twisted out of shape, recording instruments were filled with powdery snow; the variations in the magnetic field were so great that they exceeded the instruments' capacity to compensate; radio contact was often blacked out.

Nevertheless, twelve expeditions were undertaken, both by Weasel and by dog sledge, and were successfully completed within six months. One covered 375 miles in the interior, on the glacial highlands, while another discovered one of the largest colonies of Emperor penguins, the fifth to be found up to that time, on the Pointe Géologie peninsula.

On January 9, 1951, the *Commandant-Charcot*, still captained by Commander Douguet, picked up the Liotard group and replaced them with the members of Michel Barré's team, the scientific program of which was very nearly identical with that undertaken by the International Geophysical Year six years later. In April 1951, dog-sledge runs began, and on June 10, two Weasels with sledges, each with a four-man crew, arrived at Pointe Géologie to study the Emperor penguin; this was one of the first excursions ever successfully attempted in the middle of the winter night. When the team reached the rookery, the vehicles' spotlights were turned on and picked out 5,000 penguins at one time; they were pressed up one against another in an enormous, compact mass. Each penguin was incubating a single egg between its legs and the downy fold formed by its abdominal skin. Here was an exceptional spectacle indeed, and one never before seen by human eyes.

In July 1951, a serious surgical problem arose, when a member of the crew had to be operated on twice for an intestinal obstruction, each of the operations lasting two hours. With the aid of the other members of the expedition, Dr. Cendron carried out the operations successfully.

The polar ship *Tottan*, which had been chartered by the French Polar Expeditions, picked up the whole crew on February 2, 1952; their entire program had been carried out. However, during the night of January 23, at 3:20 A.M. on the twenty-fourth (twenty minutes after the hourly inspection) fire broke out and destroyed the principal building. All scientific results and baggage were, nevertheless, saved. The Barré team and the relief team under René Garcia were thus forced to put to sea again. The *Tottan* dropped three men at Pointe Géologie, thereby bringing the number of men at the winter camp commanded by Mario Marret to seven. In February 1953, everyone returned to France, leaving Adélie Coast deserted till January 1956.

In the north, the French Polar Expeditions were in the field from 1948 to 1953 under my command. Their most notable achievement was the taking of systematic seismic soundings of the Greenland glacial cap, in order to determine the profile of the rocky substratum. The peculiar conditions under which the summer thaw took place in these regions required rigorous timing on the part of the explorer and demanded that the Weasels—the mainstay of the expedition—deliver performances for which these vehicles had not been originally intended.

The M29C Weasel is an amphibious caterpillar-type vehicle borrowed from United States Army surplus supplies left in France after the war. Its weak point is its flexible caterpillar track with independent metallic links attached to two rubber treads reinforced with four cables. Certain modifications were made in it in order to facilitate its use in a polar climate; it was to be given a new body. This was a hull made of double sheets of aluminum and plywood separated by a layer of spun glass an inch thick. There was room for two men inside it. A Duralumin sledge weighing 200 pounds empty and designed to carry a load of two tons could be harnessed to each Weasel. Some sledges were set up permanently as laboratories or trailers; both metallic sledges and trailers were innovations in polar technique.

Air support was provided by planes based in Iceland, which transported either loads that could be parachuted from an altitude of 600 feet or else less-fragile equipment that could simply be released by a low-flying plane, which was again an entirely new polar technique.

A permanent base, the Central Station, was set up at the point where Wegener's *Eismitte* had been in 1930-31. The 1948 mission, whose task was to prepare the ground for future expeditions, had twenty-three members and left Rouen on May 15 aboard the ship *Force* loaded with 110 tons of equipment.

Thirty-five men, including eight who stayed through the winter, took part in the 1949 expedition. On July 1, the first convoy set out for the future Central Station. This convoy consisted of five Weasels and seven sledges, manned by a crew of twenty-two and transporting eight tons of equipment and two laboratory cabins. Despite the very unfavorable weather conditions, the western detachment succeeded in running forty-nine convoys of equipment. As for the air crew, they put in 124 hours of flight time in ten days, transporting 25 tons of fuel, 10 tons of provisions and 15 tons of equipment. When, on the twenty-fourth, the ground detachment began its retreat to the west, the station was ready for use; laboratories, supplies and housing were buried under the snow and connected by 400 feet of tunnels.

During the winter operations of 1949-50 under the direction of Robert Guillard, a minimum temperature of −87° F. and a maximum wind speed of 94 m.p.h. were registered. Relief came in July 1950; the ship *Hillevaag* (which lost her propeller in the ice floes off Cape Farewell), relayed by the *Force,* brought thirty men, including nine men for the winter camp under the direction of Paul Voguet, and 160 tons of equipment. It was during the summer of 1950 that the first round-trip crossing of the inland ice was achieved by a convoy of Weasels.

The 1951 expedition was plunged into mourning by the accident which cost the Frenchman Alain Joset and the Danish representative Jens Jarl their lives. Their train of Weasels with their towed sledges had crossed the inland ice and was approaching the west coast, in the direction of Mount Forel on August 4, 1951. The look of the snow had changed noticeably over the preceding few miles, but no crevasses had been detected. They had crossed four without suspecting they had done so; then a fifth opened up and barred the way in front of Joset's Weasel. He decided to outflank it and turned back. The snow-bridge over the last crevasse, which he had crossed safely on the journey out, gave way and the Weasel tumbled 160 feet into the void, taking its occupants and a ton and a half of equipment. When it was possible to get down to the wreckage, it was discovered that Joset and Jarl had been killed instantly. Only their notes were saved.

When the expeditions to Greenland were suspended for a time in 1952, more than 75,000 miles had been covered by the Weasels. More than half the surface of the Greenland glacial ice cap had been explored (an area twice as large as France) and a map had been drawn up—the first of its kind—of the rocky subsoil buried under 10,000 feet of ice. Thus, thanks to the efforts of, and the results obtained by, the French Polar Expeditions, results for which a high price in energy and human life had been paid, France found herself in a position to play her part in the gigantic concert of the International Geophysical Year.

26

THE FLOATING ISLANDS

On August 14, 1946, the observer aboard one of the American B-29 flying weather laboratories which crisscrossed the Arctic daily suddenly noticed an enormous, unfamiliar spot on the radar screen; it lay in the middle of the ice pack at 76° 10′ N. by 160° 10′ E. It was about 20 miles by 12 and resembled a glacial icecap surrounded by high, icy cliffs. It could only be an unknown floating island, situated at that moment about three hundred miles from Alaska. This discovery, which was carefully kept secret by the Pentagon, was going to revolutionize the techniques of polar exploration.

Lieutenant Colonel Joseph O. Fletcher of the United States Air

Force was so interested by this discovery that he devoted himself to a long series of studies and observations on the subject. He read through the whole of polar literature and noted that, in 1821, Parry had also observed a gigantic ice floe fifty feet high and that, in 1872, Nares too had made a note of floes composed of ancient ice, which he called "paleocrystic." In 1882, Greely had run into the same thing; so had Nansen; and Storkersen had lived on one (8 by 17 miles in dimension) for seven months.

A systematic investigation undertaken by the United States weather planes gave evidence of the fact that this island, called Target I, or T1, was moving. On August 21, 1950, a second island, T2, was sighted at 86° 40′ N. Finally, on August 31, T3 was discovered at 75° N. On August 1, 1951, T1 was found again to the north of Ellesmere Island, where it seemed to be immobilized; a study of the photographic documents revealed the fact that its outlines were identical with those of a bay, from which it must have broken free. Since these islands seemed to describe immense, rather regular circuits in the midst of the Arctic Ocean, and through those regions which were classified as "inaccessible," and since they passed close by the Pole, Fletcher envisaged the possibility of setting up permanent drifting observatories on them, to carry out scientific missions and to serve as rescue and directional centers for air traffic.

The Pentagon kept its secret till 1950, but the Russians, for their part, did not wait that long before they attempted to carry out the same operation. From 1947 onward, three Russian stations were functioning on the pack ice. It was in 1948 that Gakkel, using sounding techniques, discovered the Lomonosov Mountains, the peaks of which lie less than 3,250 feet below the surface. From April 1950 to April 1951, Mikhail Somov occupied a base which drifted from 76° 02′ N. by 166° 30′ W. to 81° 45′ N. by 162° 20′ W. and at which he had at his disposal a tracked snow vehicle.[1] The station was called NP2 (NP1 being that of Papanin). Later on, the Russians set up stations NP3 and NP4, both equipped with every modern device. Interstation chess games were even carried on by radio.

Fletcher thought that a base on a floating island would furnish climatic information of a crucial kind. But it was only in Decem-

---

[1] Probably of the GAZ-67 type.

ber 1950 that the Americans decided to establish a base on T3, a kidney-shaped island 5 miles by 10. Previous observation had revealed that it had covered about 1,200 miles from April 1947 to July 1950 at an average speed of a mile a day.[2] It was, moreover, slowly approaching the Pole, in whose neighborhood it would pass, if all went as expected, in March or April of 1952. Beyond this, T3 was moving very nearly along the "Ptarmigan Line," the route which the 58th Squadron followed on its way from Alaska to the Pole for weather observation missions.

Fletcher, who was then thirty-one years old and had the enthusiasm of a schoolboy, drew up his plan. It consisted of three phases: sighting and landing on T3, followed by the building of a temporary camp; the setting up of a permanent base; and, finally, the full exploitation of the island.

Just as Papanin had chosen to make his departure base on Franz Josef Land, Fletcher picked Thule as his center of operations. The tiny village of Thule, which had been dear to the hearts of Peary and Rasmussen, had grown in less than a year into the most important air base of the United States Air Force. To build it, the Americans had deployed the most colossal resources imaginable. A gigantic airlift had been organized between Westover Field, in Massachusetts, and Thule; a thousand workmen and two thousand tons of equipment and building materials were transported at the outset; their assignment was to begin by installing an airfield for heavy planes.

At the same time, the most formidable sea convoy since the Normandy landings of 1944, including fifty cargo ships and tankers, icebreakers, tugs and hundreds of miscellaneous landing craft were making their way to Thule via the Baffin Sea. An artificial harbor was built in North Star Bay, using prefabricated jetties of a more modern design than those used in the artificial harbor at Arromanches. On August 16, 1951, the cargo ships were able to tie up at the first of the 1,000-foot-long jetties. Two hundred thousand tons of building material for the airport and its substructure were unloaded by 7,500 workmen, who were paid $1,500 a month each. A boom town sprang up, with cafés, clubs, churches, movie theaters and a radio station with an antenna 400 feet high. There were telephones, an electric power station and community

---

[2] Kaare Rodahl, *North*.

heating, as well as a bus line. The whole complex covered 500 acres; it cost $300,000,000.

As for Fletcher, he had planned nothing more for the first landing on T3 than a mountain tent with double sides for from four to six men and a fireproof tent, as well as Primus stoves.

The first thing to be done was to establish the exact position of T3, and on March 14 a squadron of four Skymaster C-54's with fuel for a sixteen-hour flight took off from Thule for the north. A half hour after it had passed the Pole, T3 was sighted by radar at 88° 17′ N. by 166° 30′ W. The great departure took place on March 19, 1952. A twin-engined Dakota C-47 equipped with wheeled skis took off from the new 10,000-foot airstrip, followed by three C-54 cargo planes. Major General William D. Old, who was in command of the United States Air Force's tactical bases, joined the flight.

When T3 was sighted, Fletcher tossed a number of smoke-flares overboard onto "his" island (it was to bear his name); their smoke indicated that storm winds were blowing up. After brushing the snow several times with his plane's skis, the pilot, Captain Lew Erhart, succeeded in landing. The temperature was 58 below zero. The plane sank halfway into the deep snow.

"If you want to go back," General Old said to Fletcher, "there's still time."

"I'm staying," Fletcher groaned.

He then gave orders for the C-54's to parachute his equipment. The lightened C-47 took off, carrying the general and a *Life* reporter.

There were only three men left on T3, Colonel Fletcher, Dr. Kaare Rodahl and Captain Michael F. Brinegar, all of them sunk belly-deep in the snow at a temperature of 58 degrees below zero, in the middle of a vast sheet of ice swept by a terrifying wind. They managed to set up their tent. Then, having eaten a frozen meal, they turned in in their sleeping bags, which were heated with electric batteries. The next day they realized they would be able to build the landing strip for the C-54's which were to be sent them from Thule; they did, however, keep in contact with the Thule base through the B-29 weather planes which flew overhead. For a fortnight, they did not know what fate awaited them. The authorities hesitated to leave them where they were. But then a C-47 landed on T3 with two scientists and Tundra, Fletcher's dog. The Pentagon had given Fletcher's project the green light.

T3 became Fletcher Island, the first American floating polar station. Later on, there was a landing strip on which even a 100-ton Globemaster could land without skis. The station was evacuated in 1954, because its drift was bringing it close to the coastal Alert Station on Ellesmere Island. A new team reoccupied it in 1957, within the framework of the International Geophysical Year. In 1958, despite its 160-foot thickness, T3 broke apart and had to be evacuated under emergency conditions.

Considerable scientific results were obtained through the T3 observations, notably information concerning the configuration of the Arctic basin. On May 3, 1952, a C-47 equipped with skis and wheels took Joe Fletcher to the Pole, which then lay some 150 miles from T3. It landed there, as the planes of Papanin's expedition had done in 1937, and as Lieutenant Colonel William P. Benedict of the United States Air Force had done a few months before.

The T3 adventure persuaded the United States to increase the number of these floating stations. The United States even looked forward to precipitating the birth of new T3s by artificial means, by detaching sections of the Shelf Islands which were still connected to the land. For such islands are of considerable strategic importance. Quite apart from their usefulness as bases for the radio-direction of aircraft and for weather observation, they can be made to serve as fuel supply bases and landing fields for combat planes. They are also, thanks to their radar equipment, the advance sentinels of the West. They are, moreover, unsinkable. Thus, it is not surprising that a number of these floating islands are in existence today, and that both the United States and the U.S.S.R. keep their equipment and the positions of a certain number of them a matter of the utmost secrecy.

27

THE INTERNATIONAL GEOPHYSICAL YEAR

Followed by the trail of white smoke from its four engines, the Globemaster slowly described a large circle in the sky; below lay the South Pole. "I'll make three passes," said Lieutenant Commander Gus Shinn, the pilot of the old DC-3 *Che Sera Sera*, "one at 400 feet, one at 200, and then drag the surface at 100 feet. If it looks all right, I'll come in for a landing." Then, in an enormous sea of snow, the *Che Sera Sera* landed and came to a stop.

It was October 31, 1956, at 8:34 A.M., and the temperature was 58 below zero. Admiral George J. Dufek, the officer in charge of Operation Deep Freeze, as he got out of the airplane and trod the polar ice that only Amundsen and Scott had ever trod before him, was performing the opening act in what has been called "mankind's greatest peaceful adventure since the Renaissance": the International Geophysical Year of 1957-58.

At the time of the first International Polar Year, in 1882-83, the one in which General Greely so distinguished himself, it had been decided that, in future, projects of this kind should be organized every fifty years. The second polar year thus occurred in 1932-33 and thirty-four nations participated in it. It achieved remarkable results.

According to the original plan, then, it was in 1982-83 that the third international year was to have been organized. But the progress of science had undergone such enormous development that the need for more thorough information about our globe, and to have it right away, was soon felt. For this globe, Earth, is terribly possessive of her secrets. We had arrived at a point where we must set out on an over-all study of the earth, in its astronomical context. The era of partial exploration was over. The advance of technology had provided us with the means for carrying out a massive exploration of the planet, beginning, quite naturally, with its two poles.

The idea of pushing this exploration forward was born on April 5, 1950, in the United States, during a small dinner party at Dr. James A. Van Allen's Silver Springs, Maryland, home, to which he had invited several world-famous figures in geophysics, and particularly Professor Sydney Chapman, who was later to preside most capably over the I.G.Y. It was suggested that the interval between international years be reduced from fifty to twenty-five years and that the next one take place in 1957, a date which was all the more desirable as that year coincided with the opening of a period of intense solar activity. The idea was submitted to the International Council of Scientific Societies, which approved it and, in 1952, created a special committee for the International Geophysical Year.

In 1955, the report on the general program was unanimously approved. For the most remarkable aspect of this whole extraordinary scientific adventure was the spirit of co-operation shared by all the participating nations. Tens of thousands of scientists, from sixty-seven different countries, worked together in the most perfect harmony on a common program, at more than two thousand principal stations and an even higher number of secondary stations scattered over the face of the earth from the drifting stations at the North Pole to the station set up at the very heart of the South Pole. Observations were gathered and co-ordinated at three world centers, where all documents were immediately reproduced and sent on to the other centers. Any private organization whatever, even private persons, could obtain a copy of these results merely by paying the costs of printing.

The spirit of co-operation was total, as can easily be seen from one glance at the Antarctic, where eleven nations established stations. Russian scientists came to work at American stations and vice versa. When an Australian fell seriously ill, the Russians sent him a doctor who stayed with him until an American plane could pick him up. Likewise, when a member of Sir Vivian Fuchs's team nearly died of asphyxiation from the exhaust fumes of a Snocat engine, the American pilots flew him in bottles of oxygen, in spite of unfavorable weather conditions.

In this world-wide collaboration, the poles were more than ever before the two pivots on which the whole effort turned, through their unique geographic and climatic position, through their innate scientific interest, and, of course, through the fact that they presented the greatest difficulties and so were the site of the smallest number of observatories.

The I.G.Y. opened on July 1, 1957, at one minute past midnight and lasted officially till midnight, December 31, 1958. Its program included matters within the sphere of very nearly every scientific discipline. The practical means at its disposal were exceptional. On the technological side, the I.G.Y. marks the beginning of the total mechanization of polar techniques.

Airplanes ranged from the two-seater Auster reconnaissance plane used by the New Zealand section of the British Transantarctic Expedition to the largest transports in the world, the American expedition's four-engine Globemasters. Helicopters ranged from the French expedition's two-seater Djinns in Adélie Coast to the enormous Russian helicopters used at Mirny Station, or the Japanese expedition's S-58's. Ships were of all types and tonnages, including 8,300-ton icebreakers like the U.S.S. *Glacier* and transports of 12,500 tons like the Soviet *Ob*; caterpillar vehicles ranged from the classic Weasels and Snocats of the French Polar Expeditions and the British Transantarctic Expedition to the Americans' and Russians' 30-ton tractors.

The French Dumont d'Urville Base even had an overhead railway, as well as a ground railway. More than 500 tons of equipment was transported by air to the South Pole, and as much again was brought by heavy tractor to Byrd Station across more than 600 miles of ice riddled with crevasses, each of which could have swallowed up an entire train. Each individual room at the Russian base had a telephone, while more than one million gallons of gasoline was stored at the American McMurdo Base on Ross Island. There were washing machines, record players (including a high-fidelity set at the South Pole equipped with a supply of two hundred long-playing records), all the showers you could ask for, radar sets, electric power stations, the most varied, most complicated, most highly perfected scientific instruments. It would be difficult to make an accurate evaluation of the cost of all this, but for the Antarctic alone, it is clear that the figure must run to at least several hundreds of millions of dollars.

To get a fair idea of the extent of the operations, we need do no more than examine, only briefly, the American and Russian installations on the southern continent during the I.G.Y. Highly familiar as they were with the modern polar techniques developed in the Arctic, the Russians were among the nations best equipped to attack the Antarctic. The Russian expedition commanded by Mikhail Somov arrived at the beginning of January 1956; it comprised, among other things, the enormous freighter *Ob*, equipped with catapults for airplanes and a landing platform, and the refrigerator ship *Lena* which transported the provisions. The air fleet, composed of helicopters and planes of all sizes, was commanded by Ivan Cherevishny, a Hero of the Soviet Union. The helicopters were MI4's. The planes were heavy twin-engine Ilyushin 12's and LI2's; there was also a single-engine AN2 equipped with skis which was used on long reconnaissance flights.

The Russians called the coast Pravda and chose for their base a granite promontory on which they built a town composed of twenty-four large prefabricated buildings, set up on a 200-yard-long main street, Lenin Street. The buildings had central heating. The town's architect was named A. M. Afnasyev, and its elected mayor was G. I. Greku. The town was called Mirny, in honor of Bellingshausen's ship. There was a most impressive parking lot.

Along with special vehicles like repair trucks and bulldozers, this lot was filled mainly with C80's, KD35's and with ZIS 151 and GAZ 91 automobiles. The C80 has been the most widely used tractor in the Russian Arctic regions since 1948. Weighing 11.4 tons and with 93 horsepower it has a force of traction of nine tons. It is a sturdy, reliable vehicle with interchangeable caterpillar tracks which may be adapted to the condition of the ground. The Kirovets KD35 (with bulldozer equipment for work on the air-field) weighs 3.7 tons and has 37 horsepower. On a snowy surface, these tractors can pull a four-ton load. The wheeled automobile GAZ 69 manufactured by the Gorki Automobile Works weighs 3,350 pounds and has 55 horsepower. It is used for light haulage at the base. If need be, it can be equipped with a snowplow for leveling off landing fields. The all-terrain automobile ZIS 151 (90 horsepower; weight, 5½ tons; load, 2½ tons) is fitted out either as a repair truck or for fuel haulage or as a radio vehicle.

GAZ 47's equipped with caterpillar tracks and C80's were the vehicles which were most used for the heavy work of exploration on the continent. It was the GAZ 47 which played the largest role in the creation of the Pionerskaya Station, 250 miles inland from Mirny, although C80 tractors also participated by hauling sledge trains weighing as much as twenty tons. The C80's were equipped with superchargers which enabled them to go on working under conditions of low atmospheric pressure.

In 1957, the Russians built four more stations, including Vostok near the Geomagnetic Pole and nearly 900 miles from Mirny, and Sovietskaya in the area of the pole of relative inaccessibility 1,250 miles from Mirny. To transport the hundreds of tons of equipment required for the new stations, 400-horsepower all-terrain tractors were used. These were built at Kharkov, in the U.S.S.R., and were remarkably comfortable to travel in. Finally, in spite of all their mechanization, the Russians brought sledge dogs with them which were used on the bases.

But however great the Russian effort may have been, it seemed almost modest next to the gigantic Antarctic operations of the United States on the occasion of the I.G.Y. These were christened Operation Deep Freeze. They began in 1955 under the command of Admiral George J. Dufek, and they consisted in setting up and keeping seven American bases going. Of course, in boats and in men, Deep Freeze seemed less massive than High Jump, but in fact, thanks to the enormous progress that had been made in just a few years, it was far more important. Admiral Byrd participated in the operation as "officer in charge." But it was George J. Dufek, who was specially promoted by Congress to the rank of rear admiral, whose task it was actually to direct the project.

From 1955 onward, it consisted of 1,800 men and seven ships: icebreakers of the U.S.S. *Glacier* model, 8,600 tons and 21,000 horsepower, the most powerful then in existence, the *Edisto* and the *Eastwind;* the cargo ships *Arneb* and *Wyandotte;* the freighter *Greenville Victory;* and the tanker *Nespelen.* The ships carried light planes and helicopters. But for the first time, an air fleet flew directly from the United States to Antarctica, via New Zealand.

It consisted of eight planes: two Douglas R5D transports, which could land only on wheels; two twin-engined Neptune P2V's, patrol bombers equipped with skis on wheels; two Douglas R4D transports; a naval version of the Dakota DC-3, also with wheels on skis; and two Albatross triphibians, capable of landing on wheels, skis or pontoons. The light planes transported by ship were four DeHavilland Otters, single-engined planes designed for the Canadian wilds, and three Sikorsky HO4S-3 helicopters.

The expedition arrived at McMurdo Bay on December 17, 1955. A team led by Gordon Ebbe, the head of the naval air detachment, set off immediately by helicopter in search of a site for the first great international airport in Antarctica, where heavy planes for the various expeditions would be able to land. A spot was chosen near Hut Point, the site of Scott's base in 1901. Within forty-eight hours, an ice airstrip nearly 8,000 feet long had been opened up with bulldozers and marked out with red flags. On December 20, eight planes that had taken off from Christchurch, New Zealand, 2,500 miles away, landed without difficulty; this was the first time that a flight had been made to Antarctica from an outside base, and the first time that wheeled aircraft had landed on the ice.

The Seabees then set to work to build the two bases, Little America V and McMurdo, the task which formed Deep Freeze's objective number one for 1955-56.

Deep Freeze II (1956-57) had as its principal objective the building of five more bases: Ellsworth, Hallet, Wilkes (materials for these three could all be brought by ship), then Byrd Station, and finally, South Pole Station itself (both of which could be provisioned only by air or by dog sledge). The most spectacular of these bases was obviously the one at the South Pole, which had to be airborne entirely.

The Air Force furnished six Globemasters, capable of parachuting fourteen tons of equipment on each flight. They were based at McMurdo, but only flew over the Pole, without ever landing. A long airstrip was built on the sea ice, two miles from the McMurdo base. A special technique, which had been developed in Greenland, consisted in packing the snow with enormous rollers made from thick, hollow cylinders filled with frozen water. But as this method gave bad results, it was decided to build the airstrip on the new sea ice, which was hardened with a priming layer of sea water. The six-foot-thick snow was first cleared from an area 130 feet wide and 6,000 feet long. It took 100,000 man-hours in temperatures that went as low as —72° F.

On October 31, 1956, came Admiral Dufek's reconnaissance flight on board the *Che Sera Sera,* during the course of which he landed at the Pole while the Globemaster escort circled overhead. An American flag was planted in the snow, and a metal star was deposited as a radar guide-point; this was to be the first electronic beacon at the South Pole, by which planes arriving from McMurdo would be able to navigate.

On November 20, two R4D's landed once again at the Pole, delivering Lieutenant Bowers with eleven dogs, sledges and other essential equipment; a Globemaster parachuted a Weasel and its fuel. Bowers found by his theodolite that the exact site of the Pole was nine miles further on; as the Weasel had broken down, he made the journey there by dog sledge, as Amundsen had done forty-five years earlier. The massive parachuting operation began: in eighty-four round-trip journeys, more than 700 tons of equipment was dropped from the sky, on wide, colored parachutes. The setting up of the station began under the direction of Paul Siple, who joined Bowers, bringing a new team with him.

The seventeen members of the wintering team finally settled into an ultramodern town, which was called Amundsen-Scott. Each of the seventeen had cost Uncle Sam a million dollars. The cost was further increased by the loss of three Globemasters in accidents on the landing strip at McMurdo. Any spot of oil or the tiniest scrap of paper could bring the ice to melting point and sow the strip with hollows, making it necessary to "ice-concrete" by spreading thousands of tons of snow and water before going over the strip with the rollers. The Globemaster pilots were hindered, they said, by the fact that the McMurdo strip was marked only with oil drums painted black and orange, rather than with small fir trees, the system they had been used to in the Arctic. At the beginning of November twenty-five 6-foot-high firs were planted; they were the first trees in the Antarctic.

The mechanical equipment used for ground transport by Deep Freeze I, II, III, and IV was colossal. At the outset, it consisted of twelve D8 tractors, nine D2 tractors, three HT4's equipped with hinged arms, thirteen D315 diesel generator groups (including two which functioned nonstop at the South Pole), and two H342 diesel groups. Of the D8 tractors, ten were of the "low ground pressure" model, 23½ feet long (as opposed to 15½ for the ordinary D8). They weighed 35 tons, but the width of their caterpillar tracks reduced the pressure to a maximum of 14.2 pounds per square inch. The best machines for hauling loads were the D4 tractors, of which McMurdo had two and Little America one. The thirteen Weasels were used essentially as exploration vehicles. An army jeep with rubber tires did excellent work at McMurdo. An antitank vehicle, the *Ontos,* was tried briefly, but it soon became clear that it was too heavy, despite its 145 horsepower.

The most remarkable achievement of Deep Freeze II was the establishment of Byrd Station more than 600 miles from Little America V, all the equipment and building materials for which were transported by tractor train under the direction of Commander Frazier. After a thorough air reconnaissance had been made, a convoy set out from Little America V on November 5, 1956; it was composed of two LGPD8's, a Snocat and two Weasels.

One of the Weasels was equipped with a crevasse detector which had been developed in Greenland. It was composed of five semispherical electrodes mounted on the front of the Weasel and designed to rub over the surface of the ice. An electric current running through the electrodes enabled the operator to note variations in the conductive power of the granular ice, or firn, and thereby to detect crevasses with a high degree of accuracy. When the electrode passed over a crevasse, a small red light switched on in front of the driver.

A week after its departure, the column was halted at a point 125 miles from the base in a region which was extremely thick with crevasses. It took two weeks to find a passage 7½ miles long and 30 feet wide, which went under the name "Fashion Lane." Crevasses were dealt with by an entirely new technique; the snow bridges and lips were caved in with explosives, then the gap was filled by a bulldozer until it became possible to pass.

It was not till December that the route was judged to be in sufficiently good condition to take the greater part of the load. On December 6, a convoy composed of one Weasel and six D8 tractors, each pulling two 20-ton sledges, left Little America V. The train moved along nonstop, the teams of drivers relaying one another and eating while on the move. It arrived at Byrd Station on December 23 and was back at Little America on January 5. Twenty-three days later a second train, commanded by Major Palle Mogesson, set out. It transported 220 tons of equipment and reached Byrd a month later. The way was marked with flags and with 13-foot-high snow cairns topped with an oil drum. Gas depots had been brought by air and lay at the 280-, 340- and 560-mile markers. These depots included provisions and explosives as well as some 66,000 gallons of fuel.

But, though it is true that nothing could surpass the Americans' Antarctic performance during the I.G.Y. for scope, for sheer size, it is equally true that, in the popular imagination, Sir Vivian Fuchs and Sir Edmund Hillary's great transcontinental run was a subject of equal interest. During the winter of 1956, Hillary, the conqueror of Everest, trained his team in the mountains of southern New Zealand; then the polar ship *John Biscoe*, rechristened the *Endeavour*, transported the New Zealand crew to McMurdo Sound.

Hillary was in command of a scientific group for the I.G.Y. as well as of the New Zealand section of Vivian Fuchs's British Transantarctic Expedition. His task consisted basically in exploring, preparing and marking the last 750 miles of Fuchs's route; the latter was to set out from Shackleton base, on Filchner Ice Shelf in the Weddell Sea, and travel to Ross Island via the South Pole.

On October 14, 1957, Sir Edmund left Scott Station on Ross Island with three members of his team, to carry out his mission. His train was composed of three Ferguson tractors and a Weasel towing a camp trailer on skis and sledges loaded with provisions. The Ferguson tractors chosen by the New Zealanders were in fact overhauled farm tractors, and they had none of the comforts of the Weasel. Though they were the perfect vehicle for transport around the base, they proved ill-adapted for long runs, especially in deep snow. But thanks to the men who were handling them, they carried out their assignments with perfect success. The tracks were badly adjusted, the brake system was often insufficient and the ventilation was imperfect. The load that could be hauled varied from two tons on favorable terrain to one ton over deep snow. "In fact," Sir Edmund wrote later, "I would not at all recommend using them for a long polar run where the snow is deep and the crevasses frequent." The train was often halted by accidents and by falls into the crevasses.

On December 26, 1957, Hillary set up Depot 700, at the end-point of his run, a run which had been carried out, in spite of everything, under good conditions of safety, since the route was within the range of Hillary's own planes and of the American planes on the McMurdo-South Pole airlift.

The world-wide press coverage of him began with the famous headline in an American paper, "Conqueror of Everest Drives Toward South Pole," and ended with accusations against Sir Edmund, who was charged with having "let Fuchs down." [1] In fact, it happened that when he arrived at the site of Depot 700, a supplementary depot which had not been originally planned for and which Fuchs requested, he was nearer to the Pole than to his departure base. He then decided, with the full agreement of the leader of his expedition, to go on south. From the Pole, he was able to fly back to his base on Ross Island, where he was to wait for Fuchs's radio calls. The English press in particular presented the whole thing as a "race," a "competition," like the one between Amundsen and Scott. He then returned to the Pole to wait for Fuchs.

For his part, Sir Vivian Fuchs left Shackleton Station on the coast of the Weddell Sea after a long series of reconnaissance flights. His train consisted of three Snocats, two Weasels and a Muskeg towing sledges loaded with provisions, fuel and scientific equipment. It also included two teams of dogs. He scaled Recovery Glacier and reached the British advance station, South Ice, on December 15, 1957. A "historic race" was the farthest thing from Fuchs's mind; he was committed to a rigorous scientific program, and so his average speed over entirely unknown country was all the slower.

With something like military precision, Sir Vivian arrived within

---

[1] Hillary has even been accused of setting off the press coverage in order to advertise Ferguson tractors.

sight of the polar station at 9:00 A.M. on January 20, exactly as he had planned. Sir Edmund and Admiral Dufek greeted him warmly. Here are the historic words that were exchanged on that occasion:

"How happy I am to see you again!" Sir Vivian cried to Hillary.

"Wonderful to see you again, Bunny!" (Bunny is Fuchs's nickname), Hillary said, while shaking his hand vigorously before the reporters and cameramen.

"I was sure you would make it," said Admiral Dufek in his turn. "What do you think about a bath and a good meal?"

"I think that wouldn't be too bad an idea," Fuchs answered with a smile.

Afraid of being outrun by the winter, Fuchs decided to start off again soon afterward, and, in order to make better time, he asked the admiral to take his dogs back to McMurdo for him. On March 2, 1958, Fuchs, Hillary and their team arrived at Scott Station, which was swarming with reporters; they had brought Shackleton's dream to life. Arm in arm, the two men stood having their photographs taken. Thanks to the use of modern techniques, they had just completed the "last great journey in the world." At dessert, following the great banquet attended by everyone then at McMurdo, a telegram was brought to Vivian Ernest Fuchs; he had just been knighted by the British government, like Parry, McClintock, Nares, Ross and Shackleton before him.

Meanwhile, the French Polar Expeditions were continuing their slow, unglamorous scientific work at the two principal stations, Dumont d'Urville and Charcot. It was during the southern spring of 1956, on October 1, that Robert Gaillard set out from the coast with three Weasels and two Snocats to build the Charcot Station in the region of the South Magnetic Pole, nearly two hundred miles from the main base, on the Antarctic highland. The building used for living quarters at this station had been designed and built in France in three semicylindrical sections which were loaded onto sledges. The run took three months as a result of a long period of bad weather; a blizzard lasted uninterruptedly for nineteen days.

When the Imbert expedition arrived on the spot in January 1957, the three men who were going to winter under Jacques Dubois's direction in the heart of the Antarctic winter in this 13-by-20-foot half-cylinder found the station fully installed and were able to begin on their scientific observations immediately. During the winter of 1957, the temperature at Charcot Station went down to 80 below zero, while it never went lower than 22 below at Dumont d'Urville; at the South Pole, the Americans registered 99 below zero, and the Russians had 125 below at the Pole of Inaccessibility (in August 1958). During the winter, a member of the expedition suffered an attack of appendicitis; a successful operation was done by Dr. Goy, assisted by all the others.

In 1958, at the time of the Rouillon expedition, Dubois and his men were relieved at Charcot Station by a team headed by René Garcia. Finally, in January 1959, Rouillon was relieved by René Merle. France's scientific mission within the framework of the International Geophysical Year had been brought to a successful conclusion. The year ended on the firing of the first artificial satellite into space, an event which opened the prodigious interplanetary era.

The tally of the Geophysical Year's achievements is impressive. Submitted to the scrutiny of a myriad of scientific eyes, our planet finally offered us an entirely new portrait of herself.

For eighteen months men from all over the earth, happily reconciled in their scientific venture, united to explore the floors of the oceans, the hearts of the mountains, the depths of the volcanoes, the vastnesses of the ice floes, and the tiniest molecules of the upper atmosphere, using every technical instrument, device and piece of apparatus that had been developed over centuries of effort. The map of the ocean depths could thus be drawn up and the previously unfathomed chasms of the Pacific explored.

Several theories on the origin, formation and development of life on the earth have been brought forward, all drawing their support from the considerable sum of observations assembled during the I.G.Y.

The waters and the winds began to give up some of their secrets. True undersea rivers, whose very existence had been unsuspected, were discovered, one of which, the Cromwell Current (named for the man who died after having discovered it), is nearly 250 miles wide, with a greater volume of water than the Mississippi, a length of 8,000 miles and a speed of 2½ miles per hour.

At a depth of 6,000 feet in the Atlantic, the scientists of the I.G.Y. made a discovery which refuted all previous assumptions about the circulation of currents in that ocean. It had been thought that currents were created by the wind and were to be found mainly on the surface. But, because of the salt content and the temperature of the water, as well as the earth's rotation, which tends to accumulate more water in the west of the Atlantic than in the east, it was felt that, logically, the waters of the Gulf Stream must be replenished by a "counter-Gulf Stream," which would carry masses of cold water back from the Arctic. A series of observations in depth (made with Nansen bottles, swallow floats, and cameras which photographed the motion of ping-pong balls in depth) demonstrated the existence of a powerful and cold, southward-moving countercurrent less than 3,300 feet below the Gulf Stream.

A complete weather map was established, bringing out for the first time, the general patterns of wind currents over the surface of the globe. A map of the floor of the Arctic Ocean was drawn up, showing depths of more than 16,000 feet, mountain ranges and highlands, including the Alpha Rise, discovered by the American drifting station Alpha.

For the first time, an over-all description of the Antarctic was made. The first fact noted by the scientists was that the continent supported 40 per cent more ice than had previously been supposed. In fact, 90 per cent of the ice in the world lies on it.

During the polar night, the Antarctic air is as much as 72 degrees colder than the air over neighboring regions which are still heated by the sun; this immense difference in temperature and in barometric pressure creates violent air currents, which, added to the earth's rotation, whip around the South Pole at more than 190 miles per hour. The same phenomenon is also to be found at the North Pole, though on a more modest scale, and for the same reasons.

Thanks mainly to observations made in the polar regions, the I.G.Y. was able to bring forward a new theory for magnetic phenomena. The central nucleus of the earth, which is extremely radioactive, solid and probably composed of iron, is now thought to be surrounded by an outer nucleus; in the beginning, this metal "churn" set up a weak electric current which produced a weak electric field. The particles of metal moving through this field in turn set up new currents; the whole process resulted in the magnetic field which we may observe today, which is thought to be further influenced and disturbed by the moon and more particularly by the sun. It is believed that our terrestrial magnetic field not only picks up particles from the sun but also traps those from outer space. The origin and mechanism of the famous polar lights were also studied at great length, as were those of the aspects of solar activity which exert an influence on our life on earth.

The true character of the Antarctic continent was revealed. It was discovered that a great part of the land mass lies below sea level, and that a channel under the ice connects the Amundsen Sea with the Ross Sea, this channel running as deep as 8,200 feet below sea level. At the South Pole, the rocky subsoil lies 8,300 feet below the ice. As the Pole's altitude is 9,200 feet, it follows that the ground level at the South Pole lies 900 feet above sea level. Still, the area in which scientific exploration remains to be done is vast; as Laurence McKinley Gould, chairman of the Antarctic subcommittee of the United States Committee for the I.G.Y., has said, such exploration, "is the Antarctic's most important export."

This does not mean that the riches of the southern continent's subsoil are negligible. But they are unexploitable, for the time being. More than two hundred minerals have been identified. Coal has been found in larger or smaller quantities almost everywhere; there is also copper, gold, silver, lead, molybdenum, antimony, zinc, tin, mica, graphite and uranium. These discoveries take into account barely one per cent of the Antarctic, the thorough geological prospecting of which is yet to be carried out. Indeed, the continent, with its five and a half million square miles, covers a surface as large as that of the United States and Europe combined.

In the distant past, the Antarctic, which is now deserted and frozen over, was a verdant land covered with virgin forests, as is proven by the numerous fossils that have been found scattered over the whole face of the continent. The Antarctic peninsula and its hinterland, western Antarctica, are a prolongation of the Andes of South America, and thus have existed in their present form only from a relatively recent date.

The eastern Antarctic—that is to say, the larger part of the continent—presents the same characteristics as the south of Africa. It is of extremely ancient origin, which would lead one to suppose that this immense glacial sheet might, like the south of Africa, contain rich finds of diamonds.

Everything tends to prove that the Antarctic continent is in fact formed by two very different land masses, which must have been joined in the distant past.

Finally, although it is true that in the Antarctic fraternization and peaceful coexistence between nations have been and remain tangible realities, still we cannot hide the strategic importance it holds for a country like the United States, for example. We need do no more than think of the fact that, if the Panama Canal were ever put out of service, American ships would be forced to sail around South America and through a strait bordered by Graham Land.

For the time being, man is carrying on with his peaceful work on the enigmatic white continent, and feels no hesitation in aiding his fellows and accepting aid, a truth which is illustrated by the evacuation of the Soviet scientist Leonid Kuperov by the Americans on April 9, 1961. The Russian was at Byrd Station, carrying out a series of studies on the ionosphere, when the doctors announced that his condition was serious. It was decided that he should be evacuated to Christchurch Hospital in New Zealand. The evacuation operation took place in the middle of the polar night and winter. During this operation the first nocturnal flight and landing in the Antarctic were made. This extraordinary spirit of mutual aid is a comforting thought, when one considers, for example, the appalling stupidity of the major events in the Cold War.

The fact is that in the Antarctic there are nothing but men of good will, and that everything remains to be done. Man has just recently made his appearance there and, for the moment, is interested only in the continent's scientific aspect. The men of good will who have explored it have succeeded in persuading their governments to sign the Treaty of the Antarctic, by the terms of which they have agreed that all economic and military problems be set aside for a period of thirty years. Thus, the magnificent work of scientific exploration in common will be able to continue with complete freedom of mind for a few more years. But what will happen afterward, when the men of good will make way for the governments, the soldiers and the businessmen? For it is by no means utopian to think forward to the eventual economic development of the Antarctic. If present efforts are intensified, whole artificial towns, drawing their power from nuclear sources, may well be built in the midst of the icy desert.

The problems involved in developing Canada, at a time when Voltaire spoke of it as "a few acres of snow," were in fact more arduous than those presented by the eventual development of the

Antarctic, with the means we now have at our disposal. Since 1958, the first atomic icebreaker (the Russians' 16,000-ton, 40,000-horsepower *Lenin*), as well as the first nuclear-powered submarine (America's *Nautilus*) and helicopter, have been in operation. The McMurdo Airfield on Ross Island as well as Byrd Station in Marie Byrd Land are already getting their power from a nuclear plant.

Man has shown in the Antarctic, on an extremely small scale, what he could do, if he acted as an intelligent being. He could do as much on a world-wide scale. But, for all that, the most important requirement is that human beings should understand their calling as men; that man should cease behaving as a predatory wolf in his relations with other men, and that he should organize his affairs to make it possible to live in peace on his own planet before reaching out for others.

28

THE FIRST ATOMIC SUBMARINE

HITLER'S LIGHTNING OFFENSIVE against Russia in 1941 had brought German troops into Estonia. The armored divisions had occupied the coast of the Gulf of Finland and had blocked Soviet units in the port of Kronstadt at Leningrad. The Russian high command decided to send the submarine *K51* under the command of Vershinin into the Baltic Sea. The *K51* dove under the young ice in hopes of being able to reach the open sea. After an undersea journey of thirty-six hours, Vershinin tried to surface, to renew his air supply and to recharge his batteries, but his periscope ran against the ice. He took his vessel down to 100 feet below the surface, and rising again with the extra force provided by his long start, he tried once again to break through the ice. But the *K51* could not manage it; she was a prisoner. Fortunately, Vershinin had the time to turn back and to emerge at the moment when the whole of the gulf was beginning to freeze over.

The feat of navigating indefinitely under the ice has been one of the great dreams of modern man since the time of Jules Verne. Wilkins with his *Nautilus* in 1931 and Vershinin with his *K51* were unable to make it come true; their submarines, powered as they were by electricity drawn from storage batteries, did not have a sufficiently wide radius of action undersea to enable them to navigate freely under the ice. The German pirate subs hunting Allied convoys on their way to Murmansk also had to give up the idea.

In order to adventure safely and successfully under the ice, man had to have a submarine with a practically unlimited radius of action. Soon the competition to find one was on between the Americans and the Russians. It seemed at first that the Russians would triumph, when an article appeared in a Soviet journal describing "the exploit of the crew of a Soviet submarine under the polar ice." The exploit was not, however, an entirely submarine operation, but rather an operation in which a pocket submarine, with a bathysphere in tow, made short hops from one *polynia* (a "hole" of open water in the frozen sea) to another, under the guidance of aircraft. Before each undersea run, the submarine had to learn from its airplane escort the distance and direction to the next surfacing place. Thus, the Russian submarine, manned though it was, traversed the Arctic Ocean as a kind of guided missile rather than as a self-sufficient traveler.

It was the atomic reactor which gave the Americans the solution; capable as it was of carrying a practically unlimited fuel supply and having no need of air with which to burn it, the atomic submarine was the ideal machine for the job. And it may be said that the Americans got it only in spite of themselves; it was the obstinacy and stubbornness of one single man, Admiral Hyman G. Rickover, which finally forced the United States government to undertake the building of atomic submarines. Struggling from 1946 on, against the inertia, and sometimes even the resistance, of the Administration, the terrifying admiral, who is by now famous for the toughness of his character, managed to give his country that admirable tool, the atomic submarine.

At the outset, his project was regarded as so chimerical that his superior officer, Admiral Mills, sent it on to the Secretary of the Navy with the note in the margin: "The opinions expressed in this report reflect the personal ideas of two officers, and the Navy takes no responsibility for them." On June 14, 1952, the laying of the *Nautilus*'s first plate took place at a ceremony attended by President Truman. Rickover was still a captain and his nomination to the rank of admiral was consistently rejected by the Navy. The press and Congress intervened, and Hyman George Rickover received his two stars.

He had a very special way of choosing the officers who were to be in command of his future nuclear vessels. In his modest office in Washington he made them undergo a real psychiatric test.

"Suppose you're on a sinking ship with five other men. The conditions are that one, and only one, of you can be saved. Are you resourceful enough to talk the other five into letting you be the one?"

"U'm—yes," replied the disoriented candidate.

The Admiral gave an almost imperceptible signal, and five men burst into the room.

"All right, son," Rickover said softly. "Start talking."

Commander William R. Anderson himself, the commander of the first atomic submarine, the *Nautilus*, underwent one of the Admiral's tests, and he came out of it extremely badly. When Rickover suddenly asked him to name the books he had read in the preceding two years, he went blank and could not remember any. "Good bye," the Admiral said curtly. When he got home, Anderson sent off a list of his reading without any commentary, but without much hope either. He received a letter by return mail giving him another appointment and informing him that he had been accepted. Rickover told him later that he had crossed him off the roster of candidates and had changed his mind only on receiving the list.

The North Pole had been conquered on foot and from the air, but no one had yet been able to explore it from under the ice. There were several interesting aspects to this highly coveted victory over nature. If one glances at a map of the globe as seen from above, it will be clear that the shortest sea lane from Europe to Japan goes over the Pole, as does the shortest air lane. Up till now, every ship has had to go either east (via Suez) or west (via Panama). If it were possible for a submarine, either a cargo vessel or a passenger transport, to navigate under the polar ice pack, considerable time might be gained. It is useless, moreover, to underline the importance of a fleet of submarines armed with rockets carrying nuclear warheads, lying in ambush under the ice where they are undetectible and ready to go into action at a moment's notice.

The first test was made in 1948. The submarine *Carp*, under the command of Skip Palmer, dove under the pack in the area around Bering Strait. Experiments were made on board with the device which was going to enable the *Nautilus* to determine the thickness of the ice overhead at any given moment: the fathometer as adapted by Dr. Waldo Lyon.

The submarine uses a supersonic detector called sonar to "explore the ground" around it and to locate other submarines or the hulls of ships. It was the Frenchman Paul Langevin who invented the "asdic" (for Anti-Submarine Detection Investigation Committee) during the First World War; the ultrasonic vibrations were emitted and bounced back off the hulls of ships. But during the Second World War, a new kind of paint was discovered which would absorb the ultrasonic vibrations and so rendered this technique useless.

When the *Nautilus* set out for the Arctic, she had on board a new detection device invented—once again—by a French scientist, Professor Kastler, and based on magnetism. The metallic mass of the submarine produced a slight modification in the terrestrial magnetic field; all that was needed was to own a device that would be sensitive to this slight modification. In 1960, Sputnik III succeeded in detecting, by this method, a submerged submarine more than 560 miles away. At the present moment, this procedure has already been replaced by the famous Laser, which was stolen from the British by the Lonsdale ring of Soviet spies. With Laser, a submarine is located by means of the modifications it produces in gravity.

Sonar was used on board the *Nautilus* as an "ice detector." A pen called the "immersion indicator pen" traces a very nearly horizontal line on a recording cylinder; this line corresponds to the actual surface of the sea, whether it is free of ice or not; a second pen (the "zenithal sonar pen") traces a line corresponding to the lower surface of the ice. When the sea is free, the two lines are indistinguishable. When the submarine is under the pack, the line drawn by the zenithal sonar pen separates from the line drawn by the "surface" pen and gives the thickness of the ice at any given time. The importance of such an instrument in the location of *polynias*, or water holes, can easily be appreciated.

When the temperature falls, there first forms a sort of ice porridge, or slush, then pancake ice composed of blocks from 20 to 40 inches in diameter. These blocks freeze together to form "young ice," which is no more than 6 to 8 inches thick. At the end of winter, the ice is between 3½ and 8 feet thick; only rarely does it get to be more than 8 to 12 feet.

But it is attacked by winds and currents and breaks up, giving birth to ice floes. These floes in their turn undergo pressures which drive them into one another, smash them and heap them up in hummocks, more or less separated by unstable "rivers" or "holes" (*polynias*). Thus it was that in June 1958 the *Nautilus*, whose periscope depth is 49 feet, just missed smashing into an ice block at a depth of 157 feet; the ice was submerged to a depth of 85 feet.

The irregularity of the ice pack's profile is not the only danger involved in undersea polar navigation. On the surface it is possible to use astronomical methods in calculating one's bearings; in our own day, one can also use radiogoniometry. Under the ice, it is impossible to use either of these two procedures. Radio waves will not penetrate the water, and the ice prevents one from seeing the heavenly bodies and calculating their altitudes. Thus, the *Nautilus* would have had to navigate entirely blind, had she not had an astonishing technical novelty at her disposal: the inertial navigator. There was, of course, a gyro-compass on board, but as we shall see later, the functioning of this instrument is very uncertain in the neighborhood of the pole of rotation. But it is precisely this same rotation which enables the inertial navigator to function. This device is sensitive to the earth's rotation, which is about 1,000 miles per hour at the equator and zero at the poles. It varies inversely with the latitude. By recording this variation, the device gives a figure which can be converted into a reading of latitude.

The *Nautilus*'s equipment and the comforts available to the crew would have appealed to Jules Verne's imagination (there was a jukebox and a cinema). The absence of noise and vibration from the atomic reactor, buried behind its lead and polyethylene casing (the engine fed power into two classic turbines and two turbodynamos) was a further factor in providing for the crew's well-being. There was no danger whatever of radioactivity on board, and the least object that might be capable of producing any (like watches with luminous dials) was stored away in lead boxes.

Like Captain Nemo's *Nautilus*, Commander Anderson's had television on board, with a vertical camera transmitting the image of the under surface of the ice pack to two large screens in the central control room. Sending out ultrasonic vibrations in all directions, the *Nautilus* went under the ice pack near Point Barrow. Her average speed was about 20 knots at a depth of between 300 and 400 feet; she approached the surface only to decrease pressure and to facilitate the disposal of garbage.

On August 3, 1958, a few minutes after 11 P.M., Washington time, Commander Anderson's voice boomed over the loudspeakers: "In a few moments *Nautilus* will realize a goal long a dream of mankind—the attainment by ship of the North Geographic Pole. With continued Godspeed, in less than two days we will record an even more significant historic first—the completion of a rapid transpolar voyage from the Pacific to the Atlantic Ocean."

Then, at 11:15, came the countdown: ". . . 5 . . . 4 . . . 3 . . . 2 . . . 1. Mark! For the United States and the United States Navy, the North Pole."

On August 5, the *Nautilus* emerged from the edge of the pack, in the Greenland area and immediately sent off a message: "Top secret. *Nautilus* 90° North." Within less than a minute, United States Navy bases in Hawaii, England and Japan replied, and Anderson sent off a second message: "96 hours from Point Barrow to the Greenland Sea." Operation Sunshine was a total success, and for the first time, the world learned of an American achievement in which there was an element of surprise; this was, in a certain sense, the American answer to the Russian Sputnik.

The surprise was all the more complete when it was learned that, nine days after the *Nautilus*, a second American atomic submarine not only had reached the Pole, but had surfaced at it.

The *Skate* was officially the third of the U.S.'s atomic submarines; less heavy than the *Nautilus*, which was an experimental vessel, the *Skate* was the prototype of a new model. The crew included ten officers, eighty-seven enlisted men and nine civilians, or 106 men in all, under the command of James Calvert, who had been picked by Admiral Rickover in the spring of 1955.

The *Skate*, with a displacement of 3,000 tons, was divided into two parts, the engines in the rear, the living quarters forward, and had torpedo tubes at each end. The atomic pile was contained in a steel chamber twenty feet high. The water it heated communicated a part of its heat to a separate water system, where the steam was formed which ran the turbines. The primary water system was highly radioactive, but did not transmit this radioactivity to the secondary water. All the dangerous part was walled up behind lead and thick leaves of polyethylene plastic. Portholes made of thick leaded green glass made it possible to check the operation of the reactor. Each member of the crew carried a roll of film which was highly sensitive to radioactivity on his person. The film was developed at regular intervals to confirm the fact that the air was not contaminated.

The *Skate*, that "air-bubble surrounded by steel," as Calvert has described her, had two decks: the upper deck housed the central control room and the officers' quarters; the crew's mess, the sailors' bunks, the galley and the washrooms were on the lower deck. The crew's mess was used as a reading room, dining room, classroom and movie theater; it was equipped with a jukebox and a tape recorder, a Coca-Cola vending machine, another for coffee and a third for ice cream. The provisions included canned goods, flour, sugar, coffee, eggs, butter, vegetables, fruit and meat. A thousand bricks were provided for ballast in the nylon sacks that were used in the disposal of waste. Meals were served on white tablecloths with silver cutlery and china with a blue pattern. The traditional Thanksgiving turkey was eaten at a depth of 300 feet, with the vessel doing 20 knots. The *Skate* was equipped with a magnetic compass (which is useless under the ice), a gyroscopic compass and an inertial navigator.

Calvert's assignment was chiefly to "develop techniques for surfacing in pack ice areas." His instructions included these words: "The military usefulness of an ocean area is dependent on at least periodic access to its surface."

The *Skate*, whose crew had just learned of the *Nautilus*'s success, had a difficult part to play. She was to surface in a *polynia*, which was a feat the *Nautilus* had not managed to bring off. She found her first hole off Spitsbergen. She surfaced. The 6-by-12-foot rubber boat was inflated, and the scientists proceeded to make a set of observations on the ice. The *Skate* resumed her undersea journey in the direction of the Pole, in the vicinity of which two drifting stations, Alfa and Bravo, then lay. Calvert decided to pay a visit to Alfa Station after reaching the Pole.

On August 22, the loudspeakers echoed to Commander Calvert's voice: "5, 4, 3, 2, 1. Mark. At one-forty-seven Greenwich Time on 12 August 1958, the *Skate* has reached the northernmost part of our planet. My congratulations to each one of you, but this is only the beginning. Before we are through, we are going to demonstrate that a submarine can come into this ice pack, operate at will, surface when it wants to, and carry out whatever mission our country requires."

That afternoon, twenty-eight miles from the Pole, the *Skate* surfaced in a tiny *polynia;* her two ends were touching the ice, and only her conning tower emerged. The outside temperature: +41° F. Calvert then sent a message to Alfa Station, which was relayed by way of Manila, asking them for his exact position and for the number of *polynias* in the vicinity. Alfa replied: "85° N., 136° W. Big *polynia* 160 feet from our huts."

On Thursday, August 14, 1958, the *Skate* arrived at a point twenty-eight miles from Alfa Station. The difficulty lay in locating it exactly, since radio waves would not penetrate the water and the station was drifting. It was then just at "the pole of relative inaccessibility," according to Stefansson's definition. Calvert found a *polynia* and surfaced in order to make contact with Alfa Station.

It was agreed that the station's outboard launch would run nonstop circles in the "good" *polynia,* in order to permit the *Skate*'s sonar detector to locate it by the noise. The whole operation went off perfectly, and the unusual meeting between the men of the *Skate* and those at Alfa took place with enthusiasm. The station had been set up in 1957 for the I.G.Y. and it consisted of twenty-nine military and civilian volunteers "buried" there for six months. It was under the command of Dr. Norbert Untersteiner, who gave the submariners a grand tour of his realm; they went into ecstasies over a camera which was capable of taking photographs at depths greater than 10,000 feet.

Thanks to the co-operation of the men at Alfa, Calvert was able to telephone to the United States, to one of his chiefs, Rear Admiral F. B. Warder, in New London. The Admiral was having lunch with a number of important people when his adjutant appeared. "It's for you, Admiral. Jim Calvert is calling you from the North Pole!"

The *Skate* set out again and, after one more run toward the Pole, returned to Bergen. A ceremony took place there in the museum where Nansen's *Fram* is on display; it was attended by Joe Fletcher, the pioneer of the "floating islands." A few miles away, Sir Hubert Wilkins's old submarine, the *Nautilus,* lay six hundred feet below the surface in Bergen Fjord, dreaming doubtless of the feat she had been unable to accomplish and which the *Skate* had just carried out in her stead. To honor this memory, Calvert dispatched a telegram to Sir Hubert paying homage to "the man who showed the way."

Sir Hubert came aboard the *Skate* in Boston to spend the day.

"Now that you have everything you need," he said to Calvert, "you must go in the wintertime."

"Not much use in going if we can't get to the surface," Calvert said.

"I think you can," Wilkins replied. "Maybe you'll have to bore a hole, maybe blast. I don't know. But you'll find a way."

A few weeks later, on December 1, 1958, Sir Hubert Wilkins died of a heart attack.

In January, Calvert met Vilhjalmur Stefansson at Dartmouth College. Stefansson showed Calvert a copy of the message sent to Wilkins from the *Skate.* Wilkins had sent it on to Stefansson, and he had added a note: "Wrong addressee. Should have been sent to you." Stefansson, who was then seventy-nine years old, discussed Calvert's project for piercing the ice with him at great length, encouraging him to do with the *Skate* what whales do with their backs when they break through the ice.

Calvert did not hesitate; with the Navy's approval, the *Skate* was reinforced and improved, and it set out for the Pole for the second time within seven months, in the middle of the Arctic winter this time. The first try was a success; then, after unexpectedly meeting an enormous bed of herrings three hundred miles from the Pole, the *Skate* made a second try, which was equally successful. Everything was ready for surfacing at the Pole.

A relatively thin layer of ice was located just at the Pole, but the *Skate* had some difficulty in attacking it, for the drift of the ice was considerable; finally, the enormous submarine pierced the ice pack; the goal was reached. Then, a moving ceremony took place on the pack in memory of Sir Hubert Wilkins. His ashes were scattered in the wind, in accordance with his last wishes. The date was March 17, 1959, and the temperature stood at 22 degrees below zero.

The *Skate*'s exploit marks the final triumph of technology. Henceforward atomic submarines and icebreakers and jet planes would take possession of the Arctic where two giants confront one another in the most astonishing preventive cold war in history. Under the ice pack submarines loaded with rockets bearing nuclear warheads prowl ceaselessly: the American *Polaris* and the Soviet *Golem VI*'s. Each one of them carries more destructive power than all the bombs exploded between 1939 and 1945 combined, including those dropped on Hiroshima and Nagasaki.

The opponents go on arranging their pieces on the vast white chessboard: here an airfield, there an advance port. Little by little, the scientist is being replaced by the soldier; the beacons, the radio and radar stations make one forget the scientific stations; it is scarcely remembered that one day, not so long ago, Nansen was awarded the Nobel Peace Prize.

Still, we do have the possibility of hoping that the triumph of technology will remain the triumph of good sense. As Henri Bergson said:

> Man can sustain life on this earth only if a set of powerful tools furnishes him the leverage which the mystic calls mechanics, and only if the latter, far from implying civilization's sinking down into matter, is the means by which the progressive triumph of mind over matter, of freedom over necessity, may be carried on.

INDEX